W9-AUJ-985

KnowThis®:
Marketing Basics

Paul Christ, Ph.D.

KnowThis?
Media

KnowThis: Marketing Basics

Published By:
KnowThis Media, A Division of KnowThis LLC
615 Juniper Drive
Blue Bell, PA 19422

Publisher Website: KnowThisMedia.com
Book Website: KnowThis.com/books/marketing-basics.htm

Trademark: KnowThis is a registered trademark of KnowThis LLC

COPYRIGHT © Paul Christ, 2009

All rights reserved. No part of this publication may be reproduced, stored in a retrieval system, or transmitted in any form by any means (electronic, mechanical, photocopying, recording or otherwise) without the prior written permission of the copyright owner.

ISBN: 978-0-9820722-0-2

Printed and bound in United States of America

10 9 8 7 6 5 4 3 2 1

Contents

Why This Book?

KnowThis: Marketing Basics is produced as a direct response to many inquires from visitors to the website *KnowThis.com*. When launched in 1998, *KnowThis.com* was among the first Internet sites to address the specific needs of those involved in marketing and related fields. In short order *KnowThis.com* became a leading authority website as evidenced by high rankings on search engine queries, links on university websites, and strong site traffic.

While in the early days *KnowThis.com* was mostly a reference website offering links to materials found elsewhere on the web, it transitioned to offering original content beginning in 2004. The original material included introduction of the <u>Principles of Marketing</u> series, the most detailed look at marketing concepts that was available on the Internet.

The <u>Principles of Marketing</u> series brought a great deal of positive comments including many requests for a printed version. This book responds to these requests. **However, what is contained in this book is not simply a reproduction of content found on the website.** In fact, the material found in this book differs from the <u>Principles of Marketing</u> material in several significant ways:

- ♦ The book contains over <u>50 percent</u> new or rewritten material not found on *KnowThis.com*.
- ♦ The book contains <u>new organization</u> of topics.
- ♦ The book contains over <u>100 real-world marketing examples</u> connecting the concepts with issues facing organizations around the world.
- ♦ The book directs reader's attention to important topics through <u>formatted information boxes</u>.
- ♦ The book contains <u>additional graphics</u> not found on the website version.
- ♦ The book identifies <u>hundreds of key terms</u> either within subject headings or through the use of bolded text.
- ♦ The book offers an <u>extensive index</u> for quick look-up of marketing topics.

Who is the Book For?

KnowThis: Marketing Basics was written with several audiences in mind including:

♦ The Marketing Novice – This book is ideal for anyone who is new to marketing, as it covers all essential marketing areas. By spending time with this book the Marketing Novice will quickly gain the foundation needed to appreciate what marketers do and understand the full scope of marketing decision making. For some, reading this book may also offer insight into career options in the marketing field.

♦ The Marketing Professional – Experienced marketers will also find this book useful. Often seasoned marketers tend to focus on just a few areas of marketing as part of their day-to-day activities and this book may serve as a good refresher for areas of marketing for which they have not recently spent much time.

♦ The Marketing Educator – Teachers of marketing now have an alternative to high-priced marketing textbooks. This book offers nearly all of the same coverage found in expensive textbooks at a fraction of the price (**educators see more information below**).

Additionally, most of what is covered applies to all types of businesses including those whose objective is to make money (i.e., for-profit businesses) as well as those not driven by a profit-making motive (i.e., not-for-profit organizations).

Quality at an Affordable Cost?

Yes! *KnowThis: Marketing Basics* is written by a marketing professor and covers much of the same ground as found in much more expensive books. But it also provides insight not found in other publications and thus holds its own as a unique offering and not simply a remaking of other books.

We are able to maintain affordable pricing by using printing strategies and methods that reduce overall printing costs and inventory carrying costs. But be assured this book does not sacrifice quality. Whether this book is used in the classroom to help students learn basic concepts or used outside the classroom to assist in professional marketing activities, readers will find the material to be comprehensive, relevant, and written in a way that is intended to bridge the gap that often exists between business practice and academic textbooks.

Looking For More?

As you might guess the support website for *KnowThis: Marketing Basics* is *KnowThis.com*. Along with the usual resources found on the general site, there is also a special section for this book. The location of this section is:

KnowThis.com/books/marketing-basics.htm

Included in this section are links to many of the references cited in the book along with other resources.

For Educators

As noted, ***KnowThis: Marketing Basics*** is ideal as a textbook for an entry-level marketing course or as a supplemental reference for a more advanced class. This book covers the same ground as far more expensive textbooks while also offering new information not covered in other books. Additionally:

- This book takes a contemporary view of marketing including covering numerous new developments and how these affect marketing, such as social networks, digital signage, intellectual property, RSS feed advertising, controlled word-of-mouth promotion, neuron-research, virtual worlds, and much, much more.

- Extensive material is presented focusing on real-world examples most of which students will find to be still current and directly accessible via links on the book's support website.

- With *KnowThis.com* as the book's support website educators are directing their students to a high-quality resource that has served the marketing community since 1998.

- While the book contains over 100 real-world examples, educators will find even more examples in *KnowThis.com's* weekly updated listing of Marketing Stories. These selectively chosen stories are arranged by topic area and notices of weekly updates are available via RSS feed.

- In addition to current Marketing Stories, *KnowThis.com* has a database of thousands more stories dating back to 2004. While we cannot guarantee that all are accessible, many in fact can be located with a simple click. This database could prove quite valuable as a research resource for students and instructors.

- Slide presentations are available for those instructors who have adopted the book.

For information on obtaining exam or desk copies see KnowThis Media website at: **KnowThisMedia.com**

Would You Like to Help Us Out?

Have you found an error in the book? Is there other material you would like to see covered in a future edition? Do you have other comments? Then we would appreciate hearing from you. See the book's support webpage to find out how you can help us improve.

About the Author

Paul Christ (*pronounced with soft "i"*) holds a Ph.D. (marketing concentration) from Drexel University. He is a Professor of Marketing at West Chester University (AACSB accredited), the second largest university in the Pennsylvania State System of Higher Education and one of the largest universities in the Philadelphia region. Paul teaches MBA-level courses titled *Marketing Strategy and Customer Value*, *Marketing and Technology*, and *Business Research and Data Analysis*.

In addition to teaching Paul has held several administrative positions including currently serving as the university's MBA Program Director. Also, in 1999 he was responsible for developing one of the first E-Commerce focused MBA programs in the world.

Paul has written and presented on marketing and technology topics in numerous academic publications, conferences and other public forums and has spoken throughout the world on the topic of marketing and Internet business. Paul is editor of *KnowThis.com*, one of the Internet's leading marketing references sites. In addition to academic experience, Paul has extensive experience in various marketing and sales positions with Fortune 500 companies and served in a management position for a successful startup in the consumer electronics industry. Additionally, he has been a consultant to many marketing and technology companies, including startup Internet-based firms.

This book is lovingly dedicated to my children — Katie, Kelly, Tom, and Mark — and especially to my wife Carol whose assistance and support inspired its completion.

Chapter 1:

What is Marketing?

Welcome to the world of marketing! The main intention of ***Know This: Marketing Basics*** is to offer a straightforward examination of one of the most important, exciting, and challenging business activities crucial to nearly all organizations.

In this first chapter we lay the groundwork for our study of the field of marketing with a look at marketing's key concepts and the important tasks marketers perform. Coverage includes a close examination of the definition of marketing. A dissection of the key terms in the definition shows that marketing's primary focus is to identify and satisfy customers in a way that helps build a solid and, hopefully, sustained relationship that encourages customers to continue doing business with the marketer. We also show how marketing has evolved from a process centered on simply getting as many people as possible to purchase a product to today's highly complex efforts designed to build long-term customer relationships. Additionally, we'll see marketing is not only important to individual organizations it also carries both positive and negative influences at a broader societal level. Finally, we look at what it takes to be a successful marketer.

MARKETING DEFINED

Marketing is defined in many different ways. Some definitions focus on marketing in terms of what it means to an organization, such as being the key functional area for generating revenue, while other definitions lean more toward defining marketing in terms of its most visible tasks, such as advertising and creating new products.

There probably is no one best way to define marketing, however, whatever definition is used should have an orientation that focuses on the key to marketing success – customers.

We define marketing as follows:

> **Marketing consists of the strategies and tactics used to identify, create, and maintain satisfying relationships with customers resulting in value for both the customer and the marketer.**

Dissecting Marketing

Let's examine our definition of marketing in detail by looking at the key terms.

Strategies and Tactics

Strategies are the direction the marketing effort takes over some period of time while tactics are actionable steps or decisions made in order to follow the strategies established. For instance, if a company's strategy is to begin selling its products in a new country, the tactics may involve the marketing decisions made to carry this out. Performing strategic and tactical planning activities in advance of taking action is considered critical for long-term marketing success.

Identify

Arguably the most important marketing function involves efforts needed to gain knowledge of customers, competitors, and markets (i.e., where marketers do business). To gain knowledge marketers will continually undertake marketing research.

Create

Competition forces marketers to be creative. When marketers begin new ventures, such as building a new company, it is often based around something that is new (e.g., a new product, a new way of getting products to customers, a new advertising approach, etc.). But once something new is launched innovation does not end. Competitive pressure is continually felt by the marketer, who must respond by again devising new strategies and tactics that help the organization remain successful. For marketers, the cycle of creating something new never ends.

Maintain

Today's marketers work hard to ensure their customers return to purchase from them again and again. Long gone are the days when success for a marketer was measured simply by how many sales are made each day. Now, in most marketing situations, marketing success is evaluated not only in terms of sales but also by how long a marketer retains their customers. Consequently, marketers' efforts to attract customers do not end when a customer completes a purchase. It continues in various ways for, hopefully, a long time after the initial purchase.

• •

Microsoft found that maintaining customer relationships can be quite costly. When faced with high repair rates on a new version of its Xbox gaming system the technology giant chose to extend the warranty it offered to its customers in order to avoid future customer backlash. Doing so, however, cost the company over (US) $1 billion. (1)

• •

Satisfying Relationships

A key objective of marketing is to provide products and services that customers really want AND to make customers feel their contact with the marketer is helping build a good relationship between the two. In this way the customer becomes a partner in the transaction, not just a source of revenue for the marketer. While this concept may seem intuitive and a natural part of what all businesses should do, as Box 1-1 points out, this has not always been the case.

Value for Customer and Marketer

Value refers to the perception of benefits received for what someone must give up. For customers, value is most often measured by how much benefit they feel they are getting for their money, though the value one customer feels may differ from what another customer feels even though they purchase the same product. On the other side of the transaction, the marketer for a for-profit organization may measure value in terms of how much profit they make for the marketing efforts and resources expended. For a successful marketing effort to take place both the customer and the marketer must feel they are receiving something worthwhile in return for their efforts. Without a strong perception of value it is unlikely a strong relationship can be built.

Box 1-1

MARKETING CONCEPT

In the old days of marketing (before the 1950s) sellers of products were keen on identifying strategies and tactics that focused solely on selling more goods and services with little regard for what customers really wanted. Often this meant companies embraced a "sell-as-much-as-we-can" philosophy with little concern for building relationships for the long term.

But starting in the 1950s, companies began to see that old ways of selling were wearing thin with customers. As competition grew stiffer across most industries, organizations looked to the buyers' side of the transaction for ways to improve. What they found was an emerging philosophy suggesting that the key factor in successful marketing is understanding the needs of customers. This now famous "Marketing Concept" suggests marketing decisions should flow from FIRST knowing the customer and what they want. Only then should an organization initiate the process of developing and marketing products and services.

The Marketing Concept continues as the root of most marketing efforts. Marketers know they can no longer limit their marketing efforts to just getting customers to purchase more, they must have an in-depth understanding of who their customers are and what they want.

THE MARKETER'S TOOLKIT

In order to reach the goal of creating a relationship that holds value for customers and for the organization, marketers use a diverse Toolkit (Figure 1-1). The Toolkit represents the key tasks performed by the marketer. These tasks include:

1. Selecting Target Markets

This task involves the selection of customers identified as possessing needs the marketer believes can be addressed by its marketing efforts. In almost all cases marketers identify target markets prior to making other decisions since satisfying the needs of the target market drives all other marketing decisions. This task is discussed in detail in Chapter 5.

2. Creating Products

Marketers use tangible (e.g., goods) and intangible (e.g., services) solutions to address the needs of their target market. For many customers the product is the main reason why the customer will or will not do business with the marketer. Product decisions have several dimensions and are discussed in detail in Chapters 6 and 7.

3. Establishing Distribution

Products are only of value to the target market if they can be obtained. Selecting distribution methods that enable customers to acquire products requires very careful consideration of different distribution options which almost always requires the help of others. This task is covered in Chapters 8 and 9.

4. Developing Promotions

Most organizations must communicate information about their products to their target market. While advertising is the most notable form of promotion, there are others including sales promotion, personal selling, and public relations. In depth coverage of promotion is discussed in Chapters 10 through 15.

5. Setting Price

Marketing often results in a transaction taking place between customers and the marketing organization. While product decisions determine what the marketer will exchange with the customer, it is pricing decisions that determine what the customer will give up in order to obtain the product. Determining price can be quite complex and is addressed in detail in Chapters 16 and 17.

Figure 1-1: The Marketer's Toolkit

Characteristics of the Marketer's Toolkit

In addition to containing the five key marketing decisions, other important characteristics of the Toolkit include:

INTEGRATION OF TASKS

Each task within the Marketer's Toolkit is tightly integrated with all other tasks so that a decision in one area could, and often does, impact decisions in other areas. For instance, a change in the price of a product (e.g., lowering the price) could impact the distribution area (e.g., requires increased product shipments to retail stores).

SEQUENCE OF TASKS

While the five key marketing tasks are shown with a number, the order of decision making does not necessarily follow this sequence. However, as we will discuss, in most cases marketers should first identify target markets (#1) prior to making decisions #2 through #5 (also called the **marketing mix**) since these decisions are going to be directed toward satisfying the desired target markets.

ADDITIONAL SKILLS

To use the Toolkit properly, marketers must possess additional skills including the ability to:

- Conduct Marketing Research – As we will see in Chapter 2, marketing decisions should not be made without first committing time and resources for gathering and analyzing information through marketing research. For this reason marketing research can be viewed as the foundation of marketing and, as shown in Figure 1-1, supports all marketing decisions.

- Understand Customers – While the Marketer's Toolkit centers on making decisions that satisfy customers, marketers must take extra steps to know as much as they can about their customers. In Chapters 3 and 4 we will see what marketers do to better understand and manage their customers.

- Monitor the External Environment – As shown in Figure 1-1, options within the Marketer's Toolkit are affected by factors that are not controlled by the marketer. These factors include economic conditions, legal issues, technological developments, social/cultural changes, and many more. While not managed in the way marketers control their Toolkit, these external factors must be monitored and dealt with since these can cause considerable harm to the organization. Ignoring outside elements also can lead to missed opportunities in the market especially if competitors are the first to take advantage of the opportunities.

- Create a Marketing Plan – While some marketers may find success making decisions on the spur of the moment, most marketers must put much more thought into their decision making. As discussed in Chapter 20, developing a formal plan is a critical part of marketing.

MARKETING'S ROLE

The key objective of an organization's marketing efforts is to develop satisfying relationships with customers that benefit both the customer and the organization. These efforts lead marketing to serve an important role within most organizations and within society.

At the organizational level, marketing is a vital business function that is necessary in nearly all industries whether the organization operates as a for-profit or as a not-for-profit. For the for-profit organization, marketing is responsible for most tasks that generate revenue and profits. For the not-for-profit organization, marketing is responsible for attracting customers needed to support the not-for-profit's mission, such as raising donations or supporting a cause.

• •

Marketing is considered to be essential to the growth of almost all organizations with large sums being spent on the effort. In fact, spending by U.S. companies for just one part of marketing, advertising, is greater than the GDP of such industrial areas as Malaysia, Hong Kong, and New Zealand. (2)

• •

Marketing is also the organizational business area that interacts most frequently with the public and, consequently, what the public knows about an organization is determined by their interactions with marketers. For example, customers may believe a company is dynamic and creative based on its advertising message.

At a broader level marketing offers significant benefits to society. These include:

♦ Developing products that satisfy needs, including products that enhance society's quality of life

♦ Creating a competitive environment that helps lower product prices

♦ Developing product distribution systems that offer access to products to a large number of customers and many geographic regions

♦ Building demand for products that require organizations to expand their labor force

♦ Offering techniques having the ability to convey messages that change societal behavior in a positive way (e.g., anti-smoking advertising)

CRITICISMS OF MARKETING

While marketing is viewed as offering significant benefits to organizations and to society, the fact that marketing is a business function operating in close contact with the public opens this functional area to extensive criticism.

Among the issues cited by those who criticize marketing are:

Marketing Makes People Purchase What They Don't Need

Possibly the criticism most frequently made about marketing is that marketers are only concerned with getting customers to buy whether they need the product or not. The root of this argument stems from the belief that marketers are only out to satisfy their own needs and really do not care about the needs of their customers.

While many marketers are guilty of manipulating customers into making unwanted purchases, the vast majority understand such tactics will not lead to loyal customers and, consequently, is unlikely to lead to long-term success.

Marketers Embellish Product Claims

Marketers are often criticized for exaggerating the benefits offered by their products. This is especially the case with methods used for customer communication such as advertising. The most serious problems arise when product claims are seen as misleading customers into believing a product can offer a certain level of value that, in fact, it cannot.

But sometimes there is a fine line between what a rational person should accept as a "reasonable exaggeration" and what is considered downright misleading. Fortunately, many countries offer customers some level of protection from misleading claims since such business practices may subject the marketer to legal action. Of course, using such tactics is also likely to lead to marketing failure as customers will not be satisfied with their experience and will not return.

• •

The makers of Splenda sweetener settled a lawsuit brought by competitors who said the sweetener's slogan "Made from sugar so it tastes like sugar" was misleading and confused customers into believing the product was in some way more natural than other artificial sweeteners. (3)

• •

Marketing Discriminates in Customer Selection

A key to marketing success is to engage in a deliberate process that identifies customers who offer marketers the best chance for satisfying organizational objectives. This method, called **target marketing** (see Chapter 4), often drives most marketing decisions including product development and price setting. But some argue target marketing leads marketers to focus their efforts primarily on customers who have the financial means to make more expensive purchases. They contend this intentionally discriminates against others, especially lower income customers who cannot afford to purchase higher priced products. Additionally, they say this group ends ups being targeted with lower quality products.

While this criticism is often valid, it is worth noting that while many "lower quality" products are inferior to current high-end products, comparison of their quality to similar products from just a few years ago shows there has been significant improvement. For instance, low cost electronic equipment, such as digital cameras, offer more features compared to low cost cameras of just a few years ago. Thus, while certain customer groups may not be the target market for some new product offerings they may eventually benefit from the development of higher-end products.

Marketing Contributes to Environmental Waste

One of the loudest complaints against marketing concerns its impact on the environment through:

- the use of excessive, non-biodegradable packaging (e.g., use of plastics, placing small products in large packages, etc.)

- the continual development of resource consuming products (e.g., construction of new buildings, golf courses, shopping malls, etc.)

- the proliferation of unsightly and wasteful methods of promotions (e.g., outdoor billboards, direct mail, etc.).

Marketers have begun to respond to these concerns by introducing **green marketing** campaigns that are not only intended to appease critics but also take advantage of potential business opportunities. For example, auto makers see opportunity by creating new fuel efficient hybrid vehicles, the demand for which has accelerated in the last few years. Also, certain retailers are finding financial opportunity and promotional value by asserting their marketing muscle to encourage customers and suppliers to become more environmentally responsible. This can be seen with the world's top retailer, Wal-Mart, who now only stocks concentrated laundry detergent in an effort to conserve water and paper resources. (4) It is expected that as environmental activism gains political clout and more consumer support, marketers will see even more opportunity to market environmentally friendly products.

Marketing Encroaches on Customers' Right to Privacy

Gathering and analyzing information on the market in which marketers conduct business is a vital step in making good marketing decisions. Often the most valuable information deals with customers' buying behavior and especially determining which factors influence how customers make purchase decisions.

But to some digging deep into customer behavior crosses the line of what is considered private information. Of most concern to privacy advocates is marketers' use of methods that track user activity. In particular, they are critical of the growing use of advanced technologies allowing marketers to gain access to customer shopping and information gathering habits (see Box 1-2).

Privacy issues are not restricted to marketing research. Other areas of marketing have also experienced problems. For instance, there have been several recent incidences, most notably those involving mishandled credit card payment information, where a breach in customer privacy has placed customers at risk.

The issue of customer privacy is likely to become one of the most contentious issues marketers face in the coming years and could lead to greater legal limits on how marketers gather customer information and perform other activities.

Box 1-2

TRACKING CUSTOMERS ONLINE AND OFFLINE

Marketers have at their disposal numerous highly advanced techniques for tracking user activity both online and offline.

Online Tracking

At the most rudimentary level, marketers operating websites can determine how many people are visiting a website, what pages on the website they visit, how they arrived at the website including whether they used a search engine, where in the world they are located, and many other types of information. This information is left by visitors each time they visit a website and does not require the marketer to do much extra work to obtain the data. In fact Google, through its Analytics service, enables marketers to have access to this information for free. (5)

Some marketers do engage in questionable online research practices, such as loading tracking software onto a user's computer, without the knowledge or permission of the user. One type of software called **adware** allows marketers to monitor users' website browsing activity and use this information to deliver advertisements based on users' Internet habits.

To address online tracking concerns, several consumer U.S. advocacy groups (6) and politicians (7) are raising the prospect of legislation to limit the extent to which these techniques are used.

Offline Tracking

Privacy issues are not limited to concerns with online tracking; marketers also use techniques to track customers' offline purchase activities. One example of offline tracking occurs when retail stores match sales transactions to individual shoppers. This is easy to do when customers use purchase cards (a.k.a. loyalty cards, discount cards, club cards, etc.) as part of the buying process. This information can then be used to create individualized promotions, such as printing coupons that are based on the customer's previous buying activity.

ETHICAL AND SOCIAL CONCERNS

In addition to problems cited above, some critics also argue that the money-making motive of some marketers has encouraged many to cross the line in terms of ethical and social business behavior.

Ethical Issues

Ethics is concerned with what is right and wrong. Many people assume that only actions that violate laws are considered unethical. While it is true that illegal activity is also unethical, a business activity can be unethical even though no laws are violated. For instance, some consider it unethical for companies to aggressively promote unhealthy foods to children though such promotional practices are generally not viewed as illegal.

Sometimes the line between what is ethical and unethical is difficult to distinguish since what is right and wrong differs depending on such factors as nationality, culture, and even industry. For example, many websites offer users access at no monetary charge to their content (e.g., articles, videos, audio clips, etc.) but do so only if users register and provide contact information including an email address. Some of these sites then automatically add registrants to promotional email mailing lists. Some view the practice of automatic **opt-in** to a mailing list as being unethical since customers do not request it and are forced to take additional action to be removed from the list (**opt-out**). However, many marketers see no ethical issue with this practice and simply view adding registered users to an email list as part of the "cost" to customers for accessing material.

MARKETING CODE OF ETHICS

The call for marketers to become more responsible for their actions has led to the development of a code of ethics by many companies and professional organizations.

Company Code

A company code of ethics includes extensive coverage of how business is conducted by members of an organization. For instance, Yahoo! lays out an extensive list of what is expected of their employees in their document *The Guide to Business Conduct and Ethics@Yahoo!* (8) Among the issues covered are:

- Business Relationships ("must never take unfair advantage of others through manipulation, concealment, abuse of privileged information, misrepresentation of material facts or any other unfair dealing practice")

- Offering Gifts to Clients ("may not furnish or offer to furnish any gift that is of more than token value or that goes beyond the common courtesies")

- Receiving Gifts From Clients ("must never request or ask for gifts, entertainment or any other business courtesies")

- Business Communication ("should take care to avoid exaggeration, colorful language, guesswork, legal conclusions and derogatory remarks or characterizations of people and other companies")

Organization Code

Marketers often join professional organizations for the purpose of associating with others who share similar interests. These organizations include industry associations, whose membership is mostly limited to those who work within a particular industry, and professional services associations, whose membership consists of those who share similar job responsibilities. Marketers joining these organizations often find that a code of ethics has been developed that is intended to be followed by all organization members. For example, the Canadian Marketing Association lays out rules for its membership, which includes marketers from many for-profits and not-for-profit organizations, in its *Code of Ethics and Standards and Practices*.(9) The Code discusses such issues as:

- Accuracy of Representation of Products ("must accurately and fairly describe the product or service offered")

- Support of Claims Made About Products ("must be able to substantiate the basis for any performance claim or comparison")

- Acceptability for Using the Word "Free" ("Products or services offered without cost or obligation")

- Guidelines for Advertising Which Compares One Product to Another ("must be factual, verifiable and not misleading")

The concern over ethical behavior in marketing is one that shows little sign of abating. Those involved in marketing should take the time to fully understand the ethical implication of their decisions.

Social Responsibility in Marketing

Most marketing organizations do not intentionally work in isolation from the rest of society. Instead they find greater opportunity exists if the organization is visibly accessible and involved with the public. As we've seen, because marketing often operates as the "public face" of an organization, when issues arise between the public and the organization marketing is often at the center. In recent years the number and variety of issues raised by the public has increased. One reason for the increase is the growing perception that marketing organizations are not just sellers of product but also have an inherent responsibility to be more socially responsible, including being more responsible for its actions and more responsive in addressing social concerns.

Being socially responsible means an organization shows concern for the people and environment in which it transacts business. It also means these values are communicated and enforced by everyone in the organization and, in some cases, with outside business partners, such as those who sell products to the company (e.g., supplier of raw material for product production) and those who help the company distribute and sell to other customers (e.g., retail stores).

In addition to ensuring these values exist within the organization and its business partners, social responsibility may also manifest itself in the support of social causes that help society. For instance, marketers may sponsor charity events or produce cause-related advertising.

Marketers who are pursuing a socially responsible agenda should bear in mind such efforts do not automatically translate into increased revenue or even an improved public image. However, organizations that consistently exhibit socially responsible tendencies may eventually gain a strong reputation that could pay dividends in the form of increased customer loyalty.

• •

Many companies have created corporate positions specifically to address corporate responsibility. At Brown Forman, maker of Jack Daniels Whiskey, this position is viewed as benefiting the company on many levels including enhancing promotional opportunities. (10)

• •

THE SUCCESSFUL MARKETER

As we've seen, marketing is a critical business function operating in an environment that is highly scrutinized and continually changing. Today's marketers undertake a variety of tasks as they attempt to build customer relationships and the knowledge and skill sets needed to perform these tasks successfully are also varied. As discussed in Box 1-3, to be successful requires today's marketers not only understand marketing basics but also possess many other skills.

Box 1-3

CHARACTERISTICS OF MODERN MARKETERS

So what does it take to be a successful marketer? Basic marketing knowledge is just the beginning, for today's marketers must possess much more. Among the most important knowledge and skills needed to be successful are:

Basic Business Skills
Marketers are first and foremost business people who must perform necessary tasks required of all successful business people. These basic skills include problem analysis and decision making, oral and written communication, basic quantitative skills, and the ability to work well with others.

Understanding Marketing's Impact
Marketers must know how their decisions will impact other areas of the company and other business partners. They must realize that marketing decisions are not made in isolation and that decisions made by the marketing team could lead to problems for others in the organization. For example, making a decision to run a special sale that significantly lowers the price of a product could present supply problems if the production area is not informed well in advance of the sale.

Technology Savvy
Today's marketers must have a strong understanding of technology on two fronts. First, marketers must be skilled in using technology as part of their everyday activities. Not only must they understand how basic computer software is used to build spreadsheets or create slide presentations, but in a world where information overload is a problem marketers must investigate additional technologies that can improve their effectiveness and efficiency, such as multifunction cellphones, GPS navigation services, and web-based productivity applications. Second, marketers must understand emerging technology and applications in order to spot potential business opportunities as well as potential threats. For instance, the rapid growth of search engines requires marketers to firmly understand how these fit within an overall marketing strategy.

The Need for a Global Perspective
Thanks in large part to the Internet, nearly any company can conduct business on a global scale. Yet, just having a website that is accessible to hundreds of millions of people worldwide does not guarantee success. Marketers selling internationally must understand the nuances of international trade and cultural differences that exist between markets.

Information Seeker
The field of marketing is dynamic. Changes occur continually and often quickly. Marketers must maintain close contact with these changes through a steady diet of information.

REFERENCES

1. Edward, C., "Microsoft's Billion-Dollar Fix," *Business Week*, July 6, 2007.

2. Gupta, S. and T.J. Steenburgh, "Allocating Marketing Resources," *Harvard Business School*, January 28, 2008.

3. "Splenda Settles Lawsuit Over Sugar Claim," *MSNBC*, May 11, 2007.

4. "Wal-Mart Takes Green Approach to Detergent," *MSNBC*, September 26, 2007.

5. *Google Analytics* website.

6. Puzzanghera, J., "Tough Cookies for Web Surfers' Trying to Protect Privacy," *Los Angeles Times*, April 19, 2008.

7. Story, L., "A Push to Limit the Tracking of Web Surfers' Clicks," *New York Times*, March 20, 2008.

8. *Yahoo! Investor Relations* website.

9. *Canadian Marketing Association* website.

10. Ryssdal, K., "Corporations Find Responsibility Sells," *Marketplace - American Public Radio*, December 11, 2007.

Full text of many of the references can be accessed via links on the support website.

Chapter 2:

Marketing Research

Many organizations find the markets they serve are dynamic with customers, competitors, and market conditions continually changing. And marketing efforts that work today cannot be relied upon to be successful in the future. Meeting changing conditions requires marketers have sufficient market knowledge in order to make the right adjustments to their marketing strategy. For marketers gaining knowledge is accomplished through marketing research.

In this chapter we look at the importance of research in marketing. We explore what marketing research is and see why it is considered the foundation of marketing. Our examination includes a detailed look at the key methods marketers use to gather relevant information. Finally, we look at the trends shaping marketing research.

THE FOUNDATION OF MARKETING

Research, in general, is the process of gathering information to learn about something that is not fully known. Nearly everyone engages in some form of research. From the highly trained geologist investigating newly discovered earthquake faults to the author of best selling spy novels seeking insight into new surveillance techniques, to the model train hobbyist spending hours hunting down the manufacturer of an old electric engine, each is driven by the quest for information.

For marketers, research is not only used for the purpose of learning, it is also a critical component needed to make good decisions. Marketing research does this by giving marketers a picture of what is occurring (or likely to occur) and, when done well, offers alternative choices that can be made. For instance, good research may suggest multiple options for introducing new products or entering new markets. In most cases marketing decisions prove less risky (though they are never risk free) when the marketer can select from more than one option.

Using an analogy of a house foundation, marketing research can be viewed as the **foundation of marketing**. Just as a well-built house requires a strong foundation to remain sturdy, marketing decisions need the support of research in order to be viewed favorably by customers and to stand up to competition and other external pressures. Consequently, all areas of marketing and all marketing decisions should be supported with some level of research.

While research is key to marketing decision making, it does not always need to be elaborate to be effective. Sometimes small efforts, such as doing a quick search on the Internet, will provide the needed information. However, for most marketers there are times when more elaborate research work is needed and understanding the right way to conduct research, whether performing the work themselves or hiring someone else to handle it, can increase the effectiveness of these projects.

• •

Marketing research is important for all types of businesses including not-for-profit organizations. For instance, major museums such as the Museum of Modern Art in New York and the Detroit Institute of Arts, have directed considerable resources to learning more about their customers. They view research as a critical part of their strategy to attract more customers. (1)

• •

Research in Marketing

As noted, marketing research is undertaken to support a wide variety of marketing decisions. Table 2-1 presents a small sampling of the research undertaken by marketing decision area. Many of the issues listed under *Types of Research* are discussed in greater detail in other parts of this book.

Table 2-1: Examples of Research in Marketing

Marketing Decision	Types of Research
Target Markets	sales, market size, demand for product, customer characteristics, purchase behavior, customer satisfaction, website traffic
Product	product development, package protection, packaging awareness, brand name selection, brand recognition, brand preference, product positioning
Distribution	distributor interest, assessing shipping options, online shopping, retail store site selection
Promotion	advertising recall, advertising copy testing, sales promotion response rates, sales force compensation, traffic studies (outdoor advertising), public relations media placement
Pricing	price elasticity analysis, optimal price setting, discount options
External Factors	competitive analysis, legal environment, social and cultural trends
Other	company image, test marketing

OPTIONS FOR GATHERING RESEARCH INFORMATION

Marketers engage in a wide range of research from simple methods done spur of the moment to extensive, highly developed research projects taking months or even years to complete. To gather research marketers have three choices:

1. Acquire pre-existing research

2. Undertake new research themselves

3. Out-source the task of new research to a third party, such as a marketing research company

The first option is associated with **secondary research**, which involves accessing information that was previously collected. The last two options are associated with **primary research**, which involves the collection of original data generally for one's own use. In many instances the researcher uses both secondary and primary data collection as part of the same research project. While both secondary and primary research have advantages and disadvantages, as discussed in Box 2-1, the value in using these is dependent on how the information is collected.

Box 2-1

RISK AND DOING RESEARCH RIGHT

Marketing research is a process that investigates both organizations and people. Of course, organizations are made up of people so when it comes down to it, marketing research is a branch of the social sciences. Social science studies people and their relationships and includes such areas as economics, sociology, and psychology. To gain understanding into their fields, researchers in the social sciences use scientific methods tested and refined over hundreds of years. Many of these methods require the institution of tight controls on research projects. For instance, many companies conduct surveys (i.e., by asking questions) of a small percentage of their customers (called a **sample**) to see how satisfied they are with the company's efforts. For the information obtained from a small group of customers to be useful when evaluating how all customers feel, certain controls must be in place including controls on who should be included in the sample. Also, for results to be truly relevant, research must stand up to scrutiny using **statistical analysis**.

Thus, doing research right means the necessary controls are in place to ensure it is done correctly and increase the chance the results are relevant. Relying on results of research conducted incorrectly to make decisions could prove problematic if not disastrous. Thousands of examples exist of firms using faulty research to make decisions, including many dot-com companies that failed between 1999 and 2002. (2)

But marketers must be aware following the right procedures to produce a relevant study does not ensure the results of research will be 100 percent correct as there is always the potential results are wrong. Because of the risks associated with research, marketers are cautioned not to use the results of marketing research as the only input in making marketing decisions. Rather, smart marketing decisions require considering many factors, including management's own judgment.

But being cautious with how research is used should not diminish the need to conduct research. While making decisions without research input may work sometimes, long-term success is not likely to happen without regular efforts to collect information.

Secondary Research

By far the most widely used method for collecting data is through secondary data collection, commonly called secondary research. This process involves collecting data from either the originator or a distributor of primary research (see *Primary Research* discussion below). In other words, accessing information already gathered.

In most cases this means finding information from third-party sources such as marketing research reports, company websites, magazine articles, and other sources. But in actuality any information previously gathered, whether from sources external to the marketer's organization or from internal sources, such as previously undertaken marketing research, old sales reports, accounting records, and many others, falls under the heading of secondary research.

ADVANTAGES AND DISADVANTAGES OF SECONDARY RESEARCH:

Secondary research offers advantages and disadvantages that include:

Advantages:

- Ease of Access – In years past accessing good secondary data required marketers visit libraries or wait until a report was shipped by mail. When online access initially became an option marketers needed training to learn different rules and procedures for accessing each data source. However, the Internet has changed how secondary research is accessed by offering convenience (e.g., on-line access from many locations) and generally standardized usage methods for all data sources.

- Low Cost to Acquire – Researchers are often attracted to secondary data because getting this information is much less expensive than if the researchers had to carry out the research themselves.

- May Help Clarify Research Question – Secondary research is often used prior to larger scale primary research to help clarify what is to be learned. For instance, a researcher doing competitor analysis, but who is not familiar with competitors in a market, could access secondary sources to locate a list of potential competitors and use this information as part of his/her own primary research study.

- May Answer Research Question – As noted, secondary data collection is often used to help set the stage for primary research. In the course of doing so researchers may find the exact information they are looking for is available via secondary sources, thus eliminating the need and expense of carrying out primary research.

- <u>May Show Difficulties in Conducting Primary Research</u> – The originators of secondary research often provide details on how the information was collected. This may include discussion of difficulties encountered. For instance, a research report written by a large marketing research company reveals a high percentage of people declined to take part in the research. After obtaining this study, a marketer contemplating doing a similar study may decide it is not worth the effort given the potential difficulties in conducting the research.

Disadvantages:

- <u>Quality of Researcher</u> – As we will discuss, research conducted using primary methods is largely controlled by the marketer. However, this is not the case when it comes to data collected by others. The quality of secondary research should be scrutinized closely since the origins of the information may be questionable. Organizations relying on secondary data as an important component in their decision making must take care to critically evaluate how the information was gathered, analyzed, and presented to ensure the research was done correctly and is relevant (see Box 2-1).

- <u>Not Specific to Researcher's Needs</u> – Secondary data is often not presented in a form that exactly meets the marketer's needs. For example, a marketer obtains an expensive research report examining how different age groups feel about certain products within the marketer's industry. Unfortunately, the marketer may be disappointed to discover the way the research divides age groups (e.g., under 13, 14-18, 19-25, etc.) does not match how the marketer's company designates its age groups (e.g., under 16, 17-21, 22-30, etc). Because of this difference the results may not be useful.

- <u>Inefficient Spending for Information</u> – If the research received is not be specific to the marketer's needs, an argument can be made that research spending is inefficient. That is, the marketer may not receive a satisfactory amount of information for what is spent.

- <u>Incomplete Information</u> – Many times a researcher finds research that appears promising is in fact a "teaser" released by the research supplier. This may occur when a small portion of a study is disclosed, often for free, but the full report, which is often expensive, is needed to gain the full value of the study.

- <u>Not Timely</u> – Caution must be exercised in relying on secondary data collected well in the past. Out-of-date information generally offers little value especially for companies competing in fast changing markets.

- <u>Not Proprietary Information</u> – In most cases secondary research is not undertaken specifically for one company. Instead it is made available to many either for free or for a fee. Consequently, there is rarely an information advantage gained by those who obtain the research.

······································

It is common for companies selling online to refer to secondary research to gain insight into website traffic. Yet, online measurement is often viewed as more of an art than a science as evidenced by web research provider comScore which apparently provided estimates on Google traffic that was far different than what the search giant reported. The contradiction in numbers resulted in a major hit to comScore's stock price and raised questions concerning the validity of its methods. (3)

······································

Types of Low-Cost Secondary Research

Many marketers mistakenly believe marketing research is something that is far too expensive to do on their own. While this is true for some marketing decisions, not all marketing research must be expensive to be useful. There are secondary research sources that are easily obtainable and relatively low cost and often free. (4) These include:

TRADE ASSOCIATIONS

Trade associations are generally membership-supported organizations whose mission is to offer assistance and represent the interests of those operating in a specific industry. One of the many tasks performed by trade associations is to provide research information and industry metrics through efforts such as conducting member surveys. Accessing this information may be as simple as visiting a trade association's website, although some associations limit access to the best research to members only, in which case joining the association (if they permit) may include paying dues.

······································

An example of a trade association undertaking research can be found with the Color Marketing Group which produces research forecasting color trends, often years in advance. Members of the association then have time to plan for adjusting the colors used in their products, packaging, and promotional material. (5)

······································

GOVERNMENT SOURCES

Many national, regional and local governments offer a full range of helpful materials including information on consumers, domestic businesses, and international markets. For those operating in the United States, information available through the U.S. Government is staggering. The U.S. Government is a behemoth with agencies and offices found in more nooks and crannies than one could ever imagine and the uninitiated can spend hours on end trying to find relevant information. But once found and digested the reports are often very good.

COMPANY PROVIDED INFORMATION

If the need is for information on a specific company, and if research seekers are willing to believe what a company provides in its own literature, then value may be found in company provided information. While many materials published by organizations are promotional pieces (see *Research as Promotional Tool* discussion below), there may be good information found amongst the hype.

Options for finding information include company websites, annual reports, press releases, white papers, and presentations.

NEWS AND MEDIA SOURCES

Possibly the most widely used method for acquiring secondary research is through articles and other reports found through commercial news sources. Options include magazines, newspapers, television news, and other video/audio programming. Nearly all of these sources are available online.

ACADEMIC RESEARCH

College professors often cite industry research as part of their own scholarly efforts and they conduct their own research studies. Many of these academic works can be found in academic journals and within research centers established by many universities. The websites of these centers frequently post articles and working papers containing market data, most of which are freely accessible. An Internet search using the keywords "research center" along with industry or product keywords may yield a list.

CAUSE-RELATED GROUPS

Many non-profit groups have an organizational mission directed at supporting causes they feel are not well-supported in society. Examples include groups focusing on the environment, education, and health care. As would be expected a considerable portion of their focus looks at how business impacts these issues. Research seekers will find the best funded of these groups carry out an active marketing research agenda with many of their studies freely available on their websites.

Types of High-Cost Secondary Research

While research seekers can get lucky finding information through inexpensive means, the realty is that, in many situations, locating in-depth market information is difficult and expensive. Companies in the business of producing market studies are mostly doing so to make money and do not give the information away for free. Consequently, in many research situations, especially those in which reliable market numbers and estimates are critical, acquiring the best researched market information requires a fee.

Expensive sources of information generally include accessing reports from the originators of the research such as marketing research firms. However, since gaining access to good research can be costly, on the surface it may not seem practical for small companies or individuals to take advantage of these sources. Yet, research seekers also know that the level of detail available in a single report may be enough to provide answers to most of their questions in which case these reports can be real time savers (though marketers are cautioned against relying on a single source of information in making marketing decisions).

Also, while the cost of reports can appear prohibitive, today's reports are much more accessible than in the past when research suppliers required clients to sign up for high-priced subscription services. Purchasing a subscription would then give the client access to a large number of reports. Today many information sources permit the purchase of single research reports without the requirement to commit to a subscription.

It should be noted that some of these sources may make a limited amount of material available for free so it is worth a look no matter how much money the research seeker has to spend.

High-cost marketing research sources include (6):

MARKETING RESEARCH COMPANIES

Many companies engaged in marketing research services offer both customized research activities (i.e., produce work only for a specific client) and commercial research (i.e., produce work that nearly anyone can buy). Commercial reports produced by reputable firms are generally well researched and contain extensive product/industry metrics and statistics, including forecasts and trend analysis. Often these reports are generated by a specific researcher who has been following the market/industry for many years and produces regular updates which include offering comments and insight that go beyond the numbers. But these reports come with a high price tag. It is not uncommon to pay a large sum for a report that is only a hundred or so pages long. However, many research reports are updates of existing reports and the older reports may be available for lower cost.

FINANCIAL SERVICES COMPANIES

Financial institutions, such as brokerage firms and other financial consulting firms, are also in the business of producing original research. Financial firms assist investors by offering research reports presenting the financial firm's analysis of an industry or company including providing market metrics. While such reports may be free to a broker's clients, many reports can also be purchased by non-clients through financial portal websites.

CONSULTING FIRMS

Consulting firms consist of individuals specializing in particular business areas, such as by job function (e.g., sales training), business need (e.g., strategy development) or industry (e.g., transportation). In addition to working for individual clients, consulting firms also produce reports covering their specialties that are made available to the general public. By and large the bigger the consulting firm the more valid and reliable are the reports they produce. One group of companies to consider as a starting point is large accounting firms. Nearly all the major accounting firms now have divisions focused on management consulting. These divisions regularly make available industry reports.

MARKET INFORMATION DEALERS

The marketing research business consists of a large number of suppliers who make available many products (i.e., research studies and other documents) targeted at many buyers. To get research into the hands of buyers, the creators of the research can attempt to sell the reports themselves or they can enlist the services of companies serving an intermediary role (i.e., bring buyers and sellers together). For their services these dealers receive a percentage of the sale price.

For research seekers these dealers offer several advantages. First, they generally carry reports from many different suppliers increasing the likelihood of finding a report that meets the researcher's needs. Second, they allow for the purchase of individual reports and, in some cases, pieces of reports offered at lower cost, whereas marketing research creators often require clients to purchase a full report at full price. Third, they offer excellent search functionality making it easy to locate reports.

COMPREHENSIVE INFORMATION SOURCES

Marketers searching for extensive information or those who frequently need to locate market information may consider establishing an account with one of the major comprehensive information sources. These are the heavyweight sources of business research used by university libraries and major corporations.

Comprehensive sources offer one-stop shopping for research reports, industry news, and even government information. In fact, much of the information available from sources already mentioned is also available through comprehensive information sources. However, gaining access to these services can be prohibitively expensive. Fortunately, several comprehensive information sources are now offering pay-per-item access.

Primary Research

When marketers conduct research to collect original data for their own needs it is called primary research. This process has the marketer or someone working for the marketer designing and then carrying out a research plan. Primary research is often undertaken after the researcher has gained some insight into the issue by collecting secondary data.

While not as frequently used as secondary research, primary research still represents a significant part of overall marketing research. For many organizations, especially large firms, spending on primary research far exceeds spending on secondary research.

The primary research market consists of marketers carrying out their own research and an extensive group of companies offering their services to marketers. These companies include:

♦ Full-Service Marketing Research Firms – These companies develop and carryout the full research plan for their clients.

♦ Partial-Service Research Firms – These companies offer expertise addressing a specific part of the research plan, such as developing methods to collect data (e.g., design surveys), locating research participants or undertaking data analysis.

♦ Research Tools Suppliers – These firms provide tools used by researchers and include data collection tools (e.g., online surveys), data analysis software, and report presentation products.

Advantages and Disadvantages of Primary Research:

Primary data collection offers advantages and disadvantages that include:

Advantages:

• Addresses Specific Research Issues – Carrying out its own research allows the marketing organization to address issues specific to its own situation. Primary research is designed to collect the information the marketer wants to know and report it in ways benefiting the marketer. For example, while information reported with secondary research may not fit the marketer's needs, no such problem exists with primary research since the marketer controls the research design.

• Greater Control – Primary research enables the marketer to focus on specific issues and have a higher level of control over how the information is collected. In this way the marketer can decide such issues as size of project (e.g., how many responses), location of research (e.g., geographic area), and time frame for completing the project.

• Efficient Spending for Information – Unlike secondary research where the marketer may spend for information that is not needed, primary data collection focuses on issues specific to the researcher improving the chances research funds will be spent efficiently.

• Proprietary Information – Information collected by the marketer using primary research is its own and is generally not shared with others. Thus, information can be kept hidden from competitors and potentially offer an **information advantage** to the company that undertook the primary research.

Disadvantages:

- <u>Cost</u> – Compared to secondary research, primary data may be very expensive since there is a great deal of marketer involvement and the cost of carrying out research can be high.

- <u>Time Consuming</u> – To be done correctly, primary data collection requires the development and execution of a research plan. Going from the starting point of deciding to undertake a research project to the end point of having results is often much longer than the time it takes to acquire secondary data.

- <u>Not Always Feasible</u> – Some research projects, while potentially offering information that could prove quite valuable, are not within the reach of a marketer. Many are just too large to be carried out by all but the largest companies and some are not feasible at all. For instance, it would not be practical for McDonalds to attempt to interview every customer who visits its stores on a certain day since doing so would require hiring a huge number of researchers, an unrealistic expense. Fortunately, there are ways for McDonalds to use other methods (e.g., sampling) to meet its needs without talking to all customers.

TYPES OF PRIMARY RESEARCH

In general there are two basic types of primary research – quantitative data collection and qualitative data collection.

Quantitative Data Collection

Quantitative data collection involves the use of numbers to assess information. This information can then be evaluated using statistical analysis which offers researchers the opportunity to dig deeper into the data and look for greater meaning (see Box 2-2). Quantitative data collection comes in many forms but the most popular forms are:

- <u>Surveys</u> – This method captures information through the input of responses to a research instrument such as a questionnaire. Information can be input either by the respondents themselves (e.g., complete online survey) or the researcher can input the data (e.g. phone survey, shopping mall intercept). The main methods for distributing surveys are via postal and electronic mail, phone, website, and in-person. However, newer technologies are creating additional delivery options including through wireless devices such as smart phones.

- Tracking – With tracking research marketers monitor the behavior of customers as they engage in regular purchase or information gathering activities. Possibly the most well-known example of tracking research is used by websites as they track customer visits (see Box 1-2 in Chapter 1). But tracking research also has offline applications, especially when point-of-purchase scanners are employed such as tracking product purchases at grocery stores and automated collections on toll roads. This method of research is expected to grow significantly as more devices are introduced with tracking capability.

Box 2-2

RESEARCH BY THE NUMBERS

Primary research is collected using a **research instrument** designed to record information for later analysis. Marketing researchers use many types of instruments from basic methods that record participant responses to a survey on a piece of paper to highly advanced electronic measurement that has those participating in research hooked up to sophisticated equipment. Depending on the type of research instrument used, the researcher may be able to evaluate the results by turning responses into numbers which then allows for analysis using statistical methods (see Box 2-1).

Of course, certain information is by nature numerical. For example, asking a person their actual age or weight will result in a number. But under the right circumstances numbers can also be used to represent certain characteristics which are not on the surface considered numerical. This most often occurs with data collected within a structured and well-controlled scientific **research design**. For instance, a company researching its customers' attitudes toward products they purchased may ask a large number of customers to complete a survey. Contained in the survey is the following:

Place an "X" on the line that best indicates your impression of the overall quality of our company's products:

Poor __ __ __ __ __ __ __ *Excellent*

In this example each line, which represents a potential customer response, could be assigned a number. For example, checking the left-most line could result in the researcher entering a "1", the next line a "2", the next line a "3", and so on.

Once research is gathered for all customers completing the survey, the information for this item can then undergo statistical analysis and interesting comparisons can be made. For example, different types of customers (e.g., female vs. male, age groups, etc.) can be compared on their mean or average score for this item. Statistical analysis can then be used to determine if a difference exists.

- <u>Experiments</u> – Marketers often undertake experiments to gauge how the manipulation of one marketing variable affects another (i.e., **causal research**). The use of experiments has applications for many marketing decision areas including product testing, advertising design, setting price points, and creating packaging. (7) Unfortunately, performing highly controlled experiments can be quite costly. Some researchers have found the use of computer simulations can work nearly as well as experiments and may be less expensive, though the number of simulation applications for marketing decisions is still fairly limited.

· ·

Disney is building an experimental research laboratory to test advertising effectiveness. At the research facility subjects will be hooked up to biometric devices that, among other things, will measure heart rate and visual response to ads shown on various media outlets such as Internet, cellphone, and television. (8)

· ·

Qualitative Data Collection

Sometimes referred to as "touchy-feely" research, qualitative data collection requires researchers to interpret the information gathered, most often without the benefit of statistical support. If the researcher is well trained in interpreting respondents' comments and activities, this form of research can offer very good information. However, this data collection method may not hold the same level of relevancy as quantitative research due to the lack of scientific controls. An additional drawback of qualitative research is that it can be time consuming and expensive and only a very small portion of the marketer's desired market can participate in qualitative research. Due to the lack of strong controls in the research design using results to estimate characteristics of a larger group is more difficult.

Qualitative data collection options include:

- <u>Individual Interviews</u> – Talking to someone one-on-one allows a researcher to cover more ground than may be covered if a respondent was completing a survey. The researcher can dig deeper into a respondent's comments to find out additional details that might not emerge from initial responses. Unfortunately, individual interviewing can be quite expensive and may be intimidating to some who are not comfortable sharing details with a researcher.

- <u>Focus Groups</u> – To overcome the drawbacks associated with individual interviews, marketers can turn to focus groups. Under this research format, a group of respondents (generally numbering 8-12) are guided through discussion by a moderator. The power of focus groups as a research tool rests with the environment created by the interaction of the participants. In well run sessions, members of the group are stimulated to respond by the comments and the support of others in the group. In this way, the depth of information offered by a respondent may be much greater than that obtained through individual interviews. However, focus groups can be costly to conduct especially if participants must be paid. To help reduce costs, online options for focus groups have emerged. While there are many positive aspects to online focus groups, the fact that respondents are not physically present diminishes the benefits gained by group dynamics. However, as technology improves, in particular video conferencing, the online focus group could become a major research option.

· ·

An off-shoot of focus groups that companies, such as Del Monte Foods and Coca-Cola, are exploring as a research tool is the use of online social networks. Unlike public social networks, such by MySpace and Facebook, these private networks are organized by the companies and are populated with invited customers who assist companies by providing feedback on products. (9)

· ·

- <u>Observational Research</u> – Watching customers as they perform activities can be a very useful research method, especially when customers are observed in a natural setting (e.g., shopping in a retail store, using products at home). In fact, an emerging research technique called **ethnographic research** has researchers following customers as they shop, work, and relax at home in order to see how they make decisions, use products, and more.

TRENDS IN MARKETING RESEARCH

In recent years the evolution of marketing research has been dramatic with marketers getting access to a wide variety of tools and techniques to improve their hunt for information. Below we discuss a few important trends shaping the marketing research field:

GAINING AN INFORMATION ADVANTAGE

In its role as the foundation of marketing, marketing research is arguably the key ingredient in making marketing decisions and a critical factor in gaining advantage over competitors. Because organizations recognize the power information has in helping create and maintain customer relationships, there is an insatiable appetite to gain even more insight into customers and markets. Marketers in nearly all industries are expected to direct more resources to gathering and analyzing information especially in highly competitive markets. Many of the trends discussed below are directly related to marketers' quest to acquire large amounts of customer, competitor, and market information.

INTERNET TECHNOLOGIES

To address the need for more information, marketing companies are developing new methods for collecting data. This has led to the introduction of several new technologies to assist in the information gathering process. Many of these developments are Internet-based technologies including:

- Enhanced Tracking – As we mentioned in Chapter 1, the Internet offers an unparalleled ability to track and monitor customers. Each time a visitor accesses a website they provide marketers with extensive information including how they arrived at the website and what they did on the website. As tracking software becomes more sophisticated the use of tracking data will be a routinely used research tool.

- Improved Communication – The Internet offers a significant improvement in customer-to-company communication which is vital for marketing research. For instance, the ability to encourage customers to offer feedback on the company's products and services is easy using website popup notices and email reminders.

- Research Tools – A large number of Internet services have added options for conducting research. These include the ubiquitous search engines, tools for conducting online surveys, and access to large databases containing previous research studies (i.e., secondary research).

OTHER TECHNOLOGIES

In addition to the Internet, marketing research has benefited from other technological improvements including:

- Global Positioning Systems (GPS) – GPS enables marketers to track inventory and even track mobile sales and service personnel. Soon GPS will be a common feature of customers' communication devices, such as cellphones, offering marketers the potential to locate and track customers.

- <u>Virtual Reality and Simulations</u> – Marketers can use computer-developed virtual worlds to simulate real-world customer activity such as store shopping. While this type of research is mostly performed in a controlled laboratory setting, there are emerging virtual worlds on the Internet (e.g., Second Life) where marketers can test concepts and communicate with customers.

- <u>Data Analysis Software</u> – Research includes gathering information and it also involves analyzing what is collected. A number of software and statistical programs have been refined to give marketers greater insight into what the data really means.

- <u>Neuro-Research</u> – Companies have begun to explore the use of brain-imaging technology for marketing research. With this technique marketing researchers scan the brains of research subjects as they are exposed to neuro-stimuli, such as imagery and sound, in order to detect the effect the stimuli. (10)

AFFORDABLE RESEARCH

For many years formal research projects were considered something only the largest marketers could afford due to the expense. However, the technologies discussed above make it affordable for companies of all sizes to engage in research. For instance, surveying customers is quick and easy using one of the many online survey services which charge low fees to create, distribute, and analyze results.

MERGING OF DATA SOURCES

The wide range of technologies used to gather data has led to the creation of data centers where information is stored. Today many of these data centers are sharing information with other centers in a manner that offers the marketer a fuller picture of its customers. As we will discuss in Chapter 3, many companies have multiple contact points where customers can interact with the company (e.g., in-person, on the web, via phone call). In the past the information gathered at these points was often stored separately. Companies now see the value in knowing what customers do across all contact points and work to integrate customer information.

Additionally, some marketers go outside their own data collection and seek information on their customers from other sources, such as information provided by credit card companies. This information is then merged with the company owned information to get a fuller picture of customer activity.

PRIVACY CONCERNS

As we discussed in Chapter 1, the continual demand for customer information, along with advances in technology and the merging of information sources, has led marketing organizations to gather information in ways that raise concerns among privacy advocates and government regulators. (11) Many customers are unaware of the amount and nature of the data marketers collect. As new information gathering techniques and technologies emerge customer response to issues of privacy may determine whether these methods are feasible or forbidden.

USER COOPERATION AT ISSUE

The growing concern with privacy is leading many customers to limit their participation in a company's research activities. This includes customers choosing not to respond to company requests to take part in research studies. Customers are also becoming more aware of how their Internet activities are tracked and are responding by using techniques to restrict marketers tracking efforts. For example, marketers can place small data files called **cookies** on customers' computers and then use this to track user activity. Many customers are learning to disable cookies and, in doing so limit the marketer's ability to track customer activity.

RESEARCH AS A PROMOTIONAL TOOL

While most people do not equate marketing research with promotion, many companies are discovering research can also function as a major promotional tool. The practice of distributing company-produced research reports to potential customers and the news media has been used for a number of years in scientific and technology industries. In recent years the practice has expanded into many other fields, particularly among firms involved in consulting, healthcare, and financial industries. Such reports often provide readers with information related to product features and benefits, comparisons with competitor's offerings, and target market perceptions. These reports are produced using high quality graphs and charts backed up by carefully created narratives that proudly emphasize the company's strengths.

Unfortunately, many research reports produced for promotional reasons are not scientific; therefore, these may not carry much value. While many companies claim the research supports their products, many of these claims may, in fact, be more fluff than substance since they are not grounded in good research methods.

REFERENCES

1. Vogel, C., "Museums Refine the Art of Listening," *New York Times,* March 12, 2008.

2. For a list of dot-com failures including screen-shots see *The Museum of I-Failure* website.

3. Stelter, B., "Web Metrics and Grains of Salt," *New York Times*, April 21, 2008.

4. For an extensive list of links to low-cost secondary research websites see the **Market Research** section of *KnowThis.com*.

5. "Social Trends Color Shade-Forecasting," *MSNBC,* Aug. 30, 2007.

6. For an extensive list of links to high-cost secondary research websites see the **Market Research** section of *KnowThis.com*.

7. For an interesting look at experiments undertaken in online markets see *MarketingExperiments.com* website.

8. Nakashima, R., "Disney to Create Lab to Test Ads for ABC, ESPN," *USA Today*, May 12, 2008.

9. Steel, E., "The New Focus Groups: Online Networks," *Wall Street Journal,* January 14, 2008.

10. Baker, S., "What You Really Want to Buy," *BusinessWeek*, January 28, 2008.

11. Tessler, J., "Lawmakers Demand Info on Web Tracking Practices," *Yahoo Finance*, August 1, 2008.

Full text of many of the references can be accessed via links on the support website.

Chapter 3:

Managing Customers

In Chapter 1 we noted marketers make decisions which result in value to both the marketer and its customers. Throughout this book we emphasize the importance customers play in helping marketers meet their business objectives. To drive home this point, in Chapter 3 we concentrate our discussion on understanding customers and examining their role in the marketing process. We show that for most organizations understanding customers is necessary not only because of its effect on marketing decisions but because customers' activities influence the entire organization.

In this chapter we explore the techniques marketers use to manage customers. We begin by defining what a customer is and why they are important to an organization. We then look at what tools and strategies must be in place to skillfully manage customers, including the crucial requirement that marketers work hard to build relationships with their customers. Finally, we conclude with a discussion of how servicing customers after the sale is often just as critical as pre-sale marketing efforts.

WHAT IS A CUSTOMER?

In general terms, a customer is a person or organization that a marketer believes will benefit from the goods and services offered by the marketer's organization. As this definition suggests, a customer is not necessarily someone who is currently purchasing from the marketer. In fact, customers may fall into one of three customer groups:

EXISTING CUSTOMERS

The first group consists of customers who have purchased or otherwise used an organization's goods or services, typically within a designated period of time. For some organizations the timeframe may be short, for instance, a coffee shop may only consider someone to be an existing customer if they have purchased within the last three months. Other organizations may view someone as an existing customer even though they have not purchased in the last few years (e.g., television set manufacturer).

Existing customers are by far the most important of the three customer groups since they have a current relationship with a company and, consequently, they give a company a reason to remain in contact with them. Additionally, existing customers also represent the best market for future sales, especially if they are satisfied with the relationship they presently have with the marketer. Getting these existing customers to purchase more is significantly less expensive and time consuming than finding new customers mainly because they know and hopefully trust the marketer and, if managed correctly, are easy to reach with promotional appeals (e.g., emailing a special discount offer for a new product). Yet as discussed in Box 3-1, not all existing customers should be treated the same as some offer more value to the marketer than others.

FORMER CUSTOMERS

This group consists of those who have formerly had relations with the marketing organization typically through a previous purchase. However, the marketer no longer feels the customer is an existing customer either because they have not purchased from the marketer within a certain timeframe or through other indications (e.g., a former customer just purchased a similar product from the marketer's competitor). The value of this group to a marketer will depend on whether the customer's previous relationship was considered satisfactory to the customer or the marketer. For instance, a former customer who felt she was not treated well by the marketer will be more difficult to persuade to buy again compared to a former customer who liked the marketer but decided to buy from someone else who had a similar product that was priced lower.

Box 3-1

THE "GOOD" CUSTOMER

For marketers simply finding customers who are willing to purchase their goods or services is not enough to build a successful marketing strategy. Instead, as we note in our definition of marketing in Chapter 1, marketers should look to manage customers in a way that will "identify, create, and maintain satisfying relationships with customers." By using marketing efforts that are designed to "maintain satisfying relationships" rather than simply pursuing a quick sale, the likelihood increases that customers will be more trusting of the marketer and exhibit a higher level of satisfaction with the organization. In turn satisfied customers are more likely to become "good" customers.

For our purposes we define a "good" customer as one who holds the potential to undertake activities offering long-term value to an organization. The activities performed by "good" customers not only include purchasing products, these also include such things as:

- offering a higher level of profitability since they buy more while costing proportionally less to satisfy
- making prompt payment
- offering insight and feedback that help create new products and improve services
- voluntarily promoting the company's products to others

These activities, along with many others, represent the value (i.e., benefits for costs spent) an organization receives from its customers. In the case of "good" customers their potential for providing value should be a signal for marketers to direct additional marketing efforts in building, strengthening, and sustaining a relationship with these customers.

The fact that we place the descriptive term "good" in front of customers should not be taken lightly. Not all existing customers who currently have relationships with an organization should be treated on an equal level. Some consistently spend large sums to purchase products from an organization; others do not spend large sums but hold the potential to do so; and still others use up a large amount of an organization's resources but contribute little revenue. Clearly there are lines of demarcation between those in the existing customer category. For marketers, identifying the line that separates "good" customers from others is critical for marketing success. And in some cases, that line may result in the marketer "firing" a customer who is not considered to be offering the value sought by the marketer. (1)

POTENTIAL CUSTOMERS

The third category of customers includes those who have yet to purchase but possess what the marketer believes are the requirements to eventually become customers. As we will see in Chapter 5, the requirements to become a potential customer include such issues as having a need for a product, possessing the financial means to buy, and having the authority to make a buying decision.

Locating potential customers is an ongoing process for two reasons. First, existing customers may become former customers (e.g., decide to buy from a competitor) and must be replaced by new customers. Second, while we noted above that existing customers are the best source for future sales, it is new customers that are needed in order for a business to significantly expand. For example, a company selling only in its own country may see less room for sales growth if a high percentage of people in the country are already existing customers. In order to realize stronger growth the company may seek to sell their products in other countries where the percentage of potential customers may be quite high.

CUSTOMERS AND THE ORGANIZATION

For most organizations understanding customers is the key to success while not understanding them is likely to result in failure. It is so important that the constant drive to satisfy customers is not only a concern for those responsible for carrying out marketing tasks, it is a concern of everyone in the entire organization.

Whether someone's job involves direct contact with customers (e.g., salespeople, delivery drivers, telephone customer service representatives) or indirect contact (e.g., production, accounting), all members of an organization must appreciate the role customers play in helping the organization meets its goals. To ensure everyone understands the customer's role, many organizations continually preach a "customer is most important" message in department meetings, organizational communication (e.g., internal emails, website postings), and corporate training programs. To drive home the importance of customers, the message often contains examples of how customers impact the company. These examples include:

SOURCE OF INFORMATION AND IDEAS

Satisfying the needs of customers requires organizations maintain close contact with them. Marketers can get close to customers by conducting marketing research, such as surveys and other feedback methods (e.g., website comment forms), that encourage customers to share their thoughts and feelings. With this information marketers are able to learn what people think of their present marketing efforts and receive suggestions for making improvements. For instance, research and feedback methods can offer marketers insight into new products and services sought by their customers.

• •

When Starbucks launched a new website encouraging customers to offer their opinions of how the company can be improved, thousands of customers contributed within just a few days. The website allows customers to contribute their own ideas and vote on ideas made by others. The website also shows what ideas have been used by Starbucks. (2)

• •

AFFECTS ACTIVITIES THROUGHOUT THE ORGANIZATION

For most organizations customers not only affect decisions made by the marketing team but they are the key driver for decisions made throughout the organization. For example, customers' reaction to the design of a product may influence the type of raw materials used in the product manufacturing process. With customers impacting such a significant portion of a company, creating an environment geared to locating, understanding, and satisfying customers is imperative.

NEEDED TO SUSTAIN THE ORGANIZATION

Finally, customers are the reason an organization is in business. Without customers or the potential to attract customers, a company is not viable. Consequently, customers are not only key to revenue and profits they are also crucial to creating and maintaining jobs within the organization.

CHALLENGE OF MANAGING CUSTOMERS

While on the surface the process for managing customers may seem to be intuitive and straightforward, in reality organizations struggle to accomplish this. The challenges marketers face when it comes to managing customers include:

CUSTOMERS ARE DIFFERENT

One reason managing customers is hard is because no two customers are the same. What is appealing to one customer may not necessarily work for another. For instance, a marketer may change how it issues coupons to customers by reducing the frequency of issuing coupons by regular mail and instead directing customers to electronic coupons found on its website. The marketer makes this move to encourage customers to visit the website more often with the hope it will lead to cost savings (e.g., sending out traditional coupons by mail requires postage expense), allow the marketer to acquire more customer information (e.g., monitor their activities when they visit the website), and give the marketer the opportunity to sell more product to the customer (e.g., special promotional messages on the website). However, some long-time customers may feel electronic coupons require they do more work to acquire compared to coupons delivered through regular mail. In this example the introduction of a new feature may satisfy some customers while irritating others.

CUSTOMERS INTERACT AT DIFFERENT CONTACT POINTS

Another problem is that customers may interact with organizations at different contact points. A contact point is the method a customer uses to communicate with a company. For instance, consider the different ways customers interact with an organization:

- In-Person – Customers seek in-person assistance for their needs by visiting retail stores and other outlets, and also through discussion with company salespeople who visit customers at their place of business or in their homes.

- Telephone – Customers seeking to make purchases or have a problem solved may find it more convenient to do so through phone contact. In many companies a dedicated department, called a **call center**, handles all incoming customer inquiries.

  •

  Not all companies make it easy to contact them via telephone. In fact, online shoppers at the world's largest retailer, Wal-Mart, will not find phone contact information. Instead they must contact the company by Internet methods such as filling out a form or sending an email. (3)

  •

- Internet – The fastest growing contact point is through the Internet. The use of the Internet for purchasing (called **electronic commerce**) has exploded and is now the leading method for purchasing certain types of products including music. The Internet has also become the primary area many customers look to for help with their purchases.

- <u>Kiosks</u> – A kiosk is a standalone, interactive computer, often equipped with a touch-screen, offering customers several service options including product information, ability to make a purchase, and review of a customer's account. Kiosks are now widely used for airline check-in, banking, and, most recently, within grocery stores. (4)

- <u>In-Person Product Support</u> – Some in-person assistance is not principally intended to assist with selling but is designed to offer support once a purchase is made. Such services are handled by delivery people and service/repair technicians.

- <u>Financial Assistance</u> – Customer contact may also occur through company personnel who assist customers with financial issues. For instance, credit personnel help customers arrange the necessary funds to make a purchase while personnel in accounts receivable work with customers who are experiencing payment problems.

The challenge of ensuring customers are handled properly no matter the contact point they use is daunting for many companies. For some organizations the customer contact points cited above operate independently of others. For instance, retail stores may not be directly connected to telephone customer service. The result is that for different contact points many companies have developed different procedures and techniques for handling customers. And, for some firms, there exists little integration between contact points so customers communicating through one point one day and another point the next day may receive conflicting information. In such cases customers are likely to become frustrated and question the company's ability to provide adequate service.

Customer Relationship Management

In order to overcome the challenges faced as they attempt to cultivate and manage customers, many marketers must continually conduct marketing research to evaluate customers to determine what they want. And uncovering what customers want is made significantly easier if a company establishes methods designed to manage its customers. The most widely adopted method for managing customers is a business concept known as Customer Relationship Management (CRM). CRM is a strategic approach whose goal is to get everyone in an organization, not just the marketer, to recognize the importance of customers. Under CRM the key driver for marketing success is to treat "good" customers in a way that will increase the probability they will stay "good" customers. This is accomplished in part by ensuring a customer receives accurate information and has a consistent and satisfying experience every time he/she interacts with a company.

While CRM is generally used to manage existing customers, it also has application for other customer groups. For instance, CRM is used to help identify former customers that may hold potential to buy again. This is often possible due to the amount of information obtained and subsequently retained within a CRM system when former customers were considered existing customers. Additionally, CRM can serve an integral role in helping locate potential customers. As we will explore in Chapter 5, one method for locating potential customers is to use information contained in CRM to determine important characteristics exhibited by existing customers and use this information to pursue new customers in untapped customer markets who possess similar characteristics.

Computer technology plays a key part in carrying out CRM. A proper technology-based system is needed so that nearly anyone in an organization that comes into contact with a customer (e.g., sales force, service force, customer service representatives, accounts receivable, etc.) has access to necessary information and is well prepared to deal with the customer. For large firms with many employees, this requires the purchase of expensive CRM software along with the necessary hardware to implement CRM throughout the company. For smaller firms with only a few employees, a more cost-effective way to implement CRM is to use Internet-based services that charge monthly fees to access the technology. (5)

While the benefits of CRM are easy to appreciate, the actual execution presents many challenges. As discussed in Box 3-2, the combination of adapting to a new customer management philosophy as well as learning new technologies has presented significant obstacles for organizations implementing CRM.

CUSTOMER SERVICE AND MARKETING

As we have noted, to effectively manage customers marketers must be concerned with the entire experience a customer has with a company. While much of the value sought by customers is obtained directly from the consumption or use of goods or services they purchase (i.e., benefits from using the product), customers' satisfaction is not limited only to benefits from the actual product. Instead customers are affected by the entire purchasing experience, which is a mix of product and **non-product benefits**.

Box 3-2

CRM IS NOT ALWAYS EASY

While maintaining close and consistent relationships with customers through all contact points makes good business sense, accomplishing this has often been a challenge. Numerous problems, from technology failures and lack of communication between contact points as well as lack of adequate employee training or outright employee resistance, have derailed many CRM efforts.

For example, as we will see in Chapter 16, salespeople have been very reluctant to accept CRM since a key requirement of CRM is for members of the organization to share what they know about their customers. But for those involved in selling, what they know about their customers is often a critical component of what makes them successful. And, in organizations where salespeople compete against each other for clients, withholding valuable client information could offer an advantage to the salesperson who possesses it. Of course, this type of situation puts the company at a disadvantage if others in the company also deal with the customer, which is likely to occur especially if the salesperson leaves the company.

Though CRM is now widely adopted and is becoming an essential tool for a large number of business organizations, it still has a long way to go before it is ingrained as an essential business function within most organizations. In fact, many experts feel that a large majority of companies are still a long way from fully integrating CRM throughout their organization. (6) This suggests the full benefits of CRM are not likely to be realized for some time.

When it comes to managing customers, an important non-product benefit affecting customers' feelings about a company is customer service, which is defined as activities used by the marketer to support the purchaser's experience with a product. Customer service includes several activities including:

♦ Training – services needed to assist customers in learning how to use a product

♦ Repair – services needed to handle damaged or malfunctioning products

♦ Financial Assistance – services needed to help customers with the financial commitment required to purchase or use the product

♦ Complaint Resolution – services needed to address other problems that have arisen with customers' use of a product

45

In many industries customers' experience with a company's customer service can significantly affect their overall opinion of the product. Companies producing superior products may negatively impact their products if they back these up with shoddy service. On the other hand, many companies compete not because their products are superior to their competitors' products but because they offer a higher level of customer service. In fact, many believe customer service will eventually become the most significant benefit offered by a company because global competition (i.e., increase in similar products) makes it more difficult for a company's product to offer unique advantages.

Customer service manifests itself in several ways, with the most common being a dedicated department to handle customer issues. Whether a company establishes a separate department or spreads the function among many departments, being responsive and offering reliable service is critical and likely to be demanded by customers.

· ·

Despite the need for effective customer service, many organizations are choosing to be more selective as to which customers receive the bulk of their attention. While during the 1990s companies abided by a "customer is always right" philosophy and did their best to address the needs of all customers, this attitude is changing. (7)

· ·

Trends in Customer Service

Marketers have seen the customer service process evolve from an area receiving only marginal attention into a primary functional area. In response to customers' demands for responsive and reliable service, companies are investing heavily in innovative methods and processes to strengthen their service level. These innovations include:

INCREASED CUSTOMER SELF SERVICE

A major trend in customer service is the move by companies to encourage customers to be involved in helping solve their own service issues. This can be seen in retail industries where self-service ranges from customers placing their own grocery products in shopping bags all the way to having customers do their own checkout, including scanning products and making payment. Also, as we will soon discuss, customers needing information are being encouraged by companies to first undertake the effort themselves often by visiting special company-provided information areas (see *Website and Phone Accessible Knowledge Base* discussion below). Only after they have explored these options are customers encouraged to contact customer service personnel.

• •

A survey of 1,000 consumers by an industry consulting firm revealed that most people prefer self-check out options when shopping at retail stores. In fact, only 9 percent of those responding to the survey indicated they would refuse to use self checkout. (8)

• •

REVENUE GENERATORS

Companies maintaining a customer service staff have found these people not only help solve customer problems but they also may be in a position to convince customers to purchase more. Many companies now require sales training for their customer service personnel. At a basic level customer service representatives may be trained to ask if customers are interested in hearing about other products or services. If a customer shows interest then the representative will transfer the customer to a sales associate. At a more advanced level the representative will shift to a selling role and attempt to get the customer to commit to additional product purchases.

OUT-SOURCING

One of the most controversial developments impacting customer service is the move by many companies around the world to establish customer service functions outside of either their home country or the country in which their customers reside. Called out-sourcing, companies pursue this strategy to both reduce cost and also increase service coverage. For instance, having multiple customer service facilities around the world allows customers to talk via phone with a service person no matter what time of day. The ability to move service to another country is only viable in large part due to technological developments (see *Internet Telephone* discussion below). But such moves have raised concerns on two fronts. First, many see this trend as leading to a reduction of customer service jobs within a home country. Second, customer service personnel located off-shore may not be sufficiently trained and often lack an understanding of the conditions within the customers' local market both of which can affect service levels. At the extreme, a poorly managed move to out-source customer service can lead to a decrease in customer satisfaction which in the long-run could affect sales.

CUSTOMER SERVICE TECHNOLOGIES

As we will see throughout this book, technological innovation has significantly impacted all areas of marketing. Within customer service improvements in computer hardware and software, as well as rampant adoption of the Internet as a prime channel for connecting with customers, has led to numerous innovative methods for addressing customer needs. These methods include:

- Online Chat – Companies are finding value in using Internet chat as a way to address customer questions. (9) Typically the chat feature is presented via a pop-up browser window that appears when a customer clicks on a website link, though newer technology using computer programming, dubbed AJAX, allows for chat to take place right on a webpage and not through pop-up windows. Whether presented as a separate window or contained within a regular webpage, online chat sessions are undertaken in real-time with customers and company service people exchanging text messages. More advanced chat technology, called **collaborative browsing** or co-browsing, allows customer service representatives to manipulate a customer's web browser by sending webpages containing relevant information. For instance, retailer Land's End "pushes" webpages to customers' browsers in response to requests for clothing. In this way the service person can offer suggestions and guidance by controlling what the customer is seeing on her/his screen. (10)

- Website and Phone Accessible Knowledge Base – As part of customers' desire to be more involved in solving their own problems, companies have moved to offering technological solutions in ways that appeal to customers' desire for self service. The predominant method for doing this is by maintaining a collection of answers to commonly asked questions. The collection may be part of a Knowledge Base accessible either online, through such methods as **frequently asked questions (FAQ)**, or through a call system where an automated helper or a **virtual attendant** guides customers to an answer.

- Really Simple Syndication (RSS) – Another Internet technology rapidly gaining a place in customer service is Really Simple Syndication (RSS). Made popular by its use in Internet blogs and now widely used on most popular websites, RSS allows a company to send out information quickly, and to a large number, with little manual effort compared to traditional methods. With RSS customers are able to subscribe to a company's RSS feed and anytime the company updates information a notice is instantly sent to all subscribers. The RSS information received by subscribers includes basic details of new content, such as content title, authorship information, description, and links to the full content. Subscribers who have installed the proper software or have access to an online RSS reader will see the information appear automatically. Customer service has found RSS to be useful for: communicating product updates; technical matters, such as product defects or recalls; and general company communication, such as notification of special promotions.

- Wireless Data Access – Providing a high-level of customer service does not only occur when the customer initiates contact with an organization. Customer service takes place during any potential interaction including those that may be initiated by a company representative who is meeting face-to-face with a customer. For instance, an organization may send salespeople and other support personnel to a customer's location and their ability to address customer concerns is vital to maintaining strong customer service. To ensure field people have the most up-to-date information, many companies now equip their field teams with portable devices that can access the Internet from virtually any location. This is accomplished through wireless Internet connections enabling the field person to access company computers and tap into customer data.

- Text Messaging – Once considered a play-toy for teenagers, text messaging is quickly being adopted as a tool for customer service. Many companies and organizations, including colleges and universities, now use text messaging as a means to communicate with their customers. For instance, colleges and universities have set up instant alert security systems where students can receive a text message in the case of an on-campus emergency or weather-related problem.

- Internet Telephone – Despite the growth in the Internet as an outlet for addressing customer questions, many customers still prefer to discuss their situation with a live person through a telephone conversation. For large companies receiving thousands of calls a day a dedicated department or call center may be in place to handle customer inquiries. No matter the organization's size, the cost of maintaining telephone support services can be expensive. One major expense lies with the cost of using traditional telecommunication lines. Commonly referred to as **plain old telephone service (POTS)**, this system is more expensive because telephone lines are generally dedicated to individual users. That is, a single line can only handle one phone call, fax transmission, or computer data connection at a time. While a discussion of technical issues behind this are beyond the scope of this book, suffice to say the POTS system is inefficient since a single telephone line has the capacity to handle a far larger volume of phone and data transmission. For this reason companies have moved to a technology called **Voice over Internet Protocol (VoIP)**. With VoIP, telephone calls are delivered over the Internet with multiple phones sharing the same connection. With more people using the same line the cost per call is reduced. While the audio quality of the call may not be as reliable as POTS technology, improvements over the last few years have narrowed the quality gap to the point where most customers cannot distinguish the difference.

- Intelligent Call Routing – Another innovation associated with telephone support deals with technologies for identifying and filtering incoming customer calls. One method is the use of software that attempts to identify the caller (usually based on the incoming phone number) and then automatically directs the call for proper servicing. For instance, an appliance manufacturer may be able to distinguish between those who purchased refrigerators and those who purchased microwave ovens. But some marketers go a step further and can program their call routing system to distinguish "good" customers from others. This may result in these customers receiving preferential placement in the calling order or queue so they will be serviced before lower rated customers who sequentially called before the "good" customer.

REFERENCES

1. "When, Why, and How to Fire That Customer," *Business Week*, October/November 2007.

2. Gillespie, E.M., "Thousands of Posts Flood Starbucks Site," *San Francisco Chronicle*, April 8, 2008.

3. Noyes. K., "Wal-Mart to Online Customers: Don't Call Us," *CRM Buyer*, September 25, 2007.

4. Lewis, L., "Kiosks Bring Increased Efficiency and Sales to Supermarket Delis," *Stores*, April 2008.

5. Ransom, D., "What's CRM?" *SmartMoney*, March 31, 2008.

6. Sebor, J., "CRM Gets Serious," *CRM Magazine*, February 1, 2008.

7. Penttila, C., "Just Say No," *Entrepreneur Magazine*, October 2007.

8. Lindeman, T., "Self-Service Allows Consumers to Pile Up the Goods, Avoid Dealing with People," *Pittsburgh Post-Gazette*, November 18, 2007.

9. "Customer Service," *Internet Retailer*, July 2008.

10. "What a Five-Year-Old Has to Teach Online Shoppers," *Internet Retailer*, July 7, 2004.

Full text of many of the references can be accessed via links on the support website.

Chapter 4:

Understanding Customers

Possibly the most challenging concept in marketing deals with understanding why buyers do what they do. But such knowledge is critical for marketers since having a strong understanding of buyer behavior will help shed light on what is important to the customer and also suggest the important influences on customer decision making. Using this information, marketers can create marketing programs that they believe will be of interest to their customers.

However, factors affecting how customers make decisions are extremely complex. Buyer behavior is deeply rooted in psychology with dashes of sociology thrown in just to make things more interesting. Since every person in the world is different, it is impossible to have simple rules explaining how buying decisions are made. But those who have spent many years analyzing customer activity have presented us with useful "guidelines" in how someone decides whether or not to make a purchase.

The perspective we take in this chapter is to touch on just the basic concepts that appear to be commonly accepted as influencing customer behavior. We look at the buying behavior of both consumers (i.e., when people buy for personal reasons) and also examine factors that influence buyers' decisions in the business market.

WHY CUSTOMERS BUY

Customers make purchases in order to satisfy **needs**. Some of these needs are basic and must be filled by everyone on the planet (e.g., food, shelter), while others are not required for basic survival and vary depending on the person or organization making a purchase. It probably makes more sense to classify needs that are not a necessity as **wants** or **desires**. In fact, in many countries where the standard of living is very high, a large portion of the population's income is spent on wants and desires rather than on basic needs.

Whether the buyer is buying for personal use (i.e., consumer) or the purchase is for use by a business, it is critical for marketers to understand how their customers make decisions including the dynamics that influence the decision-making process.

We use the term customer to refer to the actual buyer, the person spending the money. But is should be pointed out the one who does the buying is not necessarily the user and others may be involved in the buying decision. For example, in planning for a family trip the mother may make the hotel reservations but others in the family may have input on the hotel choice. Similarly, a father may purchase snacks at the grocery store but his young child may be the one who selected them from the store shelf. Consequently, analysis of factors affecting why a customer buys should not be limited to only the person doing the buying transaction; others who are not performing the purchasing activity may also be involved.

. . . .

The Walt Disney Company understands that buying decisions can involve many members of a family. In fact, girls between 3 and 6 years old are an important target for Disney's line of princess products which includes movies, clothing, and fashion accessories. While the ultimate buyers may be the parents, Disney knows children will have a strong influence on what is purchased. (1)

. . . .

WHAT INFLUENCES PURCHASING

The decision-making process used by customers to make purchases is anything but straight forward. There are many factors affecting this process. The number of potential influences on customer buying behavior is limitless. However, marketers are well served to understand the key influences. By doing so they may be in a position to tailor their marketing efforts to take advantage of these influences in a way that will satisfy the customer.

The influences of purchasing break down into two main categories: Internal and External (see Fig 4-1). For the most part the influences are not mutually exclusive. Instead, they are all interconnected and work together to form who we are and how we behave. Additionally, not all influences affect all buying decisions. For example, a business buyer mulling over a purchase decision for high-priced electronics equipment that his company has never purchased before may be influenced by different factors compared to a consumer seeking to make a low-priced purchase she makes several times a week. Finally, while purchase situations facing consumers may be different than those facing business buyers in many ways the influences on the decision are similar. For this reason we present the influences as covering both consumer and business purchasing.

Figure 4-1: Influences on Customer Purchasing

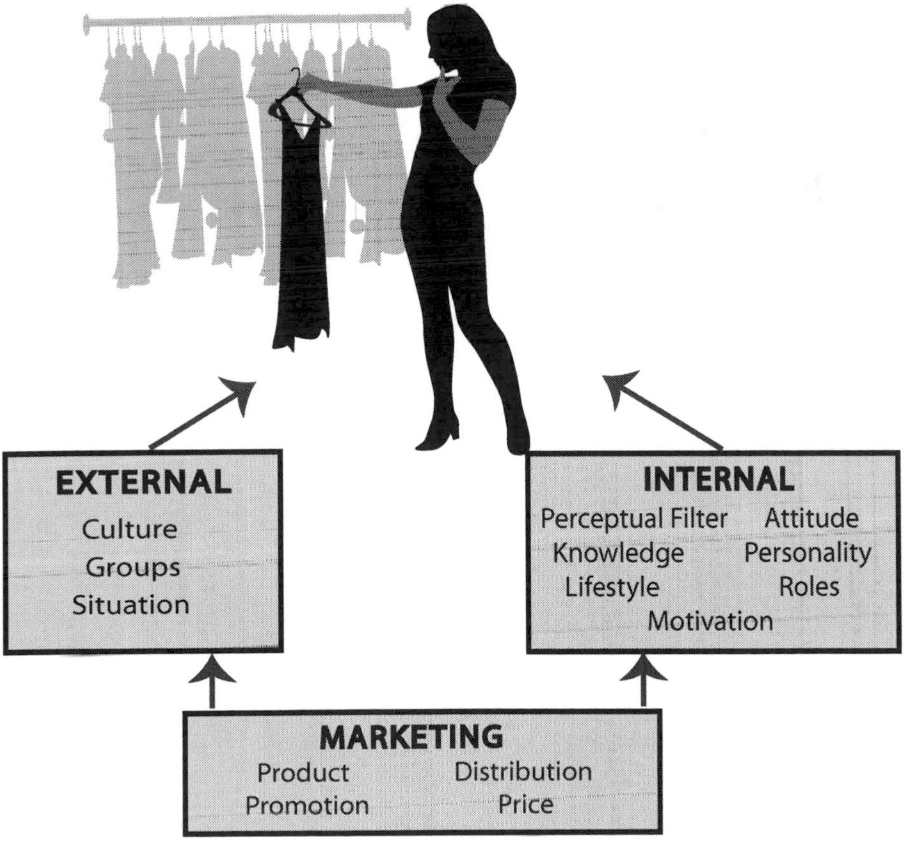

EXTERNAL
Culture
Groups
Situation

INTERNAL
Perceptual Filter   Attitude
Knowledge   Personality
Lifestyle   Roles
Motivation

MARKETING
Product   Distribution
Promotion   Price

INTERNAL INFLUENCES

We start our examination of the influences on customer purchase decisions by first looking inside ourselves to see which are the most important internal factors affecting how we make choices.

Perceptual Filter

Perception is how we see ourselves and the world we live in. However, what ends up being stored inside us does not always get there in a direct manner. Often our mental makeup results from information consciously or subconsciously filtered as we experience it, a process we refer to as a perceptual filter. To us this is our reality, though it does not mean it is an accurate reflection of what is real. Thus, perception is the way we filter stimuli (e.g., someone talking to us, reading a newspaper story) and then make sense from it.

Perception has several steps:

♦ Exposure – sensing a stimuli (e.g. seeing an advertisement)

♦ Attention – an effort to recognize the nature of a stimuli (e.g. recognizing it is an advertisement)

♦ Awareness – assigning meaning to a stimuli (e.g., it is a humorous advertisement for a particular product)

♦ Retention – adding the meaning to one's internal makeup (i.e., this product has fun advertisements)

How these steps are eventually carried out depends on a person's approach to **learning**. By learning we mean how someone changes what they know, which in turn may affect how they act. There are many theories of learning, a discussion of which is beyond the scope of this book, however, suffice to say people are likely to learn in different ways. For instance, one person may be able to focus very strongly on a certain advertisement and retain the information after being exposed only one time while another person may need to be exposed to the same advertisement many times before he/she even recognizes what it is. Customers are also more likely to retain information if a person has a strong interest in the stimuli. For example, if a person is in need of a new car they are more likely to pay attention to a new advertisement for a car while someone who does not need a car may need to see the advertisement many times before they recognize the brand of automobile. For marketers to get through customers' perceptual filters takes careful planning as outlined in Box 4-1.

Box 4-1

GETTING THROUGH THE PERCEPTUAL FILTER

Marketers spend large sums of money to get customers to have positive impression of their products. But clearly the existence of a perceptual filter suggests getting to this stage is not easy. Each stage in the perceptual filter presents challenges and opportunities:

Exposure

Exposing customers to a product can be very difficult especially when competing products are attempting to accomplish the same objective. To stand out from others requires marketers be creative and use a variety of different methods (e.g., different types of promotion) to deliver their messages. Additionally, marketers often find that a large number of attempts (e.g., frequently running advertisements) must be made before customers are exposed to their product.

Attention

Once the message reaches the customer it must be interesting in order to capture his/her attention. This often means the marketer's message must not only be engaging but must also highlight a product's benefits and how these can satisfy customers' needs. It is important to understand that being exposed to a product does not mean a customer will pay attention to it. Of course, most people experience this everyday as they are bombarded with products in stores or ads on television but they attend to only a very small percentage.

Awareness

Simply attending to the marketer's message is not enough to get a customer to retain the message. For marketers the most critical step in getting through the perceptual filter is the one that occurs with awareness where customers give meaning to what they experience. To ensure the message is getting through as intended and customers accurately interpret the facts about the product, marketers must continually monitor and respond if their message becomes distorted in ways that negatively shape its meaning. This can happen due in part to competitive activity, such as a competitor creating advertisements that position their product in a stronger light than the marketer's product, or through published comments, such as news media reports or website postings, containing negative and possibly inaccurate statements related to the marketer's product.

Retention

Finally, making sure customers are retaining positive product information requires continual customer research. If they discover the wrong information is being retained (e.g., wrong idea of how product works) then new strategies must be employed (e.g., new message delivered). Marketers can reinforce the retention process by establishing ongoing communication with the customer. This can be accomplished through such techniques as email newsletters, online chat forums, and follow-up service calls.

Knowledge

Knowledge is the sum of all information known by a person. It is the facts of the world as he/she knows it and depth of knowledge is a function of the breadth of worldly experiences and the strength of an individual's long-term memory. Obviously what exists as knowledge to an individual depends on how their perceptual filter makes sense and retains the information it is exposed to.

As we will see, when it comes to making product decisions it is likely other factors influencing customer purchase behavior are in large part shaped by what is known. Thus, developing methods (e.g., incentives) to encourage customers to accept more information (or correct information) may affect other influencing factors.

Attitude

In simple terms attitude refers to what a person feels or believes about something. Additionally, attitude may be reflected in how an individual acts based on his or her beliefs. Once formed, attitudes can be very difficult to change. If a customer has a negative attitude toward a particular issue it will take considerable effort to change what she/he believes to be true.

Marketers facing customers with negative attitudes toward their product must work to identify the key issues shaping a customer's attitude then adjust marketing decisions (e.g., advertising) in an effort to change the attitude. For companies competing against strong rivals to whom loyal customers exhibit a positive attitude, an important strategy is to work to see why customers feel positive toward the competitor and then try to meet or beat the competitor on these issues. Alternatively, a company can try to locate customers who feel negatively toward the competitor and then target its efforts to this group.

Personality

An individual's personality relates to perceived personal characteristics they consistently exhibit, especially when interacting with others. In most, but not all, cases the behaviors projected in one situation are similar to the behaviors exhibited in another situation. In this way personality is the sum of sensory experiences others get from experiencing a person (i.e., how one talks, reacts, etc.).

While one's personality is often interpreted by those we interact with, the person has his/her own vision of his/her personality, called **self concept**, which may or may not be the same has how others view them. For marketers it is important to know customers, and especially consumers, make purchase decisions to support their self concept. Using research techniques to identify how customers view themselves may give marketers insight into products and promotion options that are not readily apparent. For example, when targeting consumers a marketer may initially build marketing strategy around more obvious clues to consumption behavior such as consumers' demographic indicators (e.g., age, occupation, income). However, in-depth research may yield information showing consumers are purchasing products to fulfill self concept objectives that have little to do with the demographic category they fall into (e.g., senior citizen may be making purchases that make them feel younger). In this example, appealing to consumer's self concept needs could expand a product's customer base by including customers not initially envisioned to be in the target market.

. . . .

Credit card companies understand the importance of customers' personalities by offering options for card personalization. As an example, Bank of America's Photo Expression services allows customers to add their own pictures to their credit cards. (2)

. . . .

Lifestyle

This internal influencing factor relates to the way we live through the activities we engage in and interests we express. In simple terms it is what we value out of life. Lifestyle is often determined by how we spend our time and money. Additionally, customers often associate with others who share similar lifestyles.

In the consumer market, products and services are purchased to support consumers' lifestyles. Marketers have worked hard researching how consumers in their target markets live their lives since this information is key to developing products, suggesting promotional strategies, and even determining how best to distribute products (e.g., consumer lifestyle shows preference for shopping online).

Motivation

Motivation relates to our desire to achieve a certain outcome. Many internal factors we've already discussed can affect a customer's desire to achieve a certain outcome, but there are others. For instance, when it comes to making purchase decisions customers' motivation could be affected by such issues as financial position (e.g., *Can I afford the purchase?*), time constraints (e.g.,

Do I need to make the purchase quickly?), overall value (e.g., *Am I getting my money's worth?*), emotional attachment (e.g., *Does the product remind us of family members who have died?*), and perceived risk (e.g., *What happens if I make a bad decision?*).

Motivation is closely tied to the concept of **involvement**, which relates to how much effort the customer exerts in making a decision. Highly motivated customers will want to get mentally and physically involved in the purchase process. Not all products have a high percentage of highly involved customers (e.g., purchasing milk) but marketers who market products and services with a high level of customer involvement should prepare options to attract this group. For instance, marketers should make it easy for customers to learn about their product (e.g., information on website, free video preview) and, for some products, allow customers to experience the product (e.g., free trial) before committing to the purchase.

• •

*The practice of offering customers the opportunity to experience a product prior to purchasing appears to be growing. Dubbed **experiential marketing** the idea is to have customers immerse themselves in the product prior to making a commitment. In most cases customers experience the product at locations that are away from the marketer's location. For instance, House Party Inc, (3) offers marketers the ability to have their products be the centerpiece of hundreds of parties, often held on the same day. This method has been used by such companies as Ford, Bed Bath and Beyond, and Sunbeam. (4)*

• •

Roles

Roles represent the position we feel we hold or others feel we should hold in a group environment whether in a personal or business situation (see Box 4-2). These positions carry certain responsibilities yet it is important to understand that some of these responsibilities may be perceived and not spelled out or even accepted by others. In support of their roles, customers make product choices that vary depending on which role they are assuming. As illustration, a person who is responsible for selecting snack food for an office party his boss will attend may choose higher quality products than he would when purchasing snacks for his family.

Advertisers often show how the benefits of their products aid customers as they perform certain roles. Typically the underlying message of this promotional approach is to suggest using the advertiser's product will raise one's status in the eyes of others while using a competitor's product may have a negative effect on status.

. . . .

One major role change identified by marketing research is the growth in the purchase of household items by males. Traditionally household items, such as cleaning products, food, and kids clothing, were marketed to the female head-of-household. However, marketers of these products are increasingly targeting men who have taken on more traditional female roles. (5)

. . . .

Box 4-2

ROLES IN THE BUYING CENTER

In the business market those associated with the purchase decision are known to be part of a Buying Center, which consists of individuals within an organization performing one or more of the following roles:

- Buyer – responsible for dealing with suppliers and placing orders (e.g., purchasing agent)
- Decider – has the power to make the final purchase decision (e.g., CEO)
- Influencer – has the ability to affect what is ordered such as setting order specifications (e.g., engineers, researchers, product managers)
- User – those who will actually use the product when it is received (e.g., office staff)
- Initiator – any Buying Center member who is the first to determine that a need exists
- Gatekeeper – anyone who controls access to other Buying Center members (e.g., administrative assistant)

For marketers confronting a Buying Center it is important to first identify who plays what role. Once identified the marketer must address the needs of each member, which may differ significantly. For instance, the Decider, who may be the company president, wants to make sure the purchase will not negatively affect the company financially while the Buyer wants to be assured the product is delivered on time. The way each Buying Center member is approached and marketed to requires careful planning in order to address their unique needs.

EXTERNAL INFLUENCES

Customer purchase decisions are often affected by factors outside of their control but have direct or indirect impact on how they live and what they consume.

Culture

Culture represents the behavior, beliefs and, in many cases, the way we act which is learned by interacting with and observing other members of society. In this way much of what we do is shared behavior passed along from one member of society to another. Culture is learned from those with whom we directly interact (e.g., family, co-workers) and from those that we observe from a distance (e.g., movie stars).

Culture can be analyzed from many levels. At a broad level culture is shaped by the general behaviors, belief and the way people act shared by a very large portion of society, such as citizens of a country sharing patriotic beliefs. However, marketers are much more concerned with culture as it pertains to smaller groups or **sub-cultures**. Customers simultaneously belong to multiple sub-cultures whose cultural attributes may be different. For instance, people may simultaneously belong to different groups based on ethnicity, religious beliefs, geographic location, musical tastes, sports team allegiance, and many others. In a business situation there exist sub-cultures within an organization. For example, the organization's formal policies and procedures may be important in developing an overall corporate culture, while other sub-cultures are developed in less formal ways (e.g., members of the company bowling team).

As part of their efforts to convince customers to purchase their products, marketers often use cultural representations, especially in promotional appeals. The objective is to connect to customers using cultural references that are easily understood and often embraced by the customer. By doing so the marketer hopes customers feel comfortable with or can relate better to the product since it corresponds with their cultural values. Additionally, smart marketers use strong research efforts to identify differences in how sub-cultures behave. These efforts help pave the way for spotting trends within a sub-culture, which the marketer can capitalize on through new marketing tactics, such as developing new products.

Other Group Membership

In addition to cultural influences, customers belong to many other groups with which they share certain characteristics and which may influence purchase decisions. Some of the basic groups include:

♦ Social Class – represents the social standing one has within a society based on such factors as income level, education, and occupation

♦ Family – a person's family situation can have a strong effect on how purchase decisions are made

♦ Reference Groups – most consumers simultaneously belong to many other groups with which they associate or, in some cases, feel the need to disassociate

♦ Industry Groups – a company and many of its employees may belong to a large number of trade and community groups

Identifying and understanding the groups customers belong to is a key strategy for marketers. As Box 4-3 discusses, finding group leaders is especially important.

Box 4-3

MARKETING TO OPINION LEADERS

When appealing to groups, a key marketing strategy is to seek out group leaders and others to whom group members look to for advice or direction. Termed opinion leaders, these individuals may have influence over what others purchase if they are perceived as well-respected by the group.

Marketers may find value in researching opinion leaders to learn more about how they behave and the means by which they influence a group. For instance, research may show that an Internet blogger is viewed as an opinion leader within the marketer's industry and regularly reading the blogger's posts could yield insight on the group.

Additionally, marketers may find promotional opportunities with opinion leaders who agree to represent the company in a promotional way, such as serving as a spokesperson for the marketer's products.

Situation

A purchase decision can be strongly affected by the situation in which people find themselves. Not all situations are controllable, in which case a customer may not follow her/his normal purchase decision process. For instance, if a person needs a product quickly and a store does not carry her/his normal brand, the customer may choose a competitor's product.

Marketers can take advantage of decisions made in uncontrollable situations in at least two ways. First, the marketers can use promotional methods to reinforce a specific selection of products when the customer is confronted with a particular situation. For example, automotive services can be purchased promising to service vehicles if the user runs into problems anywhere and at anytime. Second, marketers can use marketing methods to convince customers a situation is less likely to occur if the marketer's product is used. This can be seen with financial services firms targeting business customers, where marketers explain that their clients' assets are protected in the case of unexpected economic problems.

HOW CUSTOMERS BUY

So now that we have discussed the factors influencing a customer's decision to purchase, our next task is to examine the process customers follow when making purchase decisions. Below we look at the types of decisions customers face and the steps they may take in getting to their final decision. Because consumer purchasing characteristics are different than those associated with business purchasing (see Box 4-4), we look at each separately.

Box 4-4

How Consumer and Business Purchasing Differs

It is important for marketers to understand that while the influences on purchasing are similar, the circumstances surrounding purchase decisions are quite different for consumers and businesses. The differences between these customers require marketers take a different approach when selling to business customers than they do when selling to consumers. Among the differences between consumer and business customers are:

How Decisions Are Made

In the consumer market a very large percentage of purchase decisions are made by a single person. The business market is significantly different. While single person purchasing is not unusual, especially within a small company, a significant percentage of business buying, especially within larger organizations, requires the input of many (i.e., Buying Center).

Experienced Purchasers

Organizations often employ purchasing agents or professional buyers whose job is to negotiate the best deals for their company. Unlike consumers, who often lack information when making purchase decisions, professional buyers are generally as knowledgeable about the product and the industry as the marketer who is selling to them.

Decision Making Time

Depending on the product, business purchase decisions can drag on for an extensive period. Unlike consumer markets where **impulse purchasing** (i.e., purchase decisions that are not planned) is rampant, the number of people involved in business purchase decisions results in decisions taking weeks, months, or even years.

Larger Purchases

For products regularly used and frequently purchased, businesses will often buy a larger volume at one time compared to consumer purchases. Because of this business purchasers often demand price breaks (e.g., discounts) for higher order levels.

Importance of Price

In certain business markets purchase decisions hinge on the outcome of a bidding process between competitors offering similar products and services. In these cases the decision to buy is often simply who has the lowest price. Unlike consumer markets, where customers will often purchase a particular brand with little consideration for its price, in the business market this is often not the case.

Number of Buyers

While there are several million companies worldwide operating in the overall business market, within a particular market the number is much smaller. Within some industries buyers are highly concentrated in certain geographic areas. Consequently, compared to consumer products where millions of customers make up a market, marketing efforts for the business market are confined to a smaller targeted group.

Promotional Focus

Companies who primarily target consumers often use mass advertising methods to reach an often widely dispersed market. For business-to-business marketers the size of individual orders, along with a smaller number of buyers, makes person-to-person contact by sales representatives a more effective means of promotion.

Types of Consumer Purchase Decisions

Consumers are faced with purchase decisions nearly every day. But not all decisions are treated the same. Some decisions are more complex than others requiring more effort by the consumer. Other decisions are fairly routine and require little effort. In general, consumers face four types of purchase decisions:

◆ Minor New Purchase – These purchases represent something new to a consumer but in the consumer's mind it is not a very important purchase in terms of need, money, or other reason (e.g., does not affect status within a group).

◆ Minor Re-Purchase – These are the most routine of all purchases and often the consumer returns to purchase the same product without giving much thought to other product options (i.e., consumer is loyal to a product).

◆ Major New Purchase – These purchases are the most difficult of all purchases because the product being purchased is important to the consumer but the consumer has little or no previous experience making these decisions. The consumer's lack of confidence in making this type of decision often (but not always) requires the consumer to engage in an extensive decision-making process.

◆ Major Re-Purchase – These purchase decisions are also important to the consumer but the consumer feels more confident in making the decision since they have previous experience purchasing the product.

For marketers it is important to understand how consumers treat the purchase decisions they face. If a company is targeting customers who feel a purchase decision is difficult (i.e., Major New Purchase), its marketing strategy may vary greatly compared to a company targeting customers who view the purchase decision as routine. In fact, the same company may face both situations at the same time; for some consumers the product is new, while others see the purchase as routine. The implication for marketers is that different purchase situations require different marketing efforts.

Steps in Consumer Purchasing Process

The consumer purchasing process can be viewed as a sequence of five steps (Figure 4-2). However, whether a consumer will actually carryout each step depends on the type of purchase decision that is faced. For instance, for Minor Re-Purchases the consumer may be quite loyal to the same brand and the decision is a routine one (i.e., buy the same product) with little effort needed to make a purchase decision.

In cases of routine, brand loyal purchases consumers may skip several steps in the purchasing process since they know exactly what they want allowing the consumer to move quickly to actual purchase. But for more complex decisions, such as Major New Purchases, the purchasing process can extend for days, weeks, or months. So in presenting these steps marketers should realize that, depending on the circumstances surrounding the purchase, the importance of each step may vary.

Figure 4-2: Decision Making Process

Step 1: Needs Recognized

In the first step the consumer determines that for some need he/she is not happy with his/her perceived actual level of satisfaction and seeks to improve to a perceived desired level of satisfaction. For instance, internal triggers, such as hunger or thirst, may tell the consumer that food or drink is needed. External factors can also trigger consumers' needs. Marketers are particularly good doing this through advertising, in-store displays, and even the intentional use of scent (e.g., perfume counters in retail stores). At this stage the decision-making process may stall if the consumer is not motivated to continue (see *Motivation* discussion above). However, if the consumer does have the internal drive to satisfy the need he/she will continue to the next step.

• •

Online marketers have developed several methods designed to trigger customers' recognition of a need. One widespread approach employed by such companies as Amazon and Netflix is the use of sophisticated computer-based **product recommendation systems** *offering suggestions of products a customer may find of interest. Using a technique called* **collaborative filtering***, the recommendation system suggests products based in part on purchases made by other customers who show similar behavioral patterns as the customer being targeted. (6)*

• •

Step 2: Search for Information

Assuming a consumer is motivated to satisfy her or his need, she/he will next undertake a search for information on possible solutions. The sources used to acquire this information may be as simple as remembering information from past experience (i.e., memory) or the consumer may expend considerable effort to locate information from outside sources (e.g., Internet search, talk with others, etc.). How much effort the consumer directs toward searching depends on such factors as the importance of satisfying the need, familiarity with available solutions, and the amount of time available to search. To appeal to consumers who are at the search stage, marketers should make efforts to ensure consumers can locate information related to their product. For example, for marketers whose customers rely on the Internet for information gathering, attaining high rankings in search engines for likely keyword searches done by consumers has become a critical marketing objective.

. . . .

China is second only to the United States in the number of automobiles purchased. In gathering information for their purchases, Chinese consumers tend to distrust salespeople at auto dealers and often ignore advertisements. Instead they turn to information provided by friends and family, Internet forums, and visits to auto shows to help them make their buying decision. (7)

. . . .

Step 3: Evaluate Options

Consumers' search efforts may result in a set of options from which a choice can be made. It should be noted there may be two levels to this stage. At level one the consumer may create a set of possible solutions to her/his needs (i.e., different product types) while at level two the consumer may be evaluating particular products (i.e., different individual brands) within each solution. For example, a consumer who needs to replace a television has multiple solutions to choose from such as plasma and LCD flat panel screens, as well as old-style CRT televisions. Within each solution type will be multiple brands from which to choose. Marketers need to understand how consumers evaluate product options and why some products are included while others are not. Most importantly, marketers must determine which criteria consumers are using in their selection of possible options and how each criterion is evaluated. Returning to the television example, marketing tactics will be most effective when the marketer can tailor their efforts by knowing what benefits are most important to consumers when selecting options (e.g., picture quality, brand name, screen size, price, etc.) and then determine the order of importance of each benefit.

Step 4: Purchase

In many cases the solution chosen by the consumer is the same as the product whose evaluation is the highest. However, this may change when it is actually time to make the purchase. The "intended" purchase may be altered at the time of purchase for many reasons such as: the product is out-of-stock, a competitor offers an incentive at the point-of-purchase (e.g., store salesperson mentions a competitor's offer), the customer lacks the necessary funds (e.g., credit card not working) or members of the consumer's reference group take a negative view of the purchase (e.g., friend is critical of purchase). Marketers whose product is most desirable to the consumer must make sure the transaction goes smoothly. For example, Internet retailers have worked hard to prevent consumers from abandoning online purchase (i.e., **online shopping carts**) by

67

streamlining the checkout process. For marketers whose product is not the consumer's selected product, last chance marketing efforts may be worth exploring, such as offering incentives to store personnel to "talk up" their product at the checkout line.

• •

Purchase decisions can also be affected by the purchasing environment. For example, in England retail chain Coffee Republic has found the use of contactless purchasing cards is attracting customer interest. Consumers need only wave specially-equipped credit cards in front of a payment reader without the need to enter codes or sign sales slips. Such payment systems may persuade customers to select Coffee Republic over other coffee outlets due to convenience and speed of acquiring the product. (8)

• •

Step 5: Post-Purchase Evaluation

Once the consumer has made the purchase they are faced with an evaluation of the decision. If the product performs below the consumer's expectation then he/she will re-evaluate satisfaction with the decision, which at its extreme may result in the consumer returning the product and seeking a replacement or refund while in less extreme situations the consumer will retain the purchased item but may take a negative view of the product. Such evaluations are more likely to occur in cases of expensive or highly important purchases. To help ease the concerns consumers have with their purchase evaluation, marketers need to be receptive and even encourage consumer contact. Customer service centers and follow-up marketing research are useful tools in helping to address purchasers' concerns.

Types of Business Purchase Decisions

While it would appear business customers face the same four purchase situations faced by consumers (Minor New Purchase, Minor Re-Purchase, Major New Purchase, Major Re-Purchase), the nature of the business market has led to categories that are somewhat different than those seen with consumer purchasing. This is primarily due to the differences that exist between these two markets (see Box 4-4). In particular, marketers targeting business buyers often see little value in pursuing business customers undertaking minor purchases (e.g., small orders) compared to consumer marketers who may actively pursue such customers. Consequently, while minor purchases certainly do occur, especially within small businesses, few business suppliers choose to direct their selling efforts to this type of purchase.

For buyers in business markets the types of decisions they face include:

◆ Straight Re-Purchases – These purchase situations involve routine ordering. In most cases buyers simply reorder the same products previously purchased. Many larger companies have programmed re-purchases into an automated ordering system that initiates electronic orders when inventory falls below a certain pre-determined level. For the supplier benefiting from the re-purchase this situation is ideal since the purchaser is not looking to evaluate other products. For competitors it may require extensive marketing efforts to persuade the buyer to consider other product options.

◆ Modified Re-Purchases – These purchases occur when products previously considered a Straight Re-Purchase are now under a re-evaluation process. There are many reasons why a product is moved to the status of a Modified Re-Purchase including end of purchase contract period, change in who is involved in making the purchase, supplier is removed from an approved suppliers list, mandate from top level of the organization to re-evaluate all purchasing or strong marketing efforts by competitors. In this circumstance the incumbent supplier faces the same challenges they faced when they initially convinced the buyer to make the purchase. For competitors the door is now open and they must work hard to make sure their message is heard by the decision makers.

◆ New Task Purchases – These purchases are ones the buyer has never or rarely made before. While not all New Task Purchases are considered to have equal importance, in general, the buyer will spend considerably more time evaluating alternatives than would be considered for re-purchase situations. For marketers, the goal when selling to a buyer facing a New Task Purchase is to make sure to be included in the set of evaluated products as discussed in Step 2.

Steps in Business Purchasing Process

Business purchasing follows the same five-step buying process (Figure 4-2) faced by consumers – Need Recognition, Search, Evaluate Options, Purchase, and After-Purchase Evaluation. While the steps are the same, the activities occurring within each step are quite different.

As we examine the business purchasing process it is important to keep in mind the Buying Center concept discussed in Box 4-2 since Buying Center members affect the process at different stages.

Step 1: Need Recognized

In a business environment needs arise from just about anywhere within the organization. The Buying Center concept shows Initiators are the first organizational members to recognize a need. In most situations the Initiator is also the User or Buyer. Users are inclined to identify the need for new solutions (i.e., new products) while Buyers are more likely to identify the need to re-purchase products. But marketers should also understand more companies are replacing human involvement in re-purchase decisions with automated methods, which makes it more challenging for competitors to convince buyers to replace currently purchased products. In Straight Re-Purchase situations the purchasing process often jumps from Step 1 to Step 4 and little search activity is performed.

As part of this step, a specifications document may be generated laying out the requirements of the product or service to be purchased. Several members of the Buying Center may be involved in creation of the specifications. For the marketer, establishing close contact with those who draw up the specifications may help position the marketer's product for inclusion in the search phase.

Step 2: Search for Information

The search for alternatives to consider for satisfying recognized needs is one of the most significant differences between consumer and business purchasing. Much of this has to do with an organization's motive to reduce costs. While a consumer will not search hard to save two cents on gas, a company with a large fleet of cars will. In fact, this step in the purchase process is where professional buyers make their mark. The primary intention of their search efforts is to identify multiple suppliers who meet product specifications and then, through a screening process, offer a selected group the opportunity to present their products to members of the Buying Center. Although, in some industries, online marketplaces and auction websites offer buyers access to supplier information without the need for suppliers to present to the Buying Center.

For suppliers, the key for success at this step is to make sure they are included within the search activities of the Buyer or others in the Buying Center. In some instances this may require a supplier work to be included within an approved suppliers list. In the case of online marketplaces and auction websites, suppliers should work to be included within relevant sites.

Step 3: Evaluate Options

Once the search has produced options, members of the Buying Center then choose among the alternatives. In more advanced purchase situations, members of the Buying Center evaluate each option using a checklist of features and benefits sought by the buying organization. Each feature/benefit is assigned a weight that corresponds to its importance to the purchase decision. In many cases, especially when dealing with Government and Not-For-Profit markets, suppliers must submit bids with the lowest bidder often being awarded the order, assuming products or services meet specifications.

Step 4: Purchase

To actually place the order may require the completion of paperwork (or electronic documents) such as a purchase order. Acquiring the necessary approvals can delay the order for an extended period of time. And for very large purchases, such as buildings or large equipment, financing options may need to be explored.

Step 5: Post-Purchase Evaluation

After the order is received the purchasing company may spend time reviewing the results of the purchase. This may involve the Buyer discussing product performance issues with Users. If the product is well received it may end up moving to a Straight Re-Purchase status, thus eliminating much of the evaluation process on future purchases.

REFERENCES

1. Marr, M., "Disney Reaches to the Crib to Extend Princess Magic," *Wall Street Journal*, November 19, 2007.

2. *Bank of American Photo Expressions* website.

3. *HouseParty* website.

4. Elliott, S., "Show and Tell Moves Into Living Rooms," *New York Times*, April 4, 2008.

5. "Secrets of the Male Shopper," *BusinessWeek*, September 4, 2006.

6. Taub. E.A., "Guessing the Online Customer's Next Want," *New York Times*, May 19, 2008.

7. Chen, S.J., "How China Buys Cars," *Forbes*, July 31, 2007.

8. Lomas, N., "Contactless Payments Speeds Up Coffee Drinkers," *Silicon. com*, July 28, 2008.

Full text of many of the references can be accessed via links on the support website.

Chapter 5:

Targeting Markets

In the first four chapters we saw that the essential building blocks for creating a strong marketing program rests with marketing research and a deep understanding of customers. With this groundwork in place, it is now time to turn our attention to strategic decisions undertaken by the marketer to address customers' needs and help the organization meet its objectives.

In this chapter we examine decisions affecting the selection of target markets. This is a critical point in marketing planning since all additional marketing decisions are going to be directed toward satisfying customers in the markets selected. We explore what constitutes a market and look at basic characteristics of consumer and business markets. We see not all markets are worth pursuing and marketers are often better served developing a plan identifying specific markets to target. In particular, we look at the process of market segmentation where larger markets are carved into smaller segments offering more potential. Our discussion includes methods used to identify markets holding the best potential. Finally, we discuss the important concept of product positioning and how this fits into target marketing strategy.

WHAT IS A MARKET?

The simple definition of a market is that it consists of all the people or organizations that may have an interest in purchasing a company's goods or services. In other words, a market comprises all customers who have needs that may be fulfilled by an organization's offerings. Yet just having a need is not enough to define a market. Several other factors also come into play.

The first factor is that markets consist of customers who are *qualified* to make a purchase. As spelled out in Box 5-1, customers must meet several criteria to be qualified. A second factor for defining a market is that a market can only exist if the solutions sought by customers can be satisfied with the company's offerings. If a company identifies a group of customers who are qualified to make purchases they only become a market for the company once the company is in a position to execute marketing activities designed to service those customers.

Thus, a market is defined as all people or organizations that are *qualified* to make purchases of products or services that a marketer is able to offer.

Box 5-1

CRITERIA FOR QUALIFYING CUSTOMERS

Many people may say they have a need for a California mansion overlooking the Pacific Ocean. But just because someone says they have a need for this type of property does not mean a real estate agent will automatically consider them to be a potential customer. Instead marketers are interested in customers who are qualified; they meet certain criteria which suggest they are good candidates to be the target of a company's marketing efforts.

In general, there are five basic criteria customers must meet to be considered qualified:

1. Must Seek a Solution to a Need
The customer must either consider the marketer's product to be a potential solution to a need or the marketer must believe the customer is likely to do so. In some cases, the customer may not realize or accept they have a need (e.g., "*I don't need insurance*"). These so-called **latent needs** may be unknown to the customer until something triggers them. For instance, latent needs may be triggered by exposure to certain marketing actions, such as product demonstrations, testimonials, and other promotional methods, leading the customer to decide a previously unknown need does exist.

---

2. Must be Eligible to Make a Purchase

Some marketers limit who is eligible to purchase their products. The best example is legal restrictions on who can purchase alcohol, firearms, and tobacco products. Other examples of limitations include manufacturers only selling to certain retailers (see Chapter 9) and legal firms only handling certain types of clients.

3. Must Possess the Financial Ability to Make a Purchase

In our example of the California mansion financial ability is most likely the criterion that will disqualify most people. Marketers are not likely to consider someone to be a customer if they do not have the funds to make a purchase. This is a major evaluative measure in the business market where purchasing companies lacking a strong financial position may be viewed as a risk to a supplying firm.

4. Must Have the Authority to Make the Purchase Decision

In some buying situations, the person responsible for the decision may not be the one with the need for a product. For example, in our Buying Center discussion in Chapter 4 (Box 4-2), the Decider may be the one with the power to make the decision but Users are the ones with the need for the product. In these situations, while Users may fit the criteria of need, eligibility, and financial ability, they ultimately may not have the authority to make the purchase.

5. Must be Reachable

What good are potential customers if the marketer is not able to communicate with them? When the marketer is unable to reach a customer it is not reasonable to consider them as a qualified customer even though they meet all other criteria. For example, a newly created small business marketing custom, high-end footwear may feel presidents of major companies are potential customers but establishing personal communication with these executives may prove all but impossible. Thus, it would be a stretch for these executives to reasonably be considered qualified customers.

It is important to note a customer must meet ALL criteria listed above to be considered qualified. However, in some markets the customer may have a surrogate who handles some of these qualifications. For instance, a market may consist of pre-teen customers who have a need for certain clothing items but the actual purchase may rest with the pre-teen's parents. So the parents could possibly assume one or more surrogate roles (e.g., financial ability, authority) that will result in the pre-teen being a qualified customer.

CONSUMER AND BUSINESS MARKETS

As we discussed in Chapter 4, a marketer's customers may be consumers, businesses or both. A brief profile of each of these broad markets is presented below.

Consumer Market

The consumer market is comprised of anyone who purchases goods and services for their own personal consumption or for the personal consumption of others (e.g., household members, gift for friend, etc.). Most consumer purchasing takes place at retail outlets of which there are many types (see Chapter 9), though consumers also spend in other ways, such as through auctions, flee markets, and yard sales.

For 2007 it was estimated that worldwide consumer spending (measured as private consumption expenditure) topped (US) $32 trillion (1), though this number is most likely much higher as it does not account for many unreported purchases, such as occurs with private exchanges (e.g., neighbor selling to another neighbor). In the United States, according to the *United States Bureau of Labor*, the average consumer expenditure for a household (measured as Average Annual Expenditures per Consumer Unit) was over (US) $48,000 in 2006. (2)

When marketers look at the overall consumer market for a specific geographic area they will see overall spending tends to change at slow rates from one year to the next. For instance, total consumer spending, adjusted for inflation (i.e., price increases) in developed countries may rise or fall by less than a few percentage points from one year to the next.

WHO MAKES UP THE CONSUMER MARKET

The consumer market is made up of nearly everyone in the world! This means well over 6.5 billion people exist in the consumer market. Of course not every person has the same needs and since markets are made up of people with similar needs, the consumer market can be sub-divided into a large number of categories based on needs such as food, clothing, electronics, entertainment, leisure, etc. And each of these can be further sub-divided, for instance clothing has hundreds of sub-markets such as women, men, children athletic, formal, and many, many more.

Business Market

The business market is comprised of organizations involved in the manufacture, distribution, or support of products sold or otherwise provided to other organizations. The business market easily dwarfs total spending in the consumer market even though there are far fewer buyers than in the consumer market. One estimate indicates that in 2006 total worldwide spending in the business market exceeded (US) $66 trillion. (3) This is because businesses purchase for their own needs (e.g., equipment, office supplies) and also purchase for products they sell to others (e.g., raw materials). Additionally, as we noted in Chapter 4, businesses tend to place large orders compared to consumers.

The demand by businesses for goods and services is affected by consumer purchases (called **derived demand**) and because so many organizations play a part in creating consumer items, a small swing in consumer demand can create big changes in overall business purchasing. Automobile purchases are a good example. If consumer demand for cars increases companies connected with the automobile industry also see demand for their goods and services increase (we will later refer to these companies as supply chain members). Under these conditions companies ratchet up their operations to ensure demand is met, which leads to new purchases by a large number of companies. An increase of just one or two percent for consumer demand can increase business demand for products and services by five or more percent. Unfortunately, the opposite is true if consumer demand declines. Trying to predict these swings requires businesses use marketing research to know the conditions facing their direct customers (e.g., retail stores, other businesses) as well as customers to whom they do not sell directly (e.g., final consumer).

WHO MAKES UP THE BUSINESS MARKET

There are millions of organizations worldwide selling their goods and services to other businesses. They operate in many industries and range in size from huge multinational companies with thousands of employees to one-person small businesses. For our purposes we will categorize the business market based on the general business function an organization performs rather than by industry (of which there are thousands). We break the business market down into two broad categories - Supply Chain Members and Business User Markets.

Supply Chain Members

The supply chain consists of companies engaged in activities involving product creation and delivery. Essentially the chain represents major steps needed to manufacture a product that is eventually sold as a final product.

77

The supply chain includes:

- Raw Material Suppliers – These companies are generally considered the first stage in the supply chain and provide basic products through mining, harvesting, fishing, etc., that are key ingredients in the production of higher-order products. *Example: Copper mine that extracts and refines copper from copper ore.*

- Processed Materials or Basic Component Manufacturers – Firms at this level use raw materials to produce more advanced materials or products contained within more advanced components. *Example: Electrical wire manufacturer that purchases copper.*

- Advanced Component Manufacturers – These companies use basic components to produce products offering a significant function needed within a larger product. *Example: Manufacturer of electrical power supplies purchases electrical wire.*

- Product Manufacturers – This market consists of companies purchasing both basic and advanced components and then assembling these components into a final product designated for a user. These products may or may not be sold as stand-alone products. Some may be included within larger products. *Example: Computer manufacturer purchases electrical power supplies.*

- Supporting Firms – These companies offer services at almost any point in the supply chain and also to the business user market (see *Business User Markets* discussion below). Some services are directly related to the product while others focus on areas of the business not directly related to production. *Example: A trucking company moves products from one supply chain member to another.*

Business User Markets

Several additional user markets also make purchases for their own consumption or with the intention of redistributing to others. In these purchase situations the buyer generally does not radically change the product from its purchased form. While technically these markets are also part of the supply chain, members of the business user market do not, in most cases, engage or directly assist in production activities.

The business user market consists of:

- Governments – They use purchases to assist with the functioning of the government which may include redistributing to others, such as medical supplies. *Examples: Federal, State, Local, and International governments.*

- <u>Not-For-Profits</u> – Organizations whose tax structure precludes earning profits from operations and whose mission tends to be oriented to assisting others. *Examples: Educational institutions, charities, hospitals, and industry associations.*

- <u>Resellers</u> – Also called distributors, these companies operate in both the consumer and the business markets. Their function involves purchasing large volumes of products from manufacturers (and sometimes from other resellers) and selling these products in smaller quantities. *Examples: Wholesalers, retailers and industrial distributors. (Resellers are discussed in detail in Chapters 9 and 10.).*

THE NEED FOR TARGET MARKETS

Earlier we defined a market as consisting of customers who are qualified to purchase goods or services offered by an organization. Yet as we saw in our discussion of consumer and business markets, depending on how a market is categorized, qualified customers can exist in multiple markets. With potential customers in many markets, marketers face the challenge of deciding on the best approach for reaching these customers.

For many inexperienced marketers the strategy for reaching these customers is simple: *"We will just sell to whoever wants to buy."* Yet, for most marketing organizations, the notion of marketing to ALL qualified customers is unrealistic because:

REACHING CUSTOMERS REQUIRES RESOURCES

The fact customers are qualified by no means ensures they will actually do business with the marketer. No matter where customers are located marketers must invariably spend money reaching them. In situations where qualified customers are spread throughout many markets the idea of reaching all is both ineffective and inefficient as the marketer is likely to drain resources in its quest to locate those willing to buy.

SATISFYING BASIC CUSTOMER NEEDS MAY NOT BE ENOUGH

How customers' needs are defined (Item #1 in Box 5-1) is critical to determining a market. One approach to defining needs is to identify markets as consisting of qualified customers who have a basic need that must be satisfied. For example, one could consider the beverage market as consisting of all customers that want to purchase liquid refreshment products to solve a thirst need. While this may be the largest possible market a company could hope for (it would seem to contain just about everyone in the world!) in reality there are no manufactured products that would appeal to everyone in the world since individual nutritional needs, tastes, purchase situations, economic conditions, and many other issues lead to differences in what people seek to satisfy their thirst needs.

Instead of directing resources to every conceivable customer, marketers are better off being selective in the markets they will target with their marketing efforts. **Target markets** are the markets that offer the best fit for an organization's goals and objectives. Using a target market approach an organization attempts to get the most from its resources by following a planned procedure to identify customers that appear to be the best candidates to respond to the marketer's message.

With this in mind, we now turn our attention to examining the process marketers follow to choose which markets are best to target with their marketing effort.

SELECTING TARGET MARKETS THROUGH SEGMENTATION

The market selected by a company as the target for its marketing efforts is critical since all subsequent marketing decisions will be directed toward satisfying the needs of these customers. But what approach should be taken to select markets the company will target?

As we saw in Chapter 4, marketers strive to understand as much as possible about their customers including identifying the main benefits they seek. Because people are different and seek different ways to satisfy their needs, nearly all organizations, whether for-profits or not-for-profits, must use a **market segmentation** approach to target marketing. Market segmentation divides broad markets, consisting of customers possessing different characteristics, including different needs, into smaller market segments in which customers are grouped by characteristics shared by others in the segment.

To successfully target markets using a segmentation approach, organizations should engage in the following three-step process:

1. Identify segments within the overall market.
2. Choose the segment(s) that fits best with the organization's objectives and goals.
3. Develop a marketing strategy that appeals to the selected target market(s).

Step 1: Identify Market Segments

The first step in targeting markets through market segmentation is to separate customers who make up large general markets (i.e., basic needs) into smaller groupings based on selected characteristics or variables (also referred to as **bases of segmentation**) shared by those in the group. General markets are most often associated with basic product groups, such as automobile, beverage, footwear, home entertainment, etc. The purpose of segmentation is to look deeper within the general market in order to locate customers with more specific needs (e.g., seek hybrid automobiles) AND who also share similar characteristics (e.g., college educated, support environmental issues, etc.). When grouped together these customers may form a smaller segment of the general market. By focusing marketing research on these smaller segments the marketer can learn a great deal about these customers and with this information can craft highly targeted marketing campaigns.

• •

An example of a smaller segment in the U.S. that has recently attracted marketers' attention is the adult Halloween market. The market has grown substantially in recent years with the number of adults attending Halloween parties ranking third behind parties for New Year's Eve and the Super Bowl. Marketers for such products as candy, costumes, decorations, gift cards, and beer are seeing opportunity and have increased marketing spending in this segment. (4)

• •

The variables used to segment markets can be classified into a three-stage hierarchy (Figure 5-1) with higher stages building on information obtained from lower stages in order to reach greater precision in identifying shared characteristics. More precise segmentation efforts require sufficient funding, strong research skills, and other capabilities. For instance, a marketer entering a new market may not have the ability to segment beyond the first two stages since the precision needed in Stage 3 segmentation may demand an established relationship with customers in the market.

The three-stage segmentation process presented below works for both consumer and business markets, though the variables used to segment these markets may be different. Each segmentation stage includes an explanation along with suggestions for variables the marketer should consider. This is not meant to be an exhaustive list, as other variables are potentially available, but for marketers who are new to segmentation these offer a good starting point for segmenting markets.

Figure 5-1: Stages of Segmentation

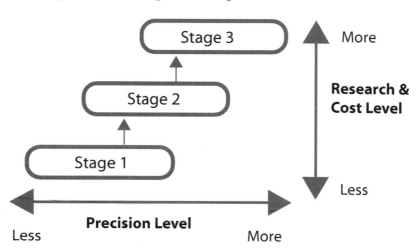

STAGE 1 SEGMENTATION VARIABLES

Stage 1 segmentation consists of variables (see Table 5-1) that can be easily identified through **demographics** (i.e., statistics describing a population), geographics (i.e., location), and financial information. For both consumer and business segmentation (see Box 5-2) this information focuses mostly on easy to obtain data from such sources as government data (e.g., census information), examining secondary data sources (e.g., news media), trade associations, and financial reporting services. While Stage 1 segmentation does not offer the segmentation benefits available with higher-level stages, the marketer benefits from accomplishing the segmentation task in a short time frame and at lower cost.

• •

An example of using demographics to segment markets can be seen with motorcycle manufacturer Harley-Davidson's efforts to target the female rider market. This market is the fastest growing segment in the motorcycle industry and Harley-Davidson appeals to this group with special products, education, and training. (5)

• •

Table 5-1: Stage 1 Segmentation Variables

Segmentation Variables Consumer Markets	Segmentation Variables Business Markets
Demographics age group (e.g., teens, retirees, young adults), gender, education level, ethnicity, income, occupation, social class, marital status	**Demographics** type (e.g., manufacturer, retailer, wholesaler), industry, size (e.g., sales volume, number of retail outlets), age (e.g., new, young growth, established growth, mature)
Geographics location (e.g., national, regional, urban/suburban/rural, international), climate	**Geographics** location (e.g., national, regional, urban/suburban/rural, international), climate **Business Arrangement** ownership (e.g.,. private versus public, independent versus chain), financial condition (e.g., credit rating, income growth, stock price, cash flow)

STAGE 2 SEGMENTATION VARIABLES

Some firms, especially companies with limited funds or those who feel they need to move quickly to get their product to market, stop the search for segmentation variables at the Stage 1 level. However, moving beyond Stage 1 segmentation offers a rich amount of customer information allowing marketers to more effectively target customers' needs. To segment using Stage 2 variables (see Table 5-2) marketers must use research techniques to gain insight into customers' current purchase situations and the environment in which customers operate. Information at this stage includes learning what options customers have chosen to satisfy their needs, what circumstances within customers' environment affect how purchases are made, and understanding local conditions impacting purchase decisions. Marketers might locate some of this information through the same sources used in Stage 1 but most variables require the marketer to engage in at least casual contact with customers in the market. This can be done through primary research methods, such as surveying the market, having sales personnel contact customers, purchasing research reports from commercial marketing research firms or hiring consultants to undertake research projects. The cost and time needed to acquire this information may be significantly greater than that of Stage 1 segmentation.

Box 5-2

FINDING BUSINESS TARGET MARKETS

On the surface segmentation of business markets may not always seem as clear as segmenting consumer markets. This can especially be a problem for marketers who are not familiar with a particular business market. For these marketers a good starting point for segmentation efforts is to utilize business classification systems set up by international governments, such as the North American Industrial Classification System (NAICS), which covers Canada, Mexico and the United States, and the International Standard Industrial Classification (ISIC), which is widely used in Europe.

These systems provide descriptions of hundreds of industry classifications. For instance, the table below shows how U.S. operators of "Golf Pro Shops" are listed in the NAICS coding system. Note the numeric sequence that occurs as one "drills down" in order to locate individual industry groups.

Level	NAICS Code	Description
Sector	45	Retail Trade
Subsector	451	Sporting Goods, Hobby, Book, and Music Stores
Industry Group	4511	Sporting Goods, Hobby, and Musical Instrument Stores
Industry	45111	Sporting Goods Stores
US Industry	451110	Golf Pro Shops

Once industry codes are known these can be used within various government and industry research reports to locate specific industry information, such as the number of firms operating in the industry, total industry sales, number of employees, and more. Additionally, these codes can be used to locate individual businesses. This can be done through business directory services specializing in listing company information, including contact data, and are generally searchable by classification code. (6)

Table 5-2: Stage 2 Segmentation Variables

Segmentation Variables Consumer Markets	Segmentation Variables Business Markets
Current Purchasing Situation brands used, purchase frequency, current suppliers **Purchase Ready** possess necessary equipment, property, knowledge, skill sets **Local Environment** cultural, political, legal	**Current Purchasing Situation** brands used, purchase frequency, current suppliers **Purchase Ready** possess necessary equipment, property, knowledge, skill sets **Local Environment** cultural, political, legal **Customers Served by the Business** identify the business' market **Business' Perceived Image** identify how targeted businesses are perceived by their customers

STAGE 3 SEGMENTATION VARIABLES

Marketers choosing to segment at the Stage 3 level face an enormous challenge in gathering useful segmentation information but, for those committed to segmenting at this level, the rewards may include gaining competitive advantage over rivals whose segmentation efforts have not dug this deep. However, the marketer must invest significant time and money to amass the detailed market intelligence needed to achieve Stage 3 segmentation. Additionally, much of what is needed at Stage 3 is information that is often well protected and not easily shared by customers. In fact, many customers are unwilling to share certain personal information (e.g., psychological) with marketers with whom they are not familiar. Consequently, segmenting on Stage 3 variables (see Table 5-3) is often not an option for marketers new to a market unless they acquire this via other means (e.g., hire a consultant who knows the market). To get access to this information marketers, who already serve the market with other products, may be able to use primary research such as focus groups, in-depth interviews, observational research, and other high level marketing research techniques.

Table 5-3: Stage 3 Segmentation Variables

Segmentation Variables Consumer Markets	Segmentation Variables Business Markets
Benefits Sought price, overall value, specific feature, ease-of-use, convenience, support services, etc.	**Benefits Sought** price, overall value, specific feature, services, profit margins, promotional assistance, etc.
Product Usage how used, why used, situation when used, used in combination with other products, etc.	**Product Usage** how used (e.g., raw material, component product, major selling item at retail level), situation when used, etc.
Purchase Conditions time of day, month or year when purchased, location of purchase, credit terms, trade-in option, etc.	**Purchase Conditions** length of sales cycle, set product specifications, bid pricing, credit terms, trade-in option, product handling, etc.
Characteristics of Individual Buyer purchase experience, how purchase is made, influencers on purchase decision, importance of purchase	**Characteristics of Buying Center** purchase experience, number of members, make-up of key influencers, willingness to assume risk
Psychographics personality, attitudes, and lifestyle combined with demographics	

Step 2: Choosing Market Segments

The second step in selecting target markets requires the marketer to critically evaluate the segments identified in Step 1 in order to select those which are most attractive. For small firms this step may not be very involved since they may lack the resources to do it effectively. So they are often left with using their own intuition or judgment to determine which segments are the most promising. For companies with the time and money to commit to this step, the results may identify the segments that are primary candidates for current marketing efforts and also present segments that are future targets for the company's offerings.

In determining whether a segment is a worthwhile target market, the marketer needs to address the following:

◆ Is the segment large enough to support the marketer's objectives? This is an especially critical question if the marketer is entering a market served by many competitors.

◆ Is the segment showing signs of growth? One of the worst situations for a marketer is to enter a market whose growth is flat or declining, especially if competitors already exist.

♦ Does the company have the necessary skills, knowledge, and expertise to service the segment? The company should understand and be able to communicate with the customers in the segment, otherwise they may face a significant learning curve in understanding how to effectively market to a segment.

♦ Does the segment meet the mission of the company? The segment should not extend too far beyond the direction the company has chosen to take.

Once one or more segments have been identified the marketer must choose the most attractive option(s) for its marketing efforts. At this point the choice becomes the firm's target market(s):

Step 3: Develop Strategy to Appeal to Target Market(s)

The results of analyzing market segments lead the marketer to consider one of the following target marketing strategies:

♦ Undifferentiated or Mass Marketing – Under this strategy the marketer attempts to appeal to one large market with a single marketing strategy. While this approach offers advantages in terms of lowering development and production costs, since only one product is marketed, there are few markets in which all customers seek the same benefits. This approach was very popular in the early days of marketing (e.g., Ford Model-T), but today few companies view this as a feasible strategy.

♦ Differentiated or Segmentation Marketing – Marketers choosing this strategy try to appeal to multiple smaller markets with a unique marketing strategy for each market. The underlying concept is that bigger markets can be divided into many sub-markets and an organization chooses different marketing strategies to reach each sub-market it targets. Most large consumer products firms follow this strategy as they offer multiple products (e.g., running shoes, basketball shoes) within a larger product category (e.g., footwear).

♦ Concentrated or Niche Marketing – This strategy combines mass and segmentation marketing by using a single marketing strategy to appeal to one or more very small markets. It is primarily used by smaller marketers who have identified small **sub-segments** of a larger segment that are not served well by larger firms that follow a segmentation marketing approach. In these situations a smaller company can do quite well marketing a single product to a narrowly defined target market.

♦ Customized or Micro Marketing – This newest target marketing strategy attempts to appeal to targeted customers with individual-ized marketing programs. For micro marketing segmentation to be effective the marketer must, to some degree, allow customers to "build-their-own" products. This approach requires extensive tech-nical capability for marketers to reach individual customers and al-low customers to interact with the marketer. The Internet has been the catalyst for this target marketing strategy. As more companies learn to utilize the Internet micro marketing is expected to flourish.

· ·

Through its NIKEiD site, Nike offers customers the opportunity to customize their own apparel. Customers can choose from a large selection of footwear, clothing, and equipment and then customize to their own needs. For instance, for some footwear products customers can adjust several different color elements including the look of the general base material, the heel, the Nike Swoosh logo, and the laces. Customization also includes the imprinting of text on the tongue of the shoe. (7)

· ·

POSITIONING PRODUCTS AND SERVICES

No matter which target marketing strategy is selected, the overall marketing strategy should involve the process of positioning the firm's offerings in ways that will appeal to targeted customers. Positioning is concerned with the per-ception customers hold regarding a product or company. In particular, it relates to marketing decisions an organization undertakes to get customers to think about a product or company in a certain way compared to its competitors.

The goal of positioning is to convince customers to believe the marketer's offerings are different in some way from its competitors on an important ben-efit sought by the market. For instance, if a customer has discovered she has a need for an affordable laptop computer, a company such as Dell may come to mind since its marketing efforts position its products as offering good value at a reasonable cost.

To position successfully the marketer must have a thorough knowledge of the key benefits sought by the market. Obviously the more effort the marketer expends on segmentation (i.e., reached Stage 3 Segmentation) the more likely it will know the benefits sought by the market. Once known, the marketer must: 1) tailor marketing efforts to ensure its offerings satisfy the most sought after benefits, and 2) communicate to the market in a way that differentiates the marketer's offerings from competitors.

For firms seeking to appeal to multiple target markets (i.e., Segmentation Marketing), positioning strategies may differ for each market. For example, a marketer may sell the same product to two different target markets, but in one market the emphasis is on styling while in another market the emphasis is on ease-of-use benefits. The important point is that the overall marketing strategy must be evaluated separately for each target market since what works well in one market may not work as well in another market.

• •

Sometimes a marketing organization, that has obtained a very favorable position within an industry, must work to change this because it no longer fits with what they do or where the industry has evolved. For example, Xerox was for many decades synonymous with the concept of photocopying. Today the company offers a full range of services of which only a small portion is photocopying. Through promotional methods, such as designing a new logo, Xerox is working to re-position the company as one that can assist with all elements of "document flow". (8)

• •

REFERENCES

1. "Bank of America Strategist Sees Coming Slump in Global Consumption," *MSN Money*, June 11, 2008.

2. "Consumer Expenditures in 2006," *Bureau of Labor Statistics - United States Department of Labor*, October 26, 2007.

3. *Visa Inc.* website.

4. Beirne, M., "Adults-Only Strategy Drives Halloween Sales to $5B," *Brandweek*, October 15, 2007.

5. Hillard, G., "Industry Embraces, Caters to Biker Chicks," *All Things Considered – National Public Radio*, October 12, 2007.

6. For a list of links to business directory services see the **Market Research** section of *KnowThis.com*.

7. *NIKEiD* website.

8. H. Deutsch, C.H., "Xerox Hopes Its New Logo Doesn't Say Copier," *New York Times*, January 7, 2008.

Full text of many of the references can be accessed via links on the support website.

Chapter 6:

Product Decisions

As we stress throughout this book, organizations attempt to provide value to a target market by offering solutions to customers' needs. These solutions include tangible or intangible (or both) product offerings marketed by an organization. In addition to satisfying the target market's needs, the product is important because it is how organizations generate revenue. It is what a for-profit company sells in order to realize profits and satisfy financial stakeholders (e.g., stockholders). Products are also important for many non-profit organizations where they are used to generate revenue needed to support operations (e.g., fund raising). Without a well-developed product strategy that includes input from the target market, a marketing organization will not have long-term success.

In this chapter we define what a product is and look at how products are categorized. We also take a close look at the key decisions marketers face as they formulate their product offerings. These decisions include: product features, branding, packaging, and labeling. We discuss each in detail and see how these impact product strategy.

WHAT IS A PRODUCT?

In marketing the term **product** is used as a catch-all word to identify solutions a marketer provides to its target market. We will use the term "product" to cover offerings that fall into one of the following categories:

GOODS

Something is considered a good if it is a tangible item. That is, it is something that is felt, tasted, heard, smelled or seen. For example, bicycles, cellphones, and donuts are all examples of tangible goods. In some cases there is a fine line between items that affect the senses and whether these are considered tangible or intangible. We often see this with digital goods accessed via the Internet, such as listening to music online or visiting an information website. In these cases there does not appear to be anything that is tangible or real since it is essentially computer code proving the solution. However, for our purposes, we distinguish these as goods since these products are built (albeit using computer code), are stored (e.g., on a computer hard drive), and generally offer the same benefits each time (e.g., quality of the downloaded song is always the same).

SERVICES

Something is considered a service if it is an offering a customer obtains through the work or labor of someone else. Services can result in the creation of tangible goods (e.g., a publisher of business magazines hires a freelance writer to write an article) but the main solution purchased is the service. Unlike goods, services are not stored, they are only available at the time of use (e.g., hair salon) and the consistency of the benefit offered can vary from one purchaser to another (e.g., not exactly the same hair styling each time).

IDEAS

Something falls into the category of an idea if the marketer attempts to convince the customer to alter his/her behavior or perception in some way. Marketing ideas is often a solution put forth by non-profit groups or governments in order to get targeted groups to avoid or change certain behavior. This is seen with public service announcements directed toward such activity as youth smoking, automobile safety, and illegal drug use.

While some marketers offer solutions providing both tangible and intangible attributes, for most organizations their primary offering is concentrated in one area. So while a manufacturer may offer intangible services or a service firm provides certain tangible equipment, these are often add-ons that support the organization's main product.

Categories of Consumer Products

Most products intended for consumer use can be further categorized as:

◆ Convenience Products – These products appeal to a very large market segment. They are generally consumed regularly and purchased frequently. Examples include most household items such as food, cleaning products, and personal care products. Because of the high purchase volume, pricing per item tends to be relatively low and consumers often see little value in shopping around since additional effort yields minimal savings. From the marketer's perspective the low price of convenience products means that profit per unit sold is very low. In order to make high profits marketers must sell in large volume. Consequently, marketers attempt to distribute these products in mass through as many retail outlets as possible (see *Mass Coverage* discussion in Chapter 8).

◆ Shopping Products – These are products consumers purchase and consume on a less frequent schedule compared to convenience products. Consumers spend more time locating these products since they are relatively more expensive than convenience products and because these may possess additional psychological benefits for purchasers, such as raising their perceived status level within their social group. Examples include many clothing products, personal services, electronic products, and household furnishings. Because consumers are purchasing less frequently and are willing to shop to locate these products, the target market for shopping products is much smaller than for convenience goods. Consequently, marketers often are more selective when choosing distribution outlets to sell these products (see *Selective Coverage* discussion in Chapter 8).

◆ Specialty Products – These are products that carry a high price tag relative to convenience and shopping products. Consumption may occur at the same rate as shopping products but consumers are much more selective. In fact, in many cases consumers know in advance which product they prefer and will not shop to compare products. But they may shop at retailers that provide the best value. Examples include high-end luxury automobiles, expensive champagne, and celebrity hair care experts. The target markets are generally very small and outlets selling the products are very limited to the point of being exclusive (see *Exclusive Coverage* discussion in Chapter 8).

> •
>
> *While most consumer convenience and shopping products can easily be purchased over the Internet, the same is not true for many high-end specialty products. For the most part, it is specialty product marketers who are not allowing their products to be sold online. They are concerned that a product which built a reputation for being unique and exclusive will lose this perception given the openness of the Internet. Additionally, they believe luxury products require the marketer to build close personal relationships with customers, something that is much easier to do in-person than over the Internet. (1)*
>
> •

In addition to the three main categories above, consumer products are classified in at least two additional ways:

◆ Emergency Products – These are products sought due to sudden events and for which pre-purchase planning is not considered. Often the decision is one of convenience (e.g., whatever works to fix a problem) or personal fulfillment (e.g., perceived to improve purchaser's image).

◆ Unsought Products – These are products whose purchase is unplanned but occur as a result of marketers' actions. Such purchase decisions are made when the customer is exposed to promotional activity, such as a salesperson's persuasion or purchase incentives, like special discounts. These promotional activities often lead customers to engage in impulse purchasing.

Categories of Business Products

Products sold within the business market fall into the following categories:

◆ Raw Materials – These are products obtained through mining, harvesting, fishing, etc., that are key ingredients in the production of higher-order products.

◆ Processed Materials – These are products created through the processing of basic raw materials. In some cases original raw materials are refined while in other cases the process combines different raw materials to create something new. For instance crops, including corn and sugar cane, can be processed to create ethanol used as fuel to power car and truck engines.

◆ Equipment – These are products used to help with production or operations activities. Examples range from conveyor belts to large buildings housing the headquarters staff of a multi-national company.

◆ Basic Components – These are products used within more advanced components and are often built with raw or processed material. Electrical wire is an example.

◆ Advanced Components – These use basic components to produce products offering a significant function needed within a larger product. By itself an advanced component is not a final product. In computers the motherboard is an example since it contains many Basic Components but without the inclusion of other products (e.g., memory chips, microprocessor, etc.) would have little value.

◆ Product Components – These are products used in the assembly of a final product though these could also function as stand alone products. Dice included as part of a children's board game is an example.

◆ MRO (Maintenance, Repair and Operating) Products – These are products used to assist with the operation of the organization but are not directly used in producing goods or services. Office supplies, parts for a truck fleet, and natural gas to heat a factory would fall into this category.

Components of a Product

On the surface it seems a product is simply a marketing offering, whether tangible or intangible, that someone wants to purchase and consume. One might believe product decisions are focused exclusively on designing and building the consumable elements of goods, services or ideas. In actuality, while decisions related to the consumable parts of the product are extremely important, the TOTAL product consists of more than what is consumed. The total product offering, and the decisions facing the marketer, can be broken down into three major parts:

Core Benefits

As we discussed in Chapter 1, customers seek to obtain value from marketers in exchange for their willingness to give up something they value, generally in the form of money. What customers obtain are solutions to their needs or stated another way, receive **benefits**. For customers benefits drive their purchase decisions (see Box 6-1). At the very heart of all product decisions is determining the core benefits a product provides. That is, the key value sought by those in the marketer's target market. From this decision, the rest of the product offering can be developed. In most cases the core benefits are offered by features of the actual product (e.g., floor cleaner) though for some customers benefits offered by other aspects or augmented features (see *Augmented Product* discussion below) of the product are also important (e.g., access to customer service).

Actual Product

For most customers, the core benefits are offered through the components that make up the actual product. When a consumer returns home from shopping and takes an item out of her shopping bag, the actual product is the item she holds in her hand. Within the actual product is the **consumable product**, which is the main good, service or idea the customer is buying. For example, while toothpaste comes in a package that makes dispensing it easy, the consumable product is the paste that is placed on a toothbrush. But marketers must understand that while the consumable product is the most critical of all product decisions, as we will soon see the actual product includes many separate product decisions, including product features, branding, packaging, labeling, and more.

Augmented Product

Marketers often surround their actual product with goods and services that provide additional value to the customer's purchase. While these factors may not be key reasons leading customers to purchase (i.e., do not offer core benefits), for some the inclusion of these items strengthens the purchase decision while for others failure to include these may cause the customer not to buy. Items considered part of the augmented product include:

- Guarantee – This provides a level of assurance that the product will perform up to expectations and if not the company marketing the product will support the customer's decision to replace, repair or return for a refund.

- Warranty – This offers customers a level of protection often extending past the guarantee period to cover repair or replacement of certain product components.

- Customer Service – As discussed in detail in Chapter 3, these services support customers through such methods as training, repair, and other types of assistance.

- Complementary Products – The value of some product purchases is enhanced with add-on products or complementary products. Such items make the main product easier to use (e.g., laptop carrybag), improve styling (e.g., cellphone face plates) or extend functionality (e.g., portable keyboard for PDAs).

Box 6-1

MARKETERS SELL BENEFITS

The benefits a customer obtains from a product are contained within the actual and augmented product through product features. Features are the separate attributes of a product. For example, for the purchase of a plasma television, features include screen size, screen resolution, surround sound, and remote control.

The benefits a customer receives from the purchase and use of the product fall into two main categories:

Functional Benefits

These are benefits derived from features that are part the consumable product. For instance, in our plasma television example, features and benefits may include:

Feature	Functional Benefit
• screen size	offers greater detail and more distant viewing
• screen resolution	provides clear, more realistic picture
• surround sound	immerses all senses in the viewing experience
• remote control	allows for greater comfort while viewing

The benefits offered by these features are called functional because they result in a benefit the user directly associates with the product. Functional benefits are often the result of materials, design, and production decisions. How the product is built can lead to benefits such as speed, ease-of-use, durability, and cost savings.

Psychological Benefits

These are benefits the customer perceives she/he receives when using the product. These benefits address psychological needs, such as status within a group, risk reduction, sense of independence, and happiness. Such benefits are developed through promotional efforts that target customer's internal makeup (see Chapter 4).

In communicating with customers, marketers should always associate a benefit with a product feature. Benefits are what customers seek; the feature is simply how the benefit is delivered. Thus, in our plasma television example, a magazine advertisement promoting the television is more effective if it speaks directly to benefits it offers such as:

> *Our new high-definition televisions offer screen resolutions* (feature) *that provide the clearest, most realistic picture* (functional benefit) *that will make your house the place to be* (psychological benefit) *for the big game!*

. . . .

Marketers selling complementary products often find themselves at the mercy of the main product. In some cases, marketers of the main product will share details with complementary product makers prior to product introduction, thus enabling the complementary products to be available at the same time as the main product. But in some cases, such as with the launch of the Apple iPhone 3G, the main product maker is reluctant to provide information in advance of the product launch. However, many complementary product makers have learned to respond quickly and can turn out compatible products within a matter of weeks of the release of the main product. (2)

. . . .

KEY PRODUCT DECISIONS

The actual product is designed to provide the core benefits sought by the target market. The marketer offers these benefits through a combination of factors making up the actual product. Below we discuss four key factors that together help shape the actual product.

Consumable Product Features

Features are characteristics of a product that offer benefits to the customer. When it comes to developing a consumable product marketers face several decisions related to product features, including:

- ◆ Features Set vs. Cost – For marketers an important decision focuses on the quantity and quality of features (i.e., features set) to include in a product. In most cases the more features included or the higher the quality level for a particular feature, the more expensive the product is to produce and market.

- ◆ Is More Better? – Even if added cost is not a major concern, the marketer must determine if more features help or hurt the target market's perception of the product. A product with too many features could be viewed as too difficult to use. This was often the case when video cassette recorders (VCR) were the principle device for taping television programs and watching rented movies. Many of the higher-level features introduced in the 1990s as the product matured, such as advanced television recording, proved too difficult for the average consumer to master.

♦ <u>Who Should Choose the Features?</u> – Historically marketers determined what features to include in a product. However, the Customized or Micro Marketing targeting strategy we discussed in the Chapter 5 offers customers the opportunity to choose their own features to custom build a product. For instance, companies offering website hosting services allow website owners to choose from a list of service options that best suit their needs. Also, for traditional products, such as clothing, companies allow customers to stylize their purchases with logos and other personalized options.

Branding

Branding involves decisions establishing an identity for a product with the goal of distinguishing it from competitors' offerings. In markets where competition is fierce and where customers may select from among many competitive products, creating an identity through branding is essential. It is particularly important in helping position the product (see Chapter 5) in the minds of the product's target market.

While consumer products companies have long recognized the value of branding, it has only been within the last 15-20 years that organizations selling in the business market have begun to focus on brand building strategies. One well-known business marketer to develop a brand is Intel, maker of component products, such as computer chips, which created a brand through its now famous "Intel Inside" slogan. Intel's success has led many others selling in the business market and even not-for-profit organizations to incorporate branding within their overall marketing strategy.

BRAND NAMES AND BRAND MARKS

At a very basic level branding is achieved through the use of unique brand names and brand marks. The brand name, which may be the individual product name or a name applied to a group or family of products, is important for many reasons, including suggesting what the product is or does (e.g., Mop-and-Glow). The name is also what we utter when we discuss the product with others. The brand mark is a design element, such as a symbol (e.g., Nike swoosh), a logo (e.g., Yahoo! graphic), a character (e.g., Keebler elves) or even a sound (e.g., Intel Inside sound), that provides visual or auditory recognition for the product.

••

Marketers are discovering there may still be value in iconic branded characters that were popular in the past but over time were replaced or demoted in favor of other promotional methods. Several companies have reintroduced these characters with the hope they can appeal to new markets. Examples include Burger King's king character, Bayer's Speedy who promotes Alka-Seltzer, and VF Corporation's Buddy Lee for its Lee jeans. (3)

••

BRANDING STRATEGY

With competition growing more intense in almost all industries, establishing a strong brand allows an organization's products to stand out and avoid potential pitfalls such as price wars. A clear understanding of branding is essential in order to build a solid product strategy. Marketers should be aware of various branding approaches that can be pursued and deployed to establish a product within the market. The purpose of these approaches is to build a brand that will exist for the long term. Making smart branding decisions in the early stages of a new product is crucial since a company may have to live with the decision for a long time.

Branding approaches include:

- <u>Individual Product Branding</u> – With this branding approach new products are assigned new names with no obvious connection to a company's existing brands. Under individual product branding the marketing organization must work hard to establish the brand in the market since it cannot ride the coattails of previously introduced brands. The chief advantage of this approach is it allows brands to stand on their own. This lessens threats that may occur to other brands marketed by the company. For instance, if a company receives negative publicity for one brand this news is less likely to rub off on the company's other brands that carry their own unique names. Under an individual branding approach, each brand builds its own separate equity (see Box 6-2) which allows the company to potentially sell off individual brands without impacting other brands owned by the company. The most famous marketing organization to follow this strategy is Procter & Gamble, which has historically introduced new brands without any link to other brands or even to the company name. (4)

- <u>Family Branding</u> – Under this branding approach new products are placed under the umbrella of an existing brand. The principle advantage of family branding is it enables the organization to rapidly build market awareness and acceptance since the brand is already established and known to the market. The potential disadvantage is that the market already has established perceptions of the brand. For instance, a company selling low-end, lower priced products may have a brand viewed as an economy brand. If the company attempts to introduce higher-end, higher priced products using the same brand name this may create customer confusion and hinder sales. Additionally, any negative publicity for one product within a brand family could spread to all other products that share the same brand name.

- Co-Branding – This approach takes the idea of individual and family branding a step further. With co-branding a marketer seeks to partner with another firm, which has an established brand, in hopes the synergy of two brands on a product is more powerful than a single brand. The partnership often has both firms sharing costs but also sharing the gains. For instance, major credit card companies, such as Visa and MasterCard, offer co-branding options to companies and organizations. The cards carry the name of a co-branded organization (e.g., university name) along with the name of the issuing bank (e.g., Citibank) and the name of the credit card company. Besides tapping into awareness for multiple brands, the co-branding strategy is designed to appeal to a larger target market, especially if each brand, when viewed separately, does not have extensive overlapping target markets with the other brand. Therefore, co-branding allows both firms to tap into market segments where they previously did not have a strong position.

• •

Another form of co-branding happens when different brands owned by the same company share the name of the product. Procter & Gamble has used this approach by combining such brands as Tide detergent with Downy fabric softener, Crest toothpaste with Scope mouthwash, and Cover Girl makeup with Olay skin care. (5)

• •

- Private Label or Store Branding – Some suppliers are in the business of producing products for other companies, including placing another company's brand name on the product. This is most often seen in the retail industry where stores or online sellers contract with suppliers to manufacture the retailer's own branded products. In some cases the supplier not only produces products for the retailer's brand but also markets its own brand so that store shelves will contain both brands. In recent years the rapid growth of private label products has resulted in more shelf space being dedicated to these products and less to branded products. (6)

- No-Name or Generic Branding – Certain suppliers provide products that are intentionally "brandless." These products are mostly basic commodity-type products consumer or business customers purchase as low price alternatives to branded products. Basic household products, such as paper products, over-the-counter medicines, such as ibuprofen, and even dog food are available in a generic form.

- Brand Licensing – Under brand licensing a contractual arrangement is created in which a company owning a brand name allows others to produce and supply products carrying the brand name. This is often seen when a brand is not directly connected with a product category. For instance, several famous children's characters, such as Sesame Street's Elmo, have been licensed to toy and food manufacturers who market products using the branded character's name and image.

ADVANTAGES OF BRANDS

A strong brand offers many advantages for marketers including:

- Enhances Product Recognition – Brands provide multiple sensory stimuli to enhance customer recognition. A brand can be visually recognizable from its packaging, logo, shape, etc. It can be recognizable via sound, such as hearing the name on a radio advertisement or verbally when someone mentions the product.

- Builds Brand Equity – Strong brands can lead to financial advantages through the concept of brand equity in which the brand itself becomes valuable. Such gains can be realized through the out-right sale of a brand or through licensing arrangements (see Box 6-2).

Box 6-2

BRAND EQUITY THROUGH INTELLECTUAL PROPERTY

When most people think of a business asset they generally think of machinery, computers, buildings, and other physical items purchased and used by a business. But companies can also create and grow their own assets that are, in essence, intangible. They principally exist as legally protected "rights" that often prevent others from doing the same thing. If managed well, such rights can become enormously valuable.

In marketing the most likely source for acquiring protected rights is through government-controlled registration systems collectively referred to as intellectual property. Intellectual property provides protection in four ways (7):

Patent
Offers legal protection for inventions, such as new products, preventing others from offering the same product for a certain period of time. For example, a company may develop certain features in a product that others can not include in their product for the period of the patent which may be as long as 20 years.

Trademark
Offers legal protection on unique words, names, symbols, and other identifiable features that distinguish one item from another. For example, a product's name, the design of a logo, special symbols, and even characters associated with a brand can be trademarked.

Copyright
Offers legal protection for original authored work, such as writings and recordings. For example, in addition to protecting authors of books and music, copyright can also be used to protect website materials, music tied to product advertising, and print advertising copy.

Trade Secret
Offers legal protection for information, tightly protected by a company, which is used within the regular course of doing business and intended to give a company an advantage over competitors. For example, the formula used to produce Coca-Cola is protected as a trade secret.

For marketers intellectual property, particularly trademarks, is important in building brand identity. As we discussed, a uniquely identified brand that is well known to a target market may occupy a position in the minds of customers that sets it apart from other brands (e.g., Apple Computers vs. PC computers) or associates it with a specific benefit (e.g., digital music player = Apple iPod). By doing this the marketer is creating a company asset from a recognizable name, symbol or other unique feature. Called brand equity, the marketer's work can lead to an asset that can grow in value and eventually offer the company a financial reward.

For example, Company A may have a well-recognized brand (Brand X) within a market but for some reason they are looking to concentrate efforts in other markets. Company B is looking to enter the same market as Brand X. If circumstances are right, Company A could sell to Company B the rights to use the Brand X name without selling any other part of the company. That is, Company A simply sells the legal rights to the Brand X name but retains all other parts of Brand X, such as the production facilities and employees. In cases of well developed brands such a transaction may carry a very large price tag. Thus, through strong branding efforts Company A achieves a large financial gain by simply signing over the rights to the name. But why would Company B seek to purchase a brand for such a high price tag? Because by buying the brand Company B has already achieved an important marketing goal – building awareness within the target market. The fact the market is already familiar with the brand allows Company B to concentrate on other marketing decisions.

• •

Companies often decide to re-name a brand. This can occur because the perception of the brand no longer matches the needs of the company. For instance, the brand may have a name that is similar to another product and is leading to customer confusion. Another reason is that the brand limits the growth of the company. FedEx discovered this when it decided to rename its Kinko's division to FedEx Office. However, the company acknowledged the loss of brand equity by writing off nearly (US) $900 million. (8)

• •

- <u>Helps Build Brand Loyalty</u> – **Brand loyal** customers are frequent and enthusiastic purchasers of a particular brand. Cultivating brand loyalty among customers is the ultimate reward for successful marketers since these customers are far less likely to switch to other brands compared to non-loyal customers.

- <u>Helps with Product Positioning</u> – Well-developed and promoted brands make product positioning efforts more effective. The result is that upon exposure to a brand (e.g., hearing it, seeing it) customers conjure up mental images or feelings of the benefits of that brand. The reverse is even better. When customers associate benefits with a particular brand, the brand may have attained a significant competitive advantage. In these situations the customer who recognizes he needs a solution to a problem (e.g., needs to bleach clothes) may automatically think of one brand that offers the solution to the problem (e.g., Clorox). This "benefit = brand" association provides a significant advantage for the brand.

- <u>Aids in Introduction of New Products</u> – A successful brand can be extended by adding new products under the earlier discussed Family Branding strategy. Such branding may allow companies to introduce new products more easily since the brand is already recognized within the market.

• •

Some marketers have found it is easier and less costly to resurrect old brands than it is to develop new ones. For example, Kellogg is re-marketing Hydrox chocolate sandwich cookies that were taken off the market in 2003. One reason for finding value in old brands is that these often have strong recognition that may aid reintroduction. Through marketing research Reserve Brands found that Eagle snacks, a dormant brand once marketed by Anheuser-Busch but off the market since the mid-1990s, still had a brand that was recognized by 6 out of 10 adults. They have now re-launched the brand hoping to attract the interest of those who remember the product. (9) & (10)

• •

Packaging

Nearly all tangible products (i.e., goods) are sold to customers in a container or package that serves many purposes, including protecting the product during shipment. In a few cases, such as with certain produce items, the final customer may purchase the product without a package but the produce marketer still faces packaging decisions when it comes to shipping its produce to others such as resellers. Consequently, for many products there are two packaging decisions – final customer package and distribution package.

Final Customer Package

This relates to the package the final customer receives in exchange for his/her payment. When the final customer makes a purchase he or she is initially exposed to the outermost container holding the product. This exterior package generally contains product information (see *Labeling* discussion below), graphic design (e.g., logo, colors scheme), special handling features (e.g., carrying handle), and other characteristics.

Depending on the type of product being purchased, there may be several components to the package holding the product. These components can be divided into the following:

- First-Level Package – This is packaging that holds the actual product (e.g., Tylenol Bottle). In some cases this packaging is minimal since it only serves to protect the product. For instance, certain frozen food products are sold to consumers in a cardboard box with the product itself contained in a plastic bag found inside the box. This plastic bag represents the first-level package. In other cases frozen food products are sold to final customers only in plastic bags. In these cases the plastic bag is the only packaging obtained by the customer.

- Second-Level Package – In some cases the first-level package is surrounded by one or more outer packages (e.g., box holding the Tylenol Bottle). This second-level package would then serve as the exterior package for the product.

- Package Inserts – Marketers use a variety of other methods to communicate with customers after they open the product package. These methods are often inserted within, or sometimes on, the product's package. Insertions include information such as instruction manuals and warranty cards, promotional incentives such as coupons, and items that add value such as recipes and software.

• •

As we discuss in Chapter 9, retailers who consumer product marketers enlist to help sell their products will consider customer packaging when making their decision to handle the product. Consequently, marketers who develop creative packaging ideas may find it easier to gain space on store shelves. For example, NXT, a newly introduced shaving gel, was able to gain space on giant U.S. retailer Target's shelf by presenting its product in a package that lights and illuminates air bubbles. From a retailer's perspective this effect can increase sales as it captures customers' attention as they walk down the aisle. (11)

• •

Distribution Package

This packaging is used to transport the final customer package through the supply chain. It generally holds multiple final customer packages and also offers a higher level of damage protection than that of customer packaging.

FACTORS TO CONSIDER WHEN MAKING PACKAGING DECISIONS

Packaging decisions are important for several reasons, including:

- Protection – Packaging is used to protect the product from damage during shipping and handling, and to lessen spoilage if the product is exposed to air or other elements.

- Visibility – Packaging design is used to capture customers' attention as they are shopping or glancing through a catalog or website. This is particularly important for customers who are not familiar with the product and in situations, such as those found in grocery stores, where a product must stand out among thousands of other products. Packaging designs that standout are more likely to be remembered on future shopping trips.

- Added Value – Packaging design and structure can add value to a product. For instance, benefits can be obtained from package structures that make the product easier to use while stylistic designs can make the product more attractive to display in the customer's home.

- Distributor Acceptance – Packaging decisions must not only be accepted by the final customer, they may also have to be accepted by distributors who sell the product for the marketer. For instance, a retailer may not accept packages unless they conform to requirements they have for storing products on its shelves.

- Cost – Packaging can represent a significant portion of a product's selling price. For example, it is estimated that in the cosmetics industry the packaging cost of some products may be as high as 40 percent of a product's selling price. Smart packaging decisions can help reduce costs and possibly lead to higher profits.

- Expensive to Create – Developing new packaging can be extremely expensive. The costs involved in creating new packaging include: graphic and structural design, production, customer testing, possible destruction of leftover old packaging, and possible advertising to inform customers of the new packaging.

- Long-Term Decision – When companies create a new package it is most often with the intention of having the design on the market for an extended period of time. In fact, changing a product's packaging too frequently can have negative effects since customers become conditioned to locating the product based on its package and may be confused if the design is altered.

- Environmental or Legal Issues – Packaging decisions must also include an assessment of its environmental impact especially for products with packages that are frequently discarded. Packages that are not easily bio-degradable could draw customer and governmental reaction. Also, caution must be exercised in order to create packages that do not infringe on another firm's intellectual property, such as copyrights, trademarks or patents.

• •

In advance of the 2008 Summer Olympics, PepsiCo Inc. began marketing its Pepsi cola product in China using a red can. While the company explained this was intended to support the host country, whose primary color is red, some marketing experts also suggest the packaging strategy is intended to disrupt customers from automatically associating red color drink packaging with Pepsi's chief rival, Coca-Cola. (12)

• •

Labeling

Most packages, whether final customer packaging or distribution packaging, are imprinted with information intended to assist the customer. For consumer products, labeling decisions are extremely important for the following reasons:

- The label is likely to be the first thing a new customer sees leading to his/her first impression of the product.

- Labels serve to capture the attention of shoppers. The use of catchy words and graphics may cause strolling customers to stop and evaluate the product.

- The label provides customers with product information to aid their purchase decision or help improve customers' experience when using the product (e.g., recipes).

- Labels generally include a universal product codes (UPC) and, in some cases, radio frequency identification (RFID) tags, making it easy for resellers, such as retailers, to process customers' purchases and manage inventory.

- For companies serving international markets or diverse cultures within a single country, bilingual or multilingual labels may be needed.

- In some countries many products, including food and pharmaceuticals, are required by law to contain certain labels, such as listing ingredients, providing nutritional information, or including usage warning information.

REFERENCES

1. de Mesa, A., "Online Luxury for the Masses," *brandchannel*, January 11, 2007.

2. Loten, A., "Apple's New iPhone: Let the Frenzy Begin," *Inc*, June 2008.

3. Elliott, S., "A 1950s Brand Mascot Fights 21st-Century Indigestion," *New York Times*, March 5, 2008.

4. *Procter* & Gamble website.

5. "Consumer Products Double Down on Brands," *MSNBC*, November 16, 2007.

6. Herr, P., "What's in Store for Store Brands," *MillwardBrown*, July 2008.

7. "What is Intellectual Property?" *United States Patent and Trademark Office* website.

8. "FedEx to Drop Kinko's Name, Take $891M Charge," *USA Today*, June 2, 2008.

9. Elliott, S., "Those Shelved Brands Start to Look Tempting," *New York Times*, August 20, 2008.

10. Walker, R., "Can a Dead Brand Live Again?" *New York Times Magazine*, May 18, 2008.

11. Newman, A.A., "A Package That Lights Up the Shelf," *New York Times*, March 4, 2008.

12. Pincott, G., "Putting the Shopper Back Into Marketing," *MillwardBrown*, December 2007.

Full text of many of the references can be accessed via links on the support website.

Chapter 7:

Managing Products

In Chapter 6 we showed marketers are confronted with many issues when building the product component of their marketing strategy. While product decisions represent just one aspect of marketers' overall activities, these decisions are often the most important because they lead directly to the reasons (i.e., benefits offered, solutions to problems) why the customer decides to choose the organization's goods, services, or ideas.

In this chapter we extend the coverage of product decisions by exploring additional product issues facing the marketer. First, we look at how companies structure their product offerings and identify the scope of a manager's responsibilities within this structure. Second, we spend a large part of this chapter covering the importance of new product development, including an analysis of the steps firms may follow to bring new products to market. Finally, we show that once new products have been established in the market numerous factors force the marketer to continually adjust its product decisions. As part of this we examine the concept of the Product Life Cycle and see how it offers valuable insight and guidance for new product decisions.

STRUCTURE OF PRODUCT MANAGEMENT

Marketers are often responsible for a wide array of decisions required to manage a company's product offerings. As we will discuss shortly, these decisions include both the creation of new products and the management of existing products. But what a marketer does on a day-to-day basis will depend on how a company structures the management of its products. Possible structures include:

PRODUCT ITEM MANAGEMENT

At this level responsibilities are associated with marketing a single product or brand. By "single" we are limiting the marketer's responsibility to one item. For instance, a startup software development company may initially market just one product. In some organizations the person in charge has the title Product Manager, though in smaller companies this person may simply be the Marketing Manager.

BRAND PRODUCT LINE MANAGEMENT

At this level responsibilities are associated with managing two or more similar product items. By "similar" we are referring to products carrying the same brand name that fit within the same product category and offer similar solutions to customers' needs. Procter & Gamble, one of the largest consumer products companies in the world, markets Tide laundry detergent in many different packaging sizes (e.g., 50oz., 100oz., 200oz.), in different forms (e.g., powder, liquid), and with different added features (e.g., softener, bleach) resulting in a product line consisting of over 100 different versions of the product. (1) Differences in the product offerings indicate these are targeted to different segments within the larger market (e.g., those preferring liquid vs. those preferring powder), however, it may also represent a choice for the same target market who may seek variety. A product line is often measured by its depth, relative to competitors, with deep product lines offering extensive product options. Brand product lines are often managed by a Brand or Product Line Manager.

CATEGORY PRODUCT LINE MANAGEMENT

At this level responsibilities are associated with managing two or more brand product lines within the same product category. In this situation the marketer may manage products offering similar basic benefits (e.g., detergent to clean clothes) but target its offerings to slightly different needs (e.g., product for tough to clean clothing vs. product to clean delicate clothing). Multiple brand product lines allow the marketer to cover the needs of more segments and, consequently, increase its chance to generate sales. Often in larger companies category product lines are the responsibility of the Product Category or Divisional Marketing Manager who may have Brand Product Managers reporting to him/her.

PRODUCT MIX MANAGEMENT

At this level responsibilities include two or more category product lines directed to different product categories. In some cases the category product lines may yield similar general solutions (e.g., cleaning) but are aimed at entirely different target markets (e.g., cleaning dishes vs. cleaning automobiles). In large companies, the product lines are very diverse and offer different solutions. For example, BIC sells writing instruments, shaving products, and butane lighters. This diversification strategy cushions against an "all-eggs-in-one-basket" risk that may come if a company directs all resources to one product category. A product mix can be classified based on its **width** (how many different category product lines) and its **depth** (how many different brand product lines within a category product line). Generally responsibility for this level belongs to a company's Vice President for Marketing.

• •

For those seeking information on marketing careers in the U.S. several websites offer good information on different career options including Salary.com (2), which offers salary information by job title, and the Occupational Employment Statistics section of the U.S. Department of Labor (3), which offers employment totals and salary information.

• •

MANAGING NEW PRODUCTS

By its nature marketing requires new ideas and successful marketers are constantly making adjustments to their marketing efforts. New ideas are essential for responding to changing market demand and competitive pressure (see Box 7-1). These changes are manifested in decisions in all marketing areas including new product development. In this section we outline what is involved in bringing new products to market.

Box 7-1

THE NEED FOR NEW PRODUCTS

New product ideas are not the sole domain of the marketing department. In fact, in many industries new products first evolve out of a dedicated research and development area, though marketers often will have an important role in the product's evolution. No matter where new products originate, new product ideas are needed for the following reasons:

Customers Change

Over time customers' needs may evolve. What attracted customer interest in the past is not guaranteed to do the same in the future. This is especially the case for products targeted to narrow age groups where not only are customers' needs changing but customers themselves change. For example, Nickelodeon, a cable television network targeted to young children and teenagers, faces a situation where customers are only in their target market for 10-12 years (from young child to early teen). The constant influx of new customers along with continually losing existing customers requires frequent evaluation of programming to ensure the network is meeting the needs of an ever changing target market.

Profit in Newer Products

Many new products earn higher profits than older products. This is often the case for products considered innovative or unique which may enjoy success and initially face little or no competition.

Keep Ahead of Competition

Fierce global competition and technological developments make it much easier for competitors to learn about products and replicate them. To stay ahead of competitors marketers must innovate and introduce new products on a consistent schedule.

Helps with Repositioning

New products can help reposition the company in customers' minds. For instance, a company with a reputation for selling low-priced products with few features may shift customers' perceptions by introducing products with more features and slightly higher pricing.

Fill Out Product Line

Companies with limited product line depth may miss out on more sales unless they add new products to fill out the line. For example, companies may have a very strong high-end and high priced product but lack a good quality, mid-price offering.

> **Expand Product Mix**
> Some firms market seasonal products that garner their highest sales during a certain time of the year or sell cyclical products whose sales fluctuate depending on economic or market factors. Expanding the firm's product mix into new areas may help offset these fluctuations. For manufacturing firms an additional benefit is realized as new products utilize existing production capacity that is under-used when seasonal or cyclical products are not being produced.

Categories of New Products

New products fall into several categories defined by the type of market the product is entering (i.e., newly created, existing but not previously targeted, existing and targeted) and the level of product innovation (i.e., radically new, new, upgrade).

Creates New Market with Radically New Product

This category is represented by new breakthrough products that are so revolutionary they create an entirely new market. A recent example is the Segway Personal Transporter. (4) Highly innovative products are rare so very few new products fall into this category.

Enters Existing but Not Previously Targeted Market with New Product

In this category a marketer introduces a new product or product line to an existing market which they did not previously target. Often these products are similar to competitors' products already available in the market but with some level of difference (e.g., different features, lower price, etc.). Microsoft's entry into the video gaming system market with their Xbox is an example.

Stays in Existing and Previously Targeted Market with New or Improved Product

Under this category the marketer attempts to improve its current market position by improving or upgrading existing products or by extending a product line by adding new products. This type of new product is seen in our earlier example of Procter & Gamble's Tide product line, which contains many product variations.

How New Products Are Obtained

Marketers have several options for obtaining new products. First, products can be developed within an organization's own research operations. For some companies, such as service firms, this may simply mean the marketer designs new service options to sell to target markets. For instance, a marketer for a mortgage company may design new mortgage packages offering borrowers different rates or payment options. At the other extreme companies may support an extensive research and development effort where engineers, scientists, or others are engaged in new product discovery.

A second way to obtain products is to acquire them from external sources. This can occur in several ways, including:

- Purchase the Product – With this option a marketer purchases the product outright from another firm that currently owns the product. The advantage is the product is already developed, which reduces the purchasing company's time and cost of trying to develop it themselves. The disadvantage is the purchase cost may be high and, under some conditions, the purchase may not include important assets (e.g., equipment, facilities, people) associated with the product.

- License the Product – Under this option the marketer negotiates with the owner of the product for the rights to market the product. This may be a particularly attractive option for companies who have to fill a new product need quickly (e.g., give a product line more depth) or it may be used as a temporary source of products while the marketer's company is developing its own product. On the negative side the arrangement may have a limited time frame at which point the licensor may decide to end the relationship leaving the marketer without a source for the product.

- Purchase Another Firm – Instead of purchasing another company's products marketers may find it easier to just purchase the whole company owning the products. One key advantage to this is that the acquisition often includes the people and resources that developed the products, which may be a key consideration if the acquiring company wants to continue to develop the acquired products.

New Product Development Process

Because introducing new products on a consistent basis is important to the future success of many organizations, marketers in charge of product decisions often follow set procedures for bringing products to market. In the scientific area this may mean the establishment of ongoing laboratory research programs for discovering new products (e.g., medicines), while other industries may pull together resources for product development on a less structured basis.

In this section we present a 7-step process comprising the key elements of new product development. While some companies may not follow a deliberate step-by-step approach, the steps are useful in showing the information input and decision making necessary to successfully develop new products. The process also shows the importance marketing research plays in developing products.

We should note that while the 7-step process works for most industries, it is less effective in developing radically new products (see *Categories of New Products* discussion above) since the target market may not provide sufficient feedback on advanced product concepts as they often find it difficult to understand radically different ideas. So while many of these steps are used to research breakthrough ideas, the marketer of radically new products should exercise caution when interpreting the results.

STEP 1: IDEA GENERATION

The first step of new product development requires gathering ideas to be evaluated as potential product options. For many companies idea generation is an ongoing process with contributions from inside and outside the organization. Many marketing research techniques are used to encourage ideas including:

- running focus groups with consumers, channel members, and the company's sales force

- encouraging customer comments and suggestions via toll-free telephone numbers, website comment boxes,or online customer forums

- gaining insight on competitive product developments through secondary data sources

· ·

French winemakers, facing a highly competitive market including aggressive marketers from Australia and South America, are responding with new product ideas that were first introduced by their competitors. One idea, sealing bottles with a screw top instead of cork, has upset traditional wine enthusiasts. Nevertheless some French wineries see this and other product changes as a necessary step to combat foreign competition. (5)

· ·

One important research technique used to generate ideas is **brainstorming** where open-minded, creative thinkers from inside and outside the company gather and share ideas. The dynamic nature of group members floating ideas, where one idea often sparks another idea, can yield a wide range of possible products that can be further explored.

STEP 2: SCREENING

In Step 2 the ideas generated in Step 1 are critically evaluated by company personnel to isolate the most attractive options. Depending on the number of ideas, screening may be done in rounds with the first round involving company executives judging the feasibility of ideas while successive rounds may utilize more advanced research techniques. As the ideas are whittled down to a few attractive options, rough estimates are made of an idea's potential in terms of sales, production costs, profit potential, and competitors' response if the product is introduced. Acceptable ideas move on to the next step.

STEP 3: CONCEPT DEVELOPMENT AND TESTING

With a few ideas in hand the marketer now seeks initial feedback from customers, distributors, and its own employees. Generally, focus groups are convened where the ideas are presented to a group, often in the form of **concept board** or **storyboard** presentations. For instance, customers may be shown a concept board displaying drawings of a product idea or even an advertisement featuring the product. In some cases focus groups are exposed to a **mock-up** of the idea, which is a physical but generally non-functional version of the product concept. During focus groups with customers the marketer seeks information including: likes and dislikes of the concept, level of interest in purchasing the product, frequency of purchase (used to help forecast demand), and price points to determine how much customers are willing to spend to acquire the product.

Step 4: Business Analysis

At this point in the new product development process the marketer has reduced a large number of ideas down to one or two options. Now in Step 4 the process becomes very dependent on marketing research as efforts are made to analyze the viability of the product ideas. The key objective at this stage is to obtain useful forecasts of market size (e.g., overall demand), operational costs (e.g., production costs), and financial projections (e.g., sales and profits). Additionally, the organization must determine if the product fits within the company's overall mission and strategy. Much effort is directed at both internal research, such as discussions with production and purchasing personnel, and external marketing research, such as customer and distributor surveys, secondary research, and competitor analysis.

Step 5: Product and Marketing Mix Development

Ideas passing through business analysis are given serious consideration for development. Companies direct their research and development teams to construct an initial design or **prototype** of the idea. Marketers begin to construct a marketing plan for the product. Once the prototype is ready the marketer seeks customer input. However, unlike the concept testing stage where customers were only exposed to the idea, in this step the customer gets to experience the real product as well as other aspects of the marketing effort, such as advertising, pricing, and distribution options (e.g., retail store, direct from company, etc.). Favorable customer reaction helps solidify the marketer's decision to introduce the product and also provides other valuable information, such as estimated purchase rates and understanding how the customer will use the product. Less favorable reaction may suggest the need for adjustments to elements of the marketing plan. Once these are made the marketer may have the customer test the product again. In addition to gaining customer feedback, this step is used to gauge the feasibility of large-scale, cost-effective production for manufactured products.

• •

Kimberly-Clark credits product testing for the success of its new Huggies Supreme Natural Fit diapers. Its testing included having parents bring their young children to a special testing center where they were outfitted with the prototype product. Periodically researchers injected saline into the diapers and then watched as the children played. The intention was to not only test for comfort but also to determine the leaking point of the product. (6)

• •

Step 6: Market Testing

Products surviving to Step 6 are ready to be tested. In some cases the marketer accepts what was learned from concept testing and skips over market testing to launch the idea as a fully marketed product. But other companies seek more input from a larger group before moving to commercialization (Step 7). The most common type of market testing makes the product available to a selective small segment of the target market (e.g., one city), which is exposed to the full marketing effort as they would be to any product they could purchase. In some cases, especially with consumer products sold at retail stores, the marketer must work hard to get the product into the **test market** by convincing distributors to purchase and place the product on their store shelves. In more controlled test markets distributors may be paid a fee if they agree to place the product on their shelves for testing. Another form of market testing for consumer products is even more controlled with customers recruited to a "laboratory" store where they are given shopping instructions. Product interest is then measured based on customers' shopping responses. Finally, there are several high-tech approaches to market testing including **virtual reality** and **computer simulations**. With virtual reality testing customers are exposed to a computer-projected environment and asked to locate and select products. With computer simulations customers may not be directly involved at all. Instead certain variables are entered into a sophisticated computer program and estimates of a target market's response are calculated.

• •

Kimberly-Clark also has developed a virtual reality facility for testing product ideas containing a large floor-to-ceiling screen displaying the interior of a store. Here research participants can move between aisles, find products, and place them in a virtual shopping cart. The software can even adjust the store layout depending on the type of retail store being evaluated. (7)

• •

Step 7: Commercialization

If market testing displays promising results the product is ready for market introduction. Some firms introduce or roll-out the product in waves with different parts of the market receiving the product on different schedules. This allows the company to ramp up production in a more controlled way and to fine tune marketing decisions as the product is distributed to new areas.

MANAGING EXISTING PRODUCTS

Marketing strategies developed for initial product introduction almost certainly need to be revised as the product settles into the market. While commercialization may be the last step in the new product development process it is just the beginning of managing the product. Adjusting the product's marketing strategy is required for many reasons including:

- changing customer tastes

- domestic and foreign competitors

- economic conditions

- technological advances

. . . .

Kraft Foods discovered that it had to reformulate its top selling Oreo cookie product in order to meet the tastes of Chinese consumers. After conducting extensive marketing research, Kraft found the Chinese consumer felt traditional Oreo cookies were too sweet and the packages too expensive. Kraft adjusted the flavor and now sells Oreos in smaller less expensive packages. (8)

. . . .

To stay on top of all possible threats the marketer must monitor all aspects of the marketing strategy and make changes as needed. Such efforts require the development and refinement of the product's marketing plan on a regular basis. In fact, marketing strategies change as a product moves through time leading to the concept called the Product Life Cycle.

The Product Life Cycle

The basic premise of the Product Life Cycle (PLC) is that products go through several stages of "life" with each stage presenting the marketer with different challenges that must be met with different marketing approaches. For example, marketers may find what works when appealing to customers early in the life of a product may be different than marketing methods used to attract customers in later stages.

There have been several attempts over the years to define the stages that make up the PLC. Unfortunately, the PLC may be different for different products, different markets, and different market conditions (e.g., economic forces).

119

Consequently, there is not a one-model-fits-all PLC. Yet there is enough evidence to suggest most products and product groups (see Box 7-2) experience patterns of activity that divide the evolution of the product into five distinct stages. As shown in Figure 7-1 these stages are:

♦ <u>Development</u> – Occurs before the product is released to the market and is principally a time for honing the product offering and preparing the market for product introduction.

♦ <u>Introduction</u> – Product is released to the market and sales begin though often gradually as the market becomes aware of the product.

♦ <u>Growth</u> – If the product is accepted it may reach a stage of rapid growth in sales and in profits.

♦ <u>Maturity</u> – At some point sales of a product may stabilize. For some products the maturity phase can be the longest stage as the product is repeatedly purchased by loyal customers. However, while overall sales may grow year-over-year, percentage sales increases may be small.

♦ <u>Decline</u> – All products eventually see demand decline as customers no longer see value in purchasing the product.

Figure 7-1: Stages of the Product Life Cycle

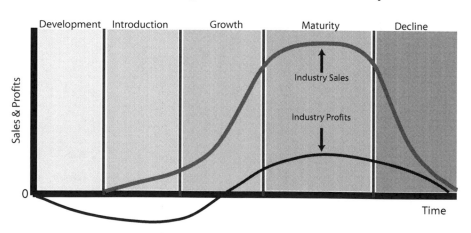

Box 7-2

LEVELS OF ANALYSIS OF THE PLC

The Product Life Cycle is commonly referenced in many business publications as a way of describing the current conditions facing a market or product. The fact it is used to describe either markets or individual products points out the need to understand the different levels of analysis for which the PLC can be used. These levels include:

Product Category

This level considers the macro market view for the general category of products that meet a general need. For instance, automobiles would be a general category that meets the need for personal motorized transportation (obviously there are others, such as motorcycles, scooters, and trucks but we will focus only on automobiles) and includes hundreds of products. Since the PLC for a product category includes sales for all products, the timeframe for the automotive PLC is quite long with the Introduction stage beginning around 1900.

Product Form

This level looks at product groupings that fall within a product category. The product form contains many different groupings that, taken together, make up the product category. These groupings include products that not only satisfy the general need of the product category, but do so by also offering additional benefits. In our example, hybrid cars would be a product form, since it satisfies the general need for personal motorized transportation and offers additional benefits in the form of fuel efficiency and environmental friendliness. Other product forms in the product category include sports cars, minivans, luxury sedans, etc. Clearly there can be a unique PLC for each form of a product. Marketers are very concerned with analysis at this level since it provides evidence for what is occurring in specific markets and for this reason is considered the most important level of analysis.

Individual Brand

This level concerns the life cycle of a specific brand within a product form. In our example this would include the Toyota Prius. While it may seem marketers would be most concerned with this level, they actually gain more value from analyzing what is happening in the overall market (i.e., product form). For instance, a marketer may make a serious mistake if she assumes the entire market has entered the Decline stage just because her company's brand has seen a sales drop. Doing so may mean a total misread of what is happening in the market and lead to the marketer missing out on additional opportunities if the market for the product form is still growing.

We should note in most cases the PLC considers what is happening for the total market (i.e., worldwide sales). However, more information could be obtained by applying the concepts of the PLC to more narrowly defined market segments, such as geographic regions or segments based on customer characteristics (e.g., by age, education level, etc.).

Adoption of New Products

The PLC is tied closely to the concept of the **Diffusion of Innovation**, which explains how information and acceptance of new products spreads through a market. Innovation is anything new that solves needs by offering a significant advantage over existing methods (e.g., other products) customers use (see Chapter 19 for a detailed discussion). Innovation can encompass both highly advanced technology products, such as new computer chips, and non-technological products, such as a new soft drink. In fact, the seminal work of the Diffusion of Innovation concept occurred in the 1950s when researchers in the agricultural industry observed how new corn seeds were adopted by farmers in the U.S. Midwest. (9)

For marketers a key concept to emerge from research on new product diffusion is the identification of adopter categories into which members of a market are likely to fall. These categories include:

Innovators

Represent a small percentage of the market that is at the forefront of adopting new products. These people are often viewed as enthusiasts and are eager to try new things, often without regard to price. While a good test ground for new products, marketers find Innovators often do not remain loyal as they continually seek new products.

Early Adopters

This group contains more members than the Innovator category. They share Innovators' enthusiasm for new products though they tend to be more practical about their decisions. They also are eager to communicate their experiences with the Early Majority (next group) and because of their influence they are important to the future success of the product (i.e., act as opinion leaders).

Early Majority

This represents the beginning of entry into the mass market (i.e., large number of potential customers). The Early Majority account for up to one-third of the overall market. The Early Majority like new things but tend to wait until they have received positive opinions from others (i.e., Early Adopters) before purchasing. Adoption by the Early Majority is key if a new product is to be profitable. On the other hand, many new products die quickly because they are not accepted beyond early trials by Innovators and Early Adopters and never reach mass market status.

Late Majority

Possibly as large as the Early Majority, this group takes a wait-and-see approach before trying something new. Marketers are likely to see their highest profits once this group starts to purchase.

Laggards

This is the last group to adopt something new and, in fact, may only do so if they have no other choice. Depending on the market this group can be large, though because of their reluctance to accept new products marketers are not inclined to direct much attention to them.

ADOPTER CATEGORIES AND THE **PLC**

The adopter categories help explain the shape of the life cycle for many products. For instance, consider how a new household cleaning product may become successful. First, Innovators may experience the product during the Development stage and then become the key targeted customers at the beginning of the Introduction stage. Early Adopters will also be targeted during the Introduction stage and their adoption will determine whether the product makes it to the Growth stage. If the product survives the Innovator and Early Adopter stages it moves to the Growth stage where acceptance by the Early Majority means the product is entering the mass market. The product can continue to be successful as it is adopted by the Late Majority and, to a much lesser extent, by Laggards. Eventually product sales decline as Innovators and Early Adopter move to something new and the cycle starts over.

It should be noted an assumption of a person's placement in a certain adopter category for one product does not imply that person will also occupy the same category for other products. For example, someone who is an Innovator for one product may be a Laggard for another. However, with research, marketers may find an individual's adopter classification for one product applies across a similar set of products. For instance, those classified as Innovators for computer hardware may have a high probability of being categorized the same for computer software. This assumption may be necessary as a software company develops its target marketing strategies in advance of the launch of a new product.

Finally, it should be noted that each adopter category may consist of multiple smaller market segments. For example, the Early Majority is made up of smaller markets that can be segmented on variables such as geography, age, income, etc.

Criticisms of the PLC

The PLC has the ability to offer marketers guidance on strategies and tactics as they manage products through changing market conditions. Unfortunately, the PLC does not offer a perfect model of markets as it contains drawbacks preventing it from being applicable to all products. Among the problems cited are:

◆ Shape of Curve – Some product forms do not follow the traditional PLC curve. For instance, clothing may go through regular up and down cycles as styles are in fashion then out then in again. **Fad products**, such as certain toys, may be popular for a period of time only to see sales drop dramatically until a future generation renews interest in the toy.

◆ Length of Stages – The PLC offers little help in determining how long each stage will last. For example, some products can exist in the Maturity stage for decades while others may be there for only a few months. Consequently, it may be difficult to determine when adjustments to the marketing plan are needed to meet the needs of different PLC stages.

◆ Competitor Reaction Not Predictable – As we discuss in greater detail in Chapter 20, the PLC suggests competitor response occurs in a somewhat consistent pattern. For example, for a new product form, the PLC says competitors will not engage in strong brand-to-brand competition until the product form has gained a foothold in the market. The logic is that until the market is established it is in the best interest of all competitors to focus on building interest in the general product form and refrain from claiming one brand is better than another. However, competitors do not always conform to theoretical models. Some will always compete on brand first and leave it to others to build market interest for the product form. Arguments can also be made that competitors will respond differently than what the PLC suggests on such issues as pricing, number of product options, and spending on declining products, to name a few.

◆ Impact of External Forces – The PLC assumes customers' decisions are primarily impacted by the marketing activities of the companies selling in the market. In fact, as we will discuss in Chapter 19, there are many other factors affecting a market which are not controlled by marketers. Such factors (e.g., social changes, technological innovation) can lead to changes in market demand at rates that are much more rapid than would occur if only marketing decisions were being changed (i.e., if everything was held constant except for the company's marketing decisions).

♦ Use for Forecasting – The impact of external forces may create challenges in using the PLC as a forecasting tool. For instance, market factors not directly associated with the marketing activities of market competitors, such as economic conditions, may have a greater impact on reducing demand than customers' interest in the product. Consequently, what may be forecasted as a decline in the market signaling a move to the Maturity stage may be the result of declining economic conditions and not a decline in customers' interest in the product. In fact, it is likely demand for the product will recover to growth levels once economic conditions improve. If a marketer follows the strict guidance of the PLC they would conclude that strategies should shift to those of the Maturity stage. Doing so may be an over-reaction that could hurt market position and profitability.

♦ Stages Not Seamlessly Connected – Some high-tech marketers question whether one stage of the PLC naturally will follow another stage. In particular, technology consultant Geoffrey Moore suggests that for high-tech products targeted to business customers a noticeable space or **chasm** occurs between the Introduction and Growth stages that can only be overcome by significantly altering marketing strategy beyond what is suggested by the PLC. (10)

While not perfect, the PLC is a marketing tool that should be well understood by marketers since its underlying message, that markets are dynamic, supports the need for frequent marketing planning (see *Planning and Strategy with the Product Life Cycle* discussion in Chapter 20). Also, for many markets the principles presented by the PLC will, in fact, prove to be very much representative of the conditions they will face in the market.

REFERENCES

1. *Tide* website.

2. *Salary.com* website.

3. *Occupational Employment Statistics* website.

4. *Segway* website.

5. "Sacrebleu! It Comes With a Straw?" *MSNBC*, April 27, 2008.

6. Yang, J.L., "Designing the iPhone for Diapers," *Fortune*, August 25, 2008.

7. Byron, E., "A Virtual View of the Store Aisle," *Wall Street Journal*, October 3, 2007.

8. Jargon, J., "Kraft Reformulates Oreo, Scores in China," *Wall Street Journal*, May 1, 2008.

9. For description of innovator categories for farmers see *High Tech Strategies* website.

10. Moore, G., <u>Crossing the Chasm, Marketing and Selling Technology Products to Mainstream Customers</u>, HarperCollins, 1991.

Full text of many of the references can be accessed via links on the support website.

Chapter 8:

Distribution Decisions

Our coverage in Chapters 6 and 7 indicate product decisions may be the most important of all marketing decisions since these lead directly to the reasons (i.e., offer benefits that satisfy needs) why customers decide to make a purchase. But having a strong product does little good if customers are not able to easily and conveniently obtain it. With this in mind we turn to the second major marketing decision area – distribution.

In this chapter we cover the basics of distribution, including defining what channels of distribution are and the purpose they serve within the overall marketing strategy. We examine the key functions and parties in a distribution system. Also, we look at the major types of channel arrangements and the factors affecting the creation of effective distribution channels. We conclude with a discussion of different distribution design options.

IMPORTANCE OF DISTRIBUTION

Distribution decisions focus on establishing the path, termed **channel of distribution**, which moves the product from the marketer to the customer. For most marketers, this means making decisions on the activities that will ultimately give customers access to and permit purchase of a marketer's product.

Distribution decisions are relevant for nearly all types of products. While it is easy to see how distribution decisions impact physical goods, such as laundry detergent or truck parts, distribution is equally important for digital goods (e.g., television programming, downloadable music), and services (e.g., income tax services). Whether a marketer is distributing products that are physical, digital or service, the bottom line is a marketer's distribution system must be both effective (i.e., delivers a good or service to the right place, in the right amount, and in the right condition) and efficient (i.e., delivers at the right time and for the right cost). As discussed in Box 8-1, creating an effective and efficient distribution system requires the marketer carefully consider the benefits offered versus the costs for establishing and maintaining the system.

Box 8-1

DISTRIBUTION TRADE-OFF ANALYSIS: SERVICE LEVEL VS. COST

As part of developing a successful distribution strategy marketers strive to provide an optimal level of service to their customers. However, "optimal" does not always translate into providing the "best" distribution service options to customers. The service level marketers offer for their distribution activities is determined using trade-off analysis.

With service level trade-off analysis, the marketer compares the number and quality of distribution features (e.g., speed of delivery, ease of placing orders, order tracking, etc.) it would like to offer versus the cost of providing the features. While customers may want quick delivery, the marketer may find fast delivery an expensive proposition that significantly reduces its profit margin.

Since most distribution activities represent a cost to the marketer, the marketer's distribution system choice may not be the "best" available in terms of getting the product into customer's hands as fast as possible. Consequently, the marketer's choice for what is optimal will be determined by analyzing distribution features and costs, and evaluating how these fit within the marketer's overall objectives.

Distribution Activities

The activities involved in establishing the channel of distribution are presented in Table 8-1. While some marketers may choose to handle all distribution activities on their own, most marketers find many of these tasks are best left to others. Whether handled by the marketer or contracted to others, these activities are crucial to having a cost-effective and efficient distribution system.

• •

Amazon is an example of a company who offers services to marketers that handle nearly all distribution tasks. Through its Fulfillment by Amazon service, Amazon manages ordering, inventory management, product handing, and shipping. All the marketing company needs to do is ship its product to an Amazon storage facility and, for a fee, Amazon handles the rest. (1)

• •

Table 8-1: Channel of Distribution Activities

Distribution Activity	Explanation
Order Processing	Includes methods for handling customer purchase requests.
Inventory Management	Includes methods to ensure the right amount of product is available to fill customer orders.
Physical Handling	Includes methods to prepare product for movement that reduces damage.
Storage	Includes facilities for holding inventory.
Shipping	Includes providing means for getting the product to customers in a timely manner.
Display	Includes having resellers place products in locations that can be seen by customers.
Promotion	Includes the need for resellers to assist in communicating products to the target market.
Selling	Includes the need for resellers to provide personal promotion to help sell product.
Information Feedback	Includes the need for methods to encourage resellers and customers to provide marketing research information to the marketer.

TYPE OF CHANNEL MEMBERS

Channel activities may be carried out by the marketer or by specialist organizations that assist with certain functions. We can classify specialist organizations into two broad categories: resellers and specialty service firms.

Resellers

These organizations, also known within some industries as **intermediaries**, **distributors**, or **dealers**, generally purchase or take ownership of products from the marketing company with the intention of selling to others. If a marketer utilizes multiple resellers within its distribution channel strategy this is called a reseller network, which is classified into several sub-categories including:

- Retailers – Organizations selling products directly to final consumers.

- Wholesalers – Organizations purchasing products from suppliers and selling these to other resellers, such as retailers or other wholesalers.

- Industrial Distributors – Firms working in the business-to-business market selling products obtained from industrial suppliers.

Specialty Service Firms

These are organizations providing additional services to help with the exchange of products but generally do not purchase the product:

- Agents and Brokers – Organizations working to bring suppliers and buyers together in exchange for a fee.

- Distribution Service Firms – Offer services aiding in the movement of products, such as assistance with transportation, storage, and order processing.

- Others – This category includes firms providing additional services, such as insurance and transportation routing assistance.

WHY DISTRIBUTION HELP IS NEEDED

As noted, distribution channels often require the assistance of others in order for the marketer to reach its target market. But why exactly does a company need others to help with the distribution of its product? Wouldn't a company that handles its own distribution functions be in a better position to exercise control over product sales and potentially earn higher profits? Also, doesn't the Internet make it much easier to distribute products, thus lessening the need for others to be involved in selling a company's product?

While on the surface it may seem to make sense for a company to operate its own distribution channel (i.e., handling all aspects of distribution) there are many factors preventing companies from doing so. While companies can do without the assistance of certain channel members, for many marketers some level of channel partnership is needed. For example, marketers who are successful without utilizing resellers to sell their product (e.g., Dell sells mostly through the Internet and not in retail stores) may still need assistance with certain parts of the distribution process (e.g., Dell uses parcel post shippers such as FedEx and UPS). In Dell's case creating its own transportation system makes little sense given how large such a system would need to be in order to service Dell's customer base. Therefore, by using shipping companies, Dell is taking advantage of the benefits these services offer to Dell and to Dell's customers.

When choosing a distribution strategy a marketer must determine what value a channel member adds to the firm's products. Remember, as we discussed in Chapter 6, customers assess a product's value by looking at many factors, including those surrounding the product (i.e., augmented product). Several surrounding features can be directly influenced by channel members, such as customer service, delivery, and availability. Consequently, selecting a channel partner involves a value analysis in the same way customers make purchase decisions. That is, the marketer must assess the benefits received from utilizing a channel partner versus the cost incurred for using the services.

• •

While we talk about marketers "selecting a channel partner" it is important to recognize that the channel member is the one who ultimately decides which products they will handle. Since a channel partner cannot handle all products, competition for gaining distribution can be quite intense and require a well developed strategy. For instance, one small company that is attempting to enter the energy drink market is employing a strategy in which it concentrates its promotional resources in a small geographic area in New York City. The hope is that once it is established in this area it can then expand to adjacent areas. (2)

• •

Benefits Offered by Channel Members:

◆ <u>Offer Cost Savings Through Specialization</u> – Members of the distribution channel are specialists in what they do and can often perform tasks better and at lower cost than companies who do not have distribution experience. Marketers attempting to handle too many aspects of distribution may end up exhausting company resources as they learn how to distribute, resulting in the company being "a jack of all trades but master of none."

◆ <u>Reduce Exchange Time</u> – Not only are channel members able to reduce distribution costs by being experienced at what they do, they often perform their job more rapidly resulting in faster product delivery. This can be seen in Box 8-2.

◆ <u>Allow Customers to Conveniently Shop for Variety</u> – Marketers have to understand what customers want in their shopping experience. Referring back to our grocery store example, consider a world without grocery stores and instead each marketer of grocery products sells through its own stores. As it is now, many customers find shopping to be a time consuming activity, but consider what would happen if customers had to visit many different retailers each week to satisfy their grocery needs. Hence, resellers within the channel of distribution serve two very important needs: 1) they give customers the products they want by purchasing from many suppliers (termed **accumulation** and **assortment** services), and 2) they make it convenient to purchase by making products available in single location.

◆ <u>Resellers Sell Smaller Quantities</u> – Channel members, and particularly resellers, allow customers to purchase in quantities that work for them. This is an especially important channel function because handling orders for small quantities is not what works best for most suppliers. Suppliers like to ship products they produce in large quantities since this is more cost effective than shipping smaller amounts (see Box 10-2 in Chapter 10). The ability of intermediaries to purchase large quantities but to resell them in smaller quantities (termed **bulk breaking**) not only makes these products available to those wanting smaller quantities, but the reseller is able to pass along to its customers a significant portion of the cost savings gained by purchasing in large volume.

Box 8-2

EFFICIENCY IN DELIVERY

Channels of distribution have evolved as a way to add efficiency to the distribution system. For instance, consider what would happen if a grocery store received direct shipment from EVERY manufacturer that sells products in the store. This delivery system would be chaotic as hundreds of trucks line up each day to make deliveries, many of which would consist of only a few boxes. On a busy day a truck may sit for hours waiting for space so it can unload its products.

Instead, a better distribution scheme may have the grocery store purchasing its supplies from a grocery wholesaler that has its own warehouse for handling simultaneous shipments from a large number of suppliers. The wholesaler distributes to the store in the quantities the store needs, on a schedule that works for the store, and often in a single truck, all of which speeds up the time it takes to get the product on the store's shelves.

♦ Create Sales – Channel partners are at the front line when it comes to creating demand for the marketer's product. In some cases resellers perform an active selling role using persuasive techniques to encourage customers to purchase a marketer's product. In other cases they encourage sales of the product through their own advertising efforts and using other promotional means, such as special product displays.

♦ Offer Access to More Customers – For marketers channel partners may offer access to more customers in a much shorter time frame than the marketer can accomplish on its own. This can be particularly beneficial to companies new to a market and do not have an established distribution network, or existing companies that have had difficulty gaining distribution using their own methods.

• •

Campbell Soup Company found that its own methods for gaining distribution for its beverage products were not meeting objectives so it sought help from Coca-Cola. The distribution arrangement between these consumer products power-houses enables Campbell to get its single-serve juice products into many more retail locations through Coca-Cola's distribution network. (3)

• •

◆ <u>Offer Financial Support</u> – Channel partners often provide programs enabling their customers to more easily purchase products by offering financial programs that ease payment requirements. These programs include allowing customers to: purchase on credit, purchase using a payment plan, delay the start of payments, and allowing trade-in or exchange options.

◆ <u>Provide Information</u> – Companies utilizing channel members for selling their products depend on these distributors to provide information that can help improve the product. High-level intermediaries, such as major retailers, may offer their suppliers real-time access to sales data, including information showing how products are selling by such characteristics as geographic location, type of customer, and product location (e.g., where located within a store, where found on a website). Even if such high-level information is not available, marketers can often count on resellers to provide feedback as to how customers are responding to products. This feedback can occur either through surveys or interviews with reseller's employees or by requesting the reseller allow the marketer to survey the reseller's customers.

Costs of Utilizing Channel Members

◆ <u>Loss of Revenue</u> – Channel members are not likely to offer services to a marketer unless they see financial gain in doing so. Firms obtain payment for their services as either direct payment (e.g., marketer pays specialty service firm for shipping costs) or, in the case of resellers, by charging their customers more than what they paid the marketer for acquiring the product (see *Markup Pricing* discussion in Chapter 18). For the latter, marketers have a good idea of what the final customer will pay for their product, which means the marketer must charge less when selling the product to resellers. In these situations marketers are not reaping the full sale price by using resellers, which they may be able to do if they sold directly to the customer.

◆ <u>Loss of Communication Control</u> – Marketers not only give up revenue when using channel partners, they may also give up control of the message being conveyed to customers. If the reseller engages in communication activities, such as when a retailer uses salespeople to sell to customers, the marketer is no longer controlling what is being said about the product. This can lead to miscommunication problems with customers, especially if the reseller embellishes or makes misstatements about the benefits the product provides. While marketers can influence what is being said by offering sales training to resellers' salespeople, they lack ultimate control of the message.

♦ Loss of Product Importance – Once a product is out of the marketer's hands the importance of that product is left up to channel members. If there are pressing issues in the channel, such as transportation problems, or if a competitor is using promotional incentives in an effort to push its product through resellers, the marketer's product may not get the attention the marketer feels it should receive.

∙∙∙

Sportswear manufacturer Nautica discovered the costs of utilizing channel members when it saw the amount of shelf space devoted to its products decline in several major U.S. retail stores. Shelf space is considered a major factor in sales success and a reduction almost always leads to lower sales. Nautica saw its products cut back primarily due to the retailers move to add its own private label line of products. (4)

∙∙∙

CHANNEL ARRANGEMENTS

The distribution channel consists of many parties each seeking to meet their own business objectives. Clearly for the channel to work well, relationships between channel members must be strong with each member understanding and trusting others on whom they depend for product distribution to flow smoothly. For instance, a small sporting goods retailer purchasing products from a wholesaler trusts the wholesaler to deliver required items on time in order to meet customer demand, while the wholesaler counts on the retailer to place regular orders and to make prompt payments.

Relationships in a channel are in large part a function of the arrangement that occurs between the members. These arrangements can be divided in two main categories: independent and dependent.

Independent Channel Arrangement

Under this arrangement a channel member negotiates deals with others that do not result in binding relationships. In other words, a channel member is free to make whatever arrangements they feel is in its best interest. This so-called **conventional distribution arrangement** often leads to significant conflict as individual members decide what is best for them and not necessarily for the entire channel. On the other hand, an independent channel arrangement is less restrictive than dependent arrangements and makes it easier for a channel member to move away from relationships they feel are not working to its benefit.

Dependent Channel Arrangement

With a dependent channel arrangement a channel member feels tied to one or more members of the distribution channel. Sometimes referred to as **vertical marketing systems** this approach makes it more difficult for an individual member to make changes to how products are distributed. However, the dependent approach provides much more stability and consistency since members are united in their goals.

The dependent channel arrangement can be broken down into three types:

Corporate

Under this arrangement a supplier operates its own distribution system in a manor that produces an integrated channel. This occurs most frequently in the retail industry where a supplier operates a chain of retail stores. Starbucks is a company that does this. They import and process coffee and then sell it under its own brand name in thousands of its own stores. (5) It should be mentioned that Starbucks also distributes its products in other ways, such as through grocery stores and mail order (see *Multi-Channel or Hybrid Systems* discussion below).

Contractual

With this approach a legal document obligates members to agree on how a product is distributed. Often times the agreement specifically spells out which activities each member is permitted to perform or not perform. This type of arrangement can occur in several formats including:

- Wholesaler-sponsored – where a wholesaler brings together and manages many independent retailers, including having the retailers operate under the same name

- Retailer-sponsored – this format also brings together retailers but the retailers are responsible for managing the relationship

- Franchised Arrangement – where a central organization controls nearly all activities of other members

- Licensing Agreement – where a central organization controls some activities of its channel members but it does not control all activities of the members

• •

While Starbucks operates over 9,000 company stores worldwide, they also license the sale of its products to thousands of businesses. Under its Licensed Store program qualified high-traffic outlets, such as hotels, universities, and large businesses, pay a fee to sell Starbucks products. (6)

• •

Administrative

In certain channel arrangements a single member may dominate the decisions within the channel. These situations occur when one channel member has achieved a significant power position (see *Channel Power* discussion below). This most likely occurs if a manufacturer has brands in strong demand by its target markets (e.g., Apple) or if a retailer has significant size and market coverage (e.g., Wal-Mart). In most cases the arrangement is understood to occur and is not bound by legal or financial arrangements.

FACTORS IN CREATING DISTRIBUTION CHANNELS

Like most marketing decisions, a great deal of research and thought must go into determining how to carry out distribution activities in a way that meets a marketer's objectives. The marketer must consider many factors when establishing a distribution system. Some factors are directly related to marketing decisions while others are affected by relationships between members of the channel.

Next we examine the key factors to consider when designing a distribution strategy. We group these into two main categories: marketing decision issues and channel relationship issues. In turn, each of these categories contains several topics of concern to marketers.

Marketing Decision Issues

Distribution strategy can be shaped by how decisions are made in other marketing areas.

PRODUCT ISSUES

The nature of the product often dictates the distribution options available especially if the product requires special handling. For instance, companies selling delicate or fragile products, such as flowers, look for shipping arrangements that are different than those sought for companies selling extremely tough or durable products, such as steel beams.

137

PROMOTION ISSUES

Besides issues related to physical handling of products, distribution decisions are affected by the type of promotional activities needed to sell the product to customers. For products needing extensive salesperson-to-customer contact (e.g., automobile purchases) the distribution options are different than for products where customers typically require no sales assistance (e.g., bread purchases).

PRICING ISSUES

The desired price at which a marketer seeks to sell its product can impact how they choose to distribute. As previously mentioned, the inclusion of resellers in a marketer's distribution strategy may affect a product's pricing since each member of the channel seeks to make a profit for their contribution to the sale of the product. If too many channel members are involved the eventual selling price may be too high to meet sales targets, in which case the marketer may explore other distribution options.

TARGET MARKET ISSUES

A distribution system is only effective if customers can obtain the product. Consequently, a key decision in setting up a channel arrangement is for the marketer to choose the approach that reaches customers in the most effective way possible. The most important decision with regard to reaching the target market is to determine the level of distribution coverage needed to effectively meet customers' needs.

Distribution Coverage

Distribution coverage is measured in terms of the **intensity** of product availability. For the most part, distribution coverage decisions are of most concern to consumer products companies, though there are many industrial products that also must decide how much coverage to give its products.

There are three main levels of distribution coverage - mass, selective, and exclusive.

- Mass Coverage – The mass coverage strategy (also known as **intensive distribution**) attempts to distribute products widely in nearly all locations in which that type of product is sold. This level of distribution is only feasible for relatively low priced products that appeal to very large target markets (e.g., consumer convenience products). A product such as Coca-Cola is a classic example since it is available in a wide variety of locations, including grocery stores, convenience stores, vending machines, hotels, and many, many more. With such a large number of locations selling the product the cost of distribution is extremely high and must be offset with very high sales volume.

- Selective Coverage – Under selective coverage the marketer deliberately seeks to limit the locations in which its product is sold. To the non-marketer it may seem strange for a marketer to not want to distribute its product in every possible location. However, the logic of this strategy is tied to the size and nature of the product's target market. Products with selective coverage appeal to smaller, more focused target markets (e.g., consumer shopping products) compared to the size of target markets for mass marketed products. Consequently, because the market size is smaller, the number of locations needed to support the distribution of the product is fewer.

- Exclusive Coverage – Some high-end products target very narrow markets having a relatively small number of customers. These customers are often characterized as "discriminating" in their taste for products and seek to satisfy some of their needs with high-quality, though expensive products. Additionally, many buyers of high-end products require a high level of customer service from the channel member from whom they purchase. These characteristics of the target market may lead the marketer to sell its products through a very select or exclusive group of resellers. Another type of exclusive distribution may not involve high-end products but rather products only available in selected locations, such as company-owned stores. While these products may or may not be higher priced compared to competitive products, the fact these are only available in company outlets gives exclusivity to the distribution.

We conclude this section by noting that while the three distribution coverage options just discussed serve as a useful guide for envisioning how distribution intensity works, the advent of the Internet has brought into question the effectiveness of these schemes. For all intents and purposes all products available for purchase over the Internet are distributed in the same way - mass coverage. So a better way to look at the three levels is to consider these as options for distribution coverage of products that are physically purchased by a customer (i.e., walk-in to purchase).

Relationship Issues

A good distribution strategy takes into account not only marketing decisions, but also considers how relationships within the channel of distribution can impact the marketer's product. In this section we examine three such issues:

CHANNEL POWER

A channel can be made up of many parties each adding value to the product purchased by customers. However, some parties (see Box 8-3) within the channel may carry greater weight than others. In marketing terms this is called channel power, which refers to the influence one party within a channel has over other channel members. When power is exerted by a channel member they are often in the position to make demands of others. For instance, they may demand better financial terms (e.g., will buy only if prices are lowered, will sell only if price is higher) or demand others members perform certain tasks (e.g., do more marketing to customers, perform more product services).

CHANNEL CONFLICT

In an effort to increase product sales, marketers are often attracted by the notion that sales can grow if the marketer expands distribution by adding additional resellers. Such decisions must be handled carefully, however, so that existing dealers do not feel threatened by the new distributors who they may feel are encroaching on their customers and siphoning potential business. For marketers, channel strategy designed to expand product distribution may in fact do the opposite if existing members feel there is a conflict in the decisions made by the marketer. If existing members sense a conflict and feel the marketer is not sensitive to their needs they may choose to stop handling the marketer's products.

· ·

Many leading consumer products manufacturers, such as Hasbro, Levi Strauss and Nike, have traditionally sold their products in retail stores but are now selling directly to customers over the Internet. To reduce the chance of creating conflict with their retailers, these companies have used strategies designed to improve overall brand awareness rather than take sales away from retailers who sell their products. (7)

· ·

NEED FOR LONG-TERM COMMITMENTS

Channel decisions have long-term consequences for marketers since efforts to establish new relationships can take an extensive period of time while ending existing relationships can prove difficult. For instance, Company A, a marketer of kitchen cabinets that wants to change distribution strategy, may decide to stop selling its product

---

Box 8-3

WHO HAS THE POWER

Channels of distribution can be dominated by certain channel members who hold something of value that is needed by other members. Examples of those holding power include:

Backend or Product Power
This occurs when a product manufacturer or service provider markets a brand that has a high level of customer demand. The marketer of the brand is often in a power position since other channel members have little choice but to carry the brand or risk losing customers. Examples include Apple and Procter & Gamble.

Middle or Wholesale Power
This occurs when an intermediary, such as a wholesaler, services a large number of smaller retailers with products obtained from a large number of manufacturers or product suppliers. In this situation the wholesaler can exert power since the small retailers are often not on their own in the position to purchase products cost-effectively and in as much variety as what is offered by the wholesaler. Examples include Do It Best (hardware stores) and Independent Grocer Alliance (grocery stores).

Front or Retailer Power
As the name suggests, the power in this situation rests with the retailer who can command major concessions from its suppliers. This type of power is most prevalent when the retailer commands a significant percentage of sales in the market it serves and others in the channel are dependent on the sales generated by the retailer. For example, to help keep costs low in a time of rising prices, Wal-Mart has demanded suppliers reassess their costs, including forcing product redesigns intended to reduce packaging and transportation costs. (8)

line through industrial supply companies that distribute cabinets to building contractors and instead sell through large retail home centers. If, in the future, Company A decides to once again enter the industrial supply market they may run into resistance since supply companies may have replaced Company A's product line with other products and, given what happened to the previous relationship, may be reluctant to deal with Company A. As another example of problems with long-term commitments, building contractors may be comfortable purchasing kitchen cabinets from industrial suppliers. If Company A decides to change its reseller network they may find it difficult to regain the building contractor customer base, who may continue to purchase from the industrial suppliers but are now purchasing products from Company A's competitors. Given these potential problems, Company A may have to give serious thought to whether breaking its long-term relationship with industrial suppliers is in the company's best interest.

OVERALL DISTRIBUTION DESIGN

Mindful of the factors affecting distribution decisions (i.e., marketing decision issues and relationship issues), the marketer may have several options to choose from when settling on a design for its distribution network. We stress the word "may" since, while in theory an option would appear to be available, marketing decision factors (e.g., product, promotion, pricing, target markets) or the nature of distribution channel relationships may not permit the marketer to pursue a particular option. For example, selling through a desired retailer may not be feasible if the retailer refuses to handle a product.

For marketers the choice of distribution design comes down to selecting between direct or indirect methods, or in some cases choosing both.

Direct Distribution System

With a direct distribution system the marketer reaches the intended final user of its product by distributing the product directly to the customer. That is, there are no other parties involved in the distribution process that take ownership of the product. The direct system can be further divided by the method of communication taking place when a sale occurs. These methods are:

- ◆ Direct Marketing Systems – With this system the customer places the order either through information gained from non-personal contact with the marketer, such as by visiting the marketer's website or ordering from the marketer's catalog, or through personal communication with a customer representative who is not a salesperson, such as through toll-free telephone ordering.

- ◆ Direct Retail Systems – This type of system exists when a product marketer also operates its own retail outlets under an independent channel arrangement. As previously discussed, Starbucks' own stores would fall into this category.

- ◆ Personal Selling Systems – The key to this direct distribution system is that a person whose main responsibility involves creating and managing sales (e.g., salesperson) is involved in the distribution process, generally by persuading the buyer to place an order. While the order itself may not be handled by the salesperson (e.g., buyer physically places the order online or by phone) the salesperson plays a role in generating the sales.

♦ Assisted Marketing Systems – Under the assisted marketing system, the marketer relies on others to help communicate the marketer's products but handles distribution directly to the customer. The classic example of assisted marketing systems is eBay which helps bring buyers and sellers together for a fee. Other agents and brokers would also fall into this category.

Indirect Distribution System

With an indirect distribution system the marketer reaches the intended final user with the help of others. These resellers generally take ownership of the product, though in some cases they may sell products on a consignment basis (i.e., only pay the supplying company if the product is sold). Under this system intermediaries may be expected to assume many responsibilities to help sell the product. Indirect methods include:

♦ Single-Party Selling System – Under this system the marketer engages another party who then sells and distributes directly to the final customer. This is most likely to occur when the product is sold through large store-based retail chains or through online retailers.

♦ Multiple-Party Selling System – This indirect distribution system has the product passing through two or more distributors before reaching the final customer. The most likely scenario is when a wholesaler purchases from the manufacturer and sells the product to retailers.

Multi-channel or Hybrid System

In cases where a marketer utilizes more than one distribution design the marketer is following a multi-channel or hybrid distribution system. As we discussed, Starbucks follows this approach as its distribution design includes using a direct retail system by selling in company-owned stores, a direct marketing system by selling via direct mail, and a single-party selling system by selling through grocery stores (they also use other distribution systems). The multi-channel approach expands distribution and allows the marketer to reach a wider market, however, as we discussed, the marketer must be careful with this approach due to the potential for channel conflict.

REFERENCES

1. *Amazon* website.

2. Martin, A., "Stumping for Shelf Space," *New York Times*, February 20, 2008.

3. "Coke Will Distribute V8, Other Campbell Soup Juices." *USA Today*, June 7, 2007.

4. Kapner, S., "Nautica Brand Losing Ground," *Fortune*, November 1 2007.

5. *Starbucks* website.

6. *Starbucks* website.

7. Meyer, A., "From Partner to Rival," *Multichannel Merchant*, July 1, 2006.

8. Kapner, S., "Wal-Mart Puts the Squeeze on Food Costs," *Fortune*, May 29, 2008.

Full text of many of the references can be accessed via links on the support website.

Chapter 9:

Retailing

In an ideal business world, most marketers would prefer to handle all their distribution activities by way of the corporate channel arrangement we discussed in Chapter 8. Such an arrangement gives the marketer total control in dealing with customers, which can make it easier to build strong, long-term relationships. Unfortunately, for many marketing organizations a corporate channel arrangement is not feasible. Whether due to high cost or lack of experience needed to run a channel efficiently, marketing organizations need third-party channel members to get their products into the hands of customers.

In this chapter we examine the role of retailers as resellers of a marketer's products. In terms of sales volume and number of employees, retailing is one of the largest sectors of most economies. We beginning by setting out reasons why selecting resellers is an important decision that should not be taken lightly. We then turn our attention to a detailed look at how retailers are classified. We show that retailing is quite diverse and marketers, who want to distribute through retailers, must be familiar with the differences that exist among different retail options.

IMPORTANCE OF RESELLERS

As we discussed in Chapter 8, marketers must often enlist the assistance of others to get their products into the hands of customers. This is especially the case for marketers selling to the final consumer through retail stores, though business-to-business marketers also face such decisions. One major type of channel member linking marketers to their customers is the reseller who purchases products from supplying firms and then resells these to its customers. Examples of resellers include retailers, wholesalers, and industrial distributors.

Choosing which resellers to aid in product distribution is important since the characteristics of a reseller, including how they handle customers, can affect how a marketer's customers view the company and the products it offers. For instance, a reseller's reputation (e.g., high-quality vs. low-quality) and customers' experience when they visit the reseller to make a purchase (e.g., how long it takes to be serviced), may impact how customers feel about the products they purchase through the reseller. Consequently, marketers must take into consideration many issues when selecting resellers including:

- Is the target market served by the reseller the same as the marketer's target market?

- Does the reseller offer the expertise needed to effectively address customers' questions regarding the marketer's product?

- Will the reseller help the marketer in promotional activities?

- Will the reseller share customer purchase information with the marketer?

- Does the reseller carry competitor's products?

Once resellers have been identified a much bigger task lies ahead for the marketer: convincing the reseller to enter a relationship. As discussed in Box 9-1, building reseller relationships requires a marketing effort that is similar to the effort used to get the final consumer to purchase.

Box 9-1

How to Establish Reseller Relationships

Convincing resellers to handle a product requires marketers use the same marketing skills they use to sell to their final customers. And, just as they do when selling to the final customer, marketers' first step when selling to resellers is to identify their needs, which are much different than those of the final customer. For instance, when it comes to selling to resellers, marketers should consider the following reseller needs:

Products
Primarily resellers seek products of interest to their customers. For instance, a buyer for a large retailer may personally not like a particular product but nonetheless will purchase it as long as customers are willing to buy. Thus, selling to resellers means the marketer must show convincing evidence the customers serviced by the reseller will purchase the products.

Delivery
Resellers want the product delivered on time and in good condition in order to meet customer demand and avoid inventory out-of-stocks. Clearly articulated distribution plans must be presented.

Profit Margin
Resellers are in business to make money so a key factor in their decision to handle a product is how much money they will make on each product sold. They expect the difference (i.e., margin) between their cost for acquiring the product from a supplier and the price they charge to sell the product to their customers will be sufficient to meet their profit objectives.

Other Incentives
Besides profit margin, resellers may want other incentives to entice them especially if they are required to give extra effort selling the product. These incentives may be in the form of additional free products or even bonuses (e.g., money, free trips) for achieving sales goals (see *Trade Sales Promotion* discussion in Chapter 14).

Packaging
Resellers want to handle products as easily as possible and want their suppliers to ship and sell products in packages that fit within their system. For example, products may need to be a certain size or design in order to fit on a store's shelf, or the shipping package must fit within the reseller's warehouse or receiving dock space. Also, many resellers are now requiring marketers to consider adding identification tags to products (e.g., RFID tags) to allow for easier inventory tracking when the product is received and also when it is sold. A major force in this is Wal-Mart which currently requires a RFID tags on shipping pallets sent to its Sam's Club outlet. By 2009 it is expected some suppliers will be required to place RFID tags on individual items. (1)

Training
Some products require the reseller to have strong knowledge of the product including demonstrating the product to customers. Marketers must consider offering training to resellers to ensure the reseller has the knowledge to present the product accurately.

Promotional Help
Resellers often seek additional help from the product supplier to promote the product to customers. Such help may come in the form of funding for advertisements, point-of-purchase product materials or in-store demonstrations.

WHAT IS RETAILING?

Retailing is defined as selling products to consumers for their personal use. A retailer is a reseller from which a consumer purchases products. In the U.S. alone there are over 1,100,000 retailers according to the *2002 U.S. Census of Retail Trade*. (2) In terms of sales volume and number of employees, retailing is one of the largest sectors of most economies.

• •

There are some who believe the number of retailers in the U.S. has exceeded the size needed to support the population. This is attributed to overbuilding of retail outlets and the expansion of retailers selling primarily over the Internet. The high number of retailers combined with a declining economy has led to store closings by such well-known retailers as Ann Taylor, Liz Claiborne, and Talbots. (3)

• •

In the majority of retail situations, the organization from which a consumer makes purchases is a reseller of products obtained from others and not the product manufacturer, though as we discussed in Chapter 8, some manufacturers do operate their own retail outlets in a corporate channel arrangement. While consumers are the retailer's buyers, a consumer does not always buy from retailers. For instance, when a consumer purchases from another consumer (e.g., eBay), the consumer purchase would not be classified as a retail purchase. This distinction can get confusing but in the U.S. and other countries the dividing line is whether the one selling to consumers is classified as a business (e.g., legal and tax purposes) or is selling as a hobby without legal business standing.

Benefits of Retailers

As a reseller, retailers offer many benefits to suppliers and customers as we discussed in Chapter 8. The major benefits for each include:

♦ <u>Access to Customers</u> – For suppliers the most important benefits relate to offering opportunities to reach their target market, build product demand through retail promotions, and provide consumer feedback to the product marketer. As discussed in Box 9-2, retailers are also marketers whose knowledge and skills are an integral part in generating sales, profits, and customer loyalty for suppliers.

Box 9-2

CONCERNS OF RETAILERS

While much of the discussion in this chapter deals with the role of retailers in the marketing strategy for consumer products companies, it important to understand that retailers face their own marketing challenges. Among the marketing issues facing retailers are:

Improving Customer Satisfaction

Retailers know that satisfied customers are loyal customers. Consequently, retailers must develop strategies intended to build relationships that result in customers returning to make more purchases.

Acquiring the Right Products

Customers will only be satisfied if they can purchase the right products to satisfy their needs. Since a large percentage of retailers do not manufacture their own products, they must seek suppliers who will supply products demanded by customers. Thus, an important objective for retailers is to identify the products customers will demand and negotiate with suppliers to obtain these products.

Presenting Products to Generate Interest

Once obtained products must be presented or merchandised to customers in a way that generates interest. Retail merchandising often requires hiring creative people who understand and can relate to the market.

Building Customer Traffic

Like any marketer, retailers must use promotional methods to build customer interest. For retailers a key measure of interest is the number of people visiting a retail location or website. Building "traffic" is accomplished with a variety of promotional techniques, such as advertising, and specialized promotional activities, such as coupons.

Creating an Attractive Layout

For store-based retailers a store's physical layout is an important component in creating a retail experience that will attract customers. The physical layout is more than just deciding in what part of the store to locate products. For many retailers designing the right shopping atmosphere (e.g., objects, light, sound) can add to the appeal of a store. Layout is also important in the online world where **website navigation and usability** may be deciding factors in whether a retail website is successful.

Finding Good Locations

Where to physically locate a retail store may help or hinder store traffic. Well placed stores with high visibility and easy access, while possibly commanding higher land usage fees, may hold significantly more value than lower cost sites that yield less traffic. Understanding the trade-off between costs and benefits of locations is an important retail decision.

Keeping Pace with Technology

Technology has invaded all areas of retailing, including customer knowledge (e.g., customer relationship management software), product movement (e.g., use of RFID tags for tracking), point-of-purchase (e.g., scanners, kiosks, self-serve checkout), web technologies (e.g., online shopping carts, purchase recommendations), and many more.

♦ <u>Access to Product</u> – For consumers the most important benefits offered by retailers relate to the ability to purchase products that may not otherwise be easily available if the consumers had to deal directly with product suppliers. In particular, retailers provide consumers with the ability to purchase small quantities of a wide assortment of products at prices that are considered reasonably affordable. Additionally, retailers are likely to locate near their target market; thereby, enabling consumers to make purchases much more conveniently than if they had to visit a product supplier's facilities.

WAYS TO CATEGORIZE RETAILERS

There are many ways retailers can be categorized depending on the characteristics being evaluated. We separate retailers based on six factors directly related to major marketing decisions:

♦ Target Markets Served

♦ Product Offerings

♦ Pricing Structure

♦ Promotional Emphasis

♦ Distribution Method

♦ Service Level

and one operational factor:

♦ Ownership

However, these groups are not meant to be mutually exclusive. In fact, in some way all retailers can be placed into each category.

Target Markets Served

The first classification looks at the type of markets a retailer intends to target. These categories are identical to the levels of distribution classification scheme discussed in Chapter 8.

♦ <u>Mass Market</u> – Mass market retailers appeal to the largest market possible by selling products of interest to nearly all consumers. With such a large market from which to draw customers, the competition among these retailers is often fierce.

♦ Specialty Market – Retailers categorized as servicing the specialty market are likely to target buyers looking for products having certain features that go beyond mass marketed products, such as customers who require more advanced product options or a higher level of customer service. While not as large as the mass market, the target market serviced by specialty retailers can be sizable.

♦ Exclusive Market – Appealing to this market means appealing to discriminating customers who are often willing to pay a premium for features found in very few products and for highly personalized services. Since this target market is small, the number of retailers addressing this market within a given geographic area may also be small.

Products Carried

Under this classification retailers are divided based on the width (i.e., number of different product lines) and depth (i.e., number of different products within a product line) of the products they carry.

♦ General Merchandisers – These retailers carry a wide range of product categories (i.e., broad width) though the number of different items within a particular product line is generally limited (i.e., shallow depth). A retailer such as Target would be considered a general merchandiser.

♦ Multiple Lines Specialty Merchandisers – Retailers classified in this category stock a limited number of product lines (i.e., narrow width) but within the categories they handle they often offer a greater selection (i.e., extended depth) than is offered by general merchandisers. For example, a consumer electronics retailer would fall into this category.

♦ Single Line Specialty Merchandisers – Some retailers limit their offerings to just one product line (i.e., very narrow width), and sometimes only one product (i.e., very shallow depth). This can be seen online where a relatively small website may sell a single product, such as computer gaming software. Another example may be a small jewelry store that only handles watches.

Distribution Method

Retailers sell in many different formats with some requiring consumers visit a physical location while others sell to customers in a virtual space. It should be noted that many retailers are not tied to a single distribution method but operate using multiple methods.

Store-Based Sellers

By far the predominant method consumers use to obtain products is to acquire these by physically visiting retail outlets (also called **brick-and-mortar stores**). Store outlets can be further divided into several categories. One key characteristic distinguishing categories is whether retail outlets are physically connected to one or more other stores:

- Stand-Alone – These are retail outlets that do not have other retail outlets connected.

- Strip-Shopping Center – A retail arrangement with two or more outlets physically connected or that share physical resources (e.g., share parking lot).

- Shopping Area – A local center of retail operations containing many retail outlets that may or may not be physically connected but are in close proximity to each other such as a city shopping district.

- Regional Shopping Mall – Consists of a large self-contained shopping area with many connected outlets.

Non-Store Sellers

Under this retail approach retailers sell products to customers who do not physically visit a retail outlet. In fact, in many cases customers make their purchase from within their own homes.

- Online Sellers – The fastest growing retail distribution method allows consumers to purchase products via the Internet. In most cases delivery is then handled by a third-party shipping service.

- Direct Marketers – Retailers principally selling via direct methods (e.g., television, catalog) may have a primary location that receives orders but does not host shopping visits. Rather, orders are received via mail or phone.

- Vending – While purchasing through vending machines does require the consumer to physically visit a location, this type of retailing is considered as non-store retailing as the vending operations are not located at the vending company's place of business.

• •

Nearly all major store-based retailers are also non-store sellers since they operate their own websites. In the U.S. websites run by retailers Best Buy, Target, and Wal-Mart are often within the top 50 websites in terms of website traffic (4), while in the U.K. retailers Argos and Tesco also operate popular sites. (5)

• •

Pricing Strategy

Retailers can be classified based on their general pricing strategy. Retailers must decide whether their approach is to use price as a competitive advantage or to seek competitive advantage in non-price ways.

♦ Discount Pricing – Discount retailers are best known for selling low priced products having a low profit margin (i.e., price minus cost). To make profits these retailers look to sell in high volume. Typically discount retailers operate with low overhead costs by vigorously controlling operational spending on such things as real estate (e.g., locate in less expensive areas), design issues (e.g., less elaborate store layout), and by offering fewer services to their customers.

♦ Competitive Pricing – The objective of some retailers is not to compete on price but alternatively not to be seen as charging the highest price. These retailers, who often operate in specialty markets, aggressively monitor the market to ensure their pricing is competitive but they do not desire to get into price wars with discount retailers. Thus, other elements of their marketing strategy (e.g., higher quality products, more attractive store setting) are used to create higher value for which the customer will pay more.

♦ Full Price Pricing – Retailers targeting exclusive markets find such markets are far less price sensitive than mass or specialty markets. In these cases the additional value added through increased operational spending (e.g., expensive locations, more attractive design, more services) justify higher retail prices. While these retailers are likely to sell in lower volume than discount or competitive pricing retailers, the profit margins for each product are much higher.

Promotional Emphasis

Retailers generate customer interest using a variety of promotional techniques, yet some retailers rely on certain methods more than others as their principle promotional approach.

- ◆ Advertising – Many retailers find traditional mass promotional methods of advertising, such as through newspapers or television, continue to be their best means for creating customer interest. Retailers selling online rely mostly on Internet advertising as their promotional method of choice.

- ◆ Direct Mail – A particular form of advertising that many retailers use for the bulk of their promotion is direct mail – advertising through postal mail. Using direct mail for promotion is the primary way catalog retailers distribute their materials and is often utilized by smaller local companies who promote using postcards and other types of mailing methods.

- ◆ Personal Selling – Retailers selling expensive or high-end products find a considerable amount of their promotional effort is spent in person-to-person contact with customers. While many of these retailers use other promotional methods, in particular advertising, the consumer-salesperson relationship is key to persuading consumers to make purchase decisions.

· ·

In addition to the promotional methods cited above, all types of retailers also use short-term promotions, called sales promotions (discussed in Chapter 14), designed to encourage customers to undertake certain activity, such as make a purchase or visit a store. One common type of sales promotion is the coupon which offers pricing discounts. Many retailers give customers coupons printed on a purchase receipt. Some customers are annoyed to discover their receipts are filled with unwanted coupons making for a long receipt even if only few items are purchased. (6)

· ·

Service Level

Retailers attract customers not only with desirable products and affordable prices, but also by offering services that enhance the purchase experience. There are at least three levels of retail service:

- ◆ Self-Service – This service level allows consumers to perform most or all of the services associated with retail purchasing. For some consumers self-service is considered a benefit while others may view it as an inconvenience. Self-service can be seen with: 1) **self-selection** services, such as online purchasing and vending machine purchases, and 2) **self-checkout** services where the consumer may get help selecting the product but they use self-checkout stations to process the purchase, including scanning and payment.

♦ Assorted-Service – The majority of retailers offer some level of service to consumers. Service includes handling the point-of-purchase transaction, product selection assistance, arrange payment plans, offer delivery, and many more.

♦ Full-Service – The full-service retailer attempts to handle nearly all aspects of the purchase to the point where all the consumer does is select the item they wish to purchase. Retailers that follow a full-price pricing strategy often follow the full-service approach as a way of adding value to a customer's purchase.

Ownership Structure

Finally, retailers can be categorized based on the ownership structure of the business.

♦ Individually Owned and Operated – Under this ownership structure an individual or corporate entity owns and operates one or a very small number of relatively small outlets.

♦ Corporate Chain – A retail chain consists of multiple retail outlets owned and operated by a single entity all performing similar retail activities. While the number of retail outlets required to be classified as a chain has never been specified, we will assume that anyone owning more than five retail locations would be considered a chain.

♦ Corporate Structure – This classification covers large retailers operating less than five locations, such as automotive dealers or furniture stores, and those operating in the non-store retail arena such as online, catalog, and vending companies.

♦ Contractually Licensed and Individually Operated – The contractual channel arrangement discussed in Chapter 8 has led to a retail ownership structure in which operators of the retail outlet are not the outright owners of the business. Instead, the arrangement often involves a legal agreement in which the owner of the retail concept allows the operator to run the owner's business concept in exchange for financial considerations, such as a percentage of revenue. This structure is most often seen in retail franchising (see *Franchise* discussion below).

RETAIL FORMATS

Now that we have presented ways in which retailers can be classified, we now use these categories to distinguish general formats or business models that best describe retail operations. These categories are designed to identify the primary format a retailer follows. In some cases, particularly with the advent of the Internet, a retailer will be involved in more than one format.

Mom-and-Pop

These represent the small, individually owned and operated retail outlets. In many cases these are family-run businesses catering to the local community often with a high level of service but relatively small product selection.

Mass Discounter

These retailers can be either general or specialty merchandisers but either way their main focus is on offering discount pricing. Compared to other store types, mass discounters offer fewer services and lower quality products.

Warehouse Store

This is a form of mass discounter that often provides even lower prices than traditional mass discounters. In addition, they often require buyers to make minimum purchases in quantities that are greater than what can be purchased at mass discount stores. These retail outlets provide few services and product selection can be limited. Furthermore, the retail design and layout is, as the name suggests, warehouse style with consumers often selecting products off the ground from the shipping package. Some forms of warehouse stores, called warehouse clubs, require customers purchase memberships in order to gain access to the outlet.

Specialty Store

A step above the boutique store is the specialty store, which is generally represented by mid-sized stores carrying more depth than the boutique store. The service level of specialty stores is not as focused as it is with a boutique, though customer service is a key element to their success.

Boutique

This retail format is best represented by a small store carrying very specialized and often high-end merchandise. In many cases a boutique is a full-service retailer following a full-price pricing strategy.

Category Killer

Many major retail chains have taken what were previously narrowly focused, small specialty store concepts and have expanded them to create large specialty stores. These so-called "category killers" have been found in such specialty areas as electronics (e.g., Best Buy), office supplies (e.g., Staples), and sporting goods (e.g., Sports Authority).

Department Store

These retailers are general merchandisers offering mid-to-high quality products and a strong level of services, though in most cases these retailers would not fall into the full-service category. While department stores are classified as general merchandisers some carry a more selective product line. For instance, while Sears carries a wide range of products from hardware to cosmetics, Nordstrom focuses its products on clothing and personal care products.

· ·

In the U.S. department stores, such as Macy's and Bloomingdales, have experienced declines in sales to children and teens principally due to the growth of specialty retailers such as Aéropostale and Urban Outfitters. Also, department stores face a perception problem as many young people view these stores as mostly being for their parents. To attract this market back to their stores, department stores have altered their product offerings to include trendier items and redesigned store interiors. (7)

· ·

Catalog Retailer

Retailers such as Lands' End and LL Bean have built their businesses by having customers place orders after seeing products that appear in a mailed catalog. Orders are then delivered by a third-party shipper.

Convenience Store

As the name implies these general merchandise retailers cater to offering customers an easy purchase experience. Convenience is offered in many ways, including through easily accessible store locations, small store size that allows for quick shopping, and fast checkout. The product selection offered by these retailers is very limited and pricing can be high.

Franchise

As noted in Chapter 8, a franchise is a form of contractual channel in which one party, the franchisor, controls the business activities of another party, the franchisee. Under these arrangements, an eligible franchisee agrees to pay for the right to use the franchisor's business methods and other important business aspects, such as the franchise name. Franchises offer several advantages as discussed in Box 9-3.

Box 9-3

FRANCHISING BASICS

Starting a retail operation is a dream for many aspiring entrepreneurs. But the risks involved can be substantial. Whether starting a store-based or online retail outlet, the costs associated with creating a presence, such as opening a store or building a website and acquiring inventory, can be high. But even for retailers having the financial resources to establish a retail location, they still face the major hurdle of gaining customer recognition. In fact, opening a store may be easy compared to promotional efforts needed to build store traffic.

Because of the risk involved in building a retail outlet, acquiring a franchise may be an attractive option for entrepreneurs looking to move quickly from initial investment to producing revenue. Franchises hold many advantages, including the fact that success rates tend to be much higher than for businesses that are started in more traditional ways, especially when joining a well-established franchise operation. Franchise business opportunities are available in a wide variety of categories and include such well-known names as Subway, Dunkin' Donuts, 7-Eleven, and Holiday Inn. (8)

Under a franchise arrangement, a **franchisor** (i.e., franchise owner) allows others, known as **franchisees**, to employ its business model in exchange for a fee which generally includes a portion of the generated revenue. For instance, McDonalds is a well-known franchisor that allows individuals to use the McDonalds name and methods to deliver food to consumers. Payment is usually in the form of a one-time, upfront franchise fee and also an on-going percentage of revenue.

While the cost to the franchisee may be quite high and there are often many restrictions on what the franchisee can do, this form of retailing offers several advantages including: 1) allowing the franchisee to open a retail outlet that may already be known to local customers, and 2) being trained in how to operate the business, which may allow the franchisee to be successful much faster than if they attempted to start a business on his/her own. For the franchisor, in addition to added revenue, the franchise model allows for faster expansion since funds needed to expand the business (e.g., acquiring retail space, local advertising) are often supported by the franchisee's up-front franchise fee.

---

e-tailer

Possibly the most publicized retail model to evolve in the last 50 years is the retailer that principally sells via the Internet. There are thousands of online-only retail sellers of which Amazon is the most famous. These retailers offer shopping convenience including being open for business all day, every day. Electronic retailers or e-tailers also have the ability to offer a wide selection of product since all they really need to attract orders is a picture and description of the product. That is, they may not need to have the product on-hand the way physical stores do. Instead an e-tailer can wait until an order is received from a customer before placing its own order with its suppliers. This cuts down significantly on the cost of maintaining products in-stock.

· ·

In the early days of e-commerce some pundits suggested online retailing would be limited to non-personalized products that do not require the customer to see, feel, or try before purchasing. Zappos is one company that has proven this to be wrong. Zappos' principle product is shoes, a product that most would consider highly personalized. Yet with free shipping and free returns to go along with a huge inventory the company has enjoyed tremendous success. (9)

· ·

Vending

Within this category are automated methods allowing consumers to make purchases and quickly acquire products. While most consumers are well aware of vending machines for the purchase of smaller items, such as beverages and snack foods, newer devices are entering the market containing more expensive and bulkier products, such as music players, software, flowers, and cologne. (10) These systems require the vending machine have either Internet or telecommunications access to permit purchase using credit cards.

Retailing Format Summary

Below in Table 9-1 we summarize each retail format by using the seven categorization characteristics. The characteristics identified for each format should be viewed as the "most likely" case for that format and are not necessarily representative of all retailers that fall into this format.

Table 9-1: Retailing Format Summary

Format	Target Market	Products Carried	Pricing Strategy	Promotion Emphasis	Distribution	Service Level	Ownership Structure
Mom-and-Pop	mass specialty	general specialty	competitive	advertising direct mail	stand-alone strip center shopping area	assorted	individually owned/oper.
Mass Discounter	mass	general	discount	advertising	stand-alone strip-center	self	corp. chain
Warehouse Store	mass	general	discount	advertising	stand-alone	self	corp. chain
Specialty	specialty	specialty	full competitive	selling advertising	shopping area shopping mall	full	corp. chain
Boutique	specialty exclusive	specialty	full	selling	stand-alone strip center shopping area	full	individually owned/oper. corp. chain
Category Killer	mass	specialty	discount competitive	advertising	stand-alone strip center	assorted	corp. chain
Department Store	specialty	general	competitive	advertising	shopping area shopping mall	assorted	corp. chain
Catalog	mass specialty	general specialty	discount competitive	direct mail	direct marketer	assorted	corp. structure
Convenience	mass	general	full	advertising	stand-alone	self	individually owned/oper. corp. chain
Franchise	mass	specialty	competitive	advertising	stand-alone strip center	assorted	contractual
e-tailer	mass specialty	general specialty	discount full competitive	advertising	online seller	self	corp. structure.
Vending	mass	specialty	full	none	vending	self	corp. structure

REFERENCES

1. Johannes, A., "Wal-Mart to Require Item-Level Tags," *Promo Magazine*, March 1, 2008.

2. "2002 Census of Retail Trade," *United States Census Bureau*.

3. Gross. D., "America Has Too Many Stores," *Slate*, February 16, 2008.

4. Top 100 U.S. Websites, *Alexa.com*.

5. Top 100 U.K. Websites, *Alexa.com*.

6. Rouvalis, C., "Loaded With Coupons and Surveys, Receipts Grow Longer, Aggravating Many," *Pittsburgh Post-Gazette*, July 24, 2007.

7. O'Donnell, J. and E. Kutz, "USA Big Retailers Seek Teens and Parents," *USA Today*, April 17, 2008.

8. For a list of top franchises see *Entrepreneur Magazine* website.

9. Cornish, A., "Zappos Proves Shoes Do Sell Online," *National Public Radio*, July 14, 2007.

10. McConnon, A., "The Va Va Vooming of Vending Machines," *Business-Week*, January 22, 2008.

Full text of many of the references can be accessed via links on the support website.

Chapter 10:

Wholesaling and Product Movement

As we saw in Chapter 9, it is more the rule than the exception that marketers are not able to handle all distribution activities on their own. Instead, to get products into the hands of customers often requires the assistance of third-party service firms. In addition to retailers, marketers should be aware of others whose expertise in certain facets of distribution can prove quite beneficial.

In this chapter we first examine another reselling group - wholesalers - and see how they come into play when a marketer attempts to reach the final customer. We show wholesalers exist in many formats, affect a wide range of industries, and offer different sets of features and benefits depending on the markets they serve. In the second half of the chapter we examine the tasks that must be carried out in order to physically move products to customers. In some cases the marketer will take on the responsibility of carrying out some functions, while other tasks may be assigned to distribution service providers. Whether handled by the marketer or contracted to others, these functions are crucial to having a cost-effective and efficient distribution system. It is worth noting that while most product movement is concerned with moving tangible products, some of the issues covered here are also applicable to intangible products, such as services, and to digital products.

WHAT IS WHOLESALING?

Wholesaling is a distribution channel function where one organization buys from supply firms with the primary intention of redistributing to other organizations. A wholesaler is an organization providing the necessary means to: 1) allow suppliers to reach organizational buyers, and 2) allow certain business buyers to purchase products which they may not be able to otherwise purchase. According to the *2002 U.S. Census of Wholesale Trade*, there are over 430,000 wholesale operations in the United States. (1)

While many large retailers and even manufacturers have centralized facilities and carry out the same tasks as wholesalers, we do not classify these as wholesalers since these relationships only involve one other party, the buyer. Thus, a distinguishing characteristic of wholesalers is they offer distribution activities for both a supplying party and for a purchasing party. For our discussion of wholesalers we will primarily focus on wholesalers who sell to other resellers, such as retailers.

Benefits of Wholesalers

The benefits wholesalers offer to members of the channel can be significant and involve most of channel member benefits we discussed in Chapter 8, though specific benefits vary by type of wholesaler. Yet there are two particular benefits – one for suppliers and one for retailers – that are common to most wholesale operations and are worth further discussion:

♦ Provide Access to Products – Wholesalers are in business to provide products and services to buyers (e.g., retailers) who either cannot purchase directly from suppliers because their purchase quantities are too low to meet the supplier's minimum order requirements or, if they purchase directly from suppliers, will pay higher prices compared to bigger retailers who obtain better pricing by purchasing in greater quantities. Since wholesalers sell to a large number of buyers their order quantities may match those of large retailers, which may allow them to obtain lower prices from suppliers. Wholesalers can then pass these lower prices along to their buyers, which can enable smaller retailers to remain competitive with larger rivals. In this way transacting through wholesalers is often the only way certain retailers can stay in business.

♦ Provide Access to Markets – Providing smaller retailers access to products they cannot acquire without wholesaler help offers a benefit for suppliers as well since it opens additional market opportunities for suppliers. That is, suppliers can have their products purchased and made available for sale across a wide number of retail outlets. More importantly, for a company offering a new product, convincing a few wholesalers to stock a new product may make it easier to gain traction in the market as the wholesaler can yield power with the smaller retailers convincing them to stock the new product. Considering a wholesaler can serve hundreds of small retail customers, the marketing efforts required to persuade a single wholesaler to adopt a new product may be far more efficient compared to efforts needed to convince hundreds of individual store owners to stock the new product.

Despite the benefits they offer, wholesalers face many challenges which may be changing how they perform their tasks. The challenges are discussed in Box 10-1.

Box 10-1

CONCERNS OF WHOLESALERS

The wholesale industry has served an important role in the distribution process for well over 100 years, yet the challenges they face today are raising the stakes as many wholesalers fight to maintain their market position. Some of the issues facing today's wholesalers include:

Disintermediation
The growth of the Internet as a communication and distribution channel has led many to conclude that wholesaling will lose its importance as manufacturers and final buyers learn to transact directly. This so called "disintermediation" of marketing channels is a real concern to some wholesalers, especially those that do not function as a dominate party within a distribution channel. For example, assume a retailer operating a gift card store uses a wholesaler only to purchase a specific manufacturer's products. In this situation if the manufacturer begins to offer direct purchasing to smaller customers the wholesaler may have little leverage in efforts to retain the retailer as a customer. In instances of disintermediation wholesalers face the challenge of creating greater value for their services with the intention of making the retailer's decision to switch more difficult.

Facility Location
Wholesalers who are heavily involved in product shipment may spend considerable time evaluating sites to locate facilities. For organizations needing very large facilities, the decision as to where to locate becomes more difficult and more expensive the closer the location is to major metropolitan areas. In fact, land costs in some regions of the world have risen so high that utilizing this space for wholesal-

---

ing operations may not be feasible. In addition to land costs, facility location is also affected by access to adequate transportation such as roads, seaports, airports, and rail terminals. Areas with available land often lack the infrastructure needed to run wholesale facilities unless expensive and time-consuming improvements (e.g., build highway, extend rail line, etc) are made.

Transportation Costs

For wholesalers involved in transporting products, the worldwide rise in fuel costs has forced a close examination of how they handle product distribution. Transportation expense can represent a significant portion of overall distribution costs and these higher costs are often passed on to customers in the form of higher product prices. For example, grocery retailers in Hawaii, who receive many produce products from wholesalers located on the U.S. mainland, have seen a large increase in food costs due to escalating fuel prices. (2) However, high transportation expense also presents opportunities for wholesalers that work hard to control fuel costs with such methods as: using equipment and delivery vehicles that are more fuel efficient, utilizing computer routing software to determine less costly delivery routes, and offering greater incentives to customers to accept deliveries during less congested times of the day.

Adapting to New Technologies

In addition to technologies to lower fuel costs, other technologies that assist the distribution process are offering both advantages and disadvantages to wholesalers. New technologies, such as radio frequency identification tags (RFID) placed on shipped products, allow wholesalers to maintain tighter control over their distribution activities. But gaining the benefits associated with these new distribution technologies can be expensive in terms of acquiring and learning to use.

Offering Non-Product Assistance

Wholesalers are finding that offering access to products is not enough to satisfy buyers. Many customers also want wholesalers to offer additional value-added services such as employee training (e.g., teach selling skills), promotional support (e.g., financial support for advertising), and assistance in managing their operations (e.g., building an online store). Keeping pace with the services demanded by customers requires constant research and communication with customers.

WAYS TO CATEGORIZE WHOLESALERS

In Chapter 9 we showed how retailers can be categorized using different characteristics. Wholesalers can likewise be grouped together, though the characteristics are slightly different.

For our purposes we will separate wholesale operations based on four marketing decisions:

♦ Products Carried

♦ Promotional Activities

♦ Distribution Method

♦ Service Level

and one legal factor:

♦ Product Ownership

As we discussed with our retailer categorization, these grouping schemes are not meant to be mutually exclusive. Consequently, a wholesaler can be evaluated on each characteristic.

Products Carried

Similar to how retailers can be categorized, wholesalers can also be classified by the width and depth of the product lines they handle. The categories include:

♦ General Merchandise – Wholesalers carrying a very broad line of products fall into the general merchandise wholesaler category. Like general merchandise retailers, the product lines these wholesalers carry may not offer many options (i.e., shallow depth). These wholesalers tend to market to smaller general merchandise retailers, such as convenience or mom-and-pop stores.

♦ Specialty Merchandise – Wholesalers focusing on narrow product lines, but offering deep selection within the lines, fall into the specialty merchandise category. Most specialty merchandise wholesalers direct their marketing efforts to specific industries. For example, specialty wholesalers supply industries such as electronics, seafood, and pharmaceuticals.

• •

The website Wholesale Central provides links to over 1,400 wholesalers selling more than 50 product categories. For instance, the website lists over 25 wholesalers selling perfume products. For the most part, companies listed only sell to other businesses, such as retailers, and not to consumers. (3)

• •

Promotional Activities

Wholesalers can be separated based on the importance promotion plays in generating demand for products handled by the wholesaler. Two basic categories exist:

◆ Extensive Promotion – The main job of some wholesalers is to actively locate buyers. This occurs most often where a wholesaler is hired to find buyers for a supplier's products or where the wholesaler is very aggressive in finding new customers for its business. Under these arrangements the most common promotional activity is personal selling through a sales force, though advertising may also be used.

◆ Limited Promotion – Nearly all wholesalers engage in some promotional activities. Even in situations where a wholesaler dominates a channel and clients have little choice but to acquire products from the wholesaler, some promotion will still occur. For instance, at times a wholesaler may need to use its salespeople to persuade buyers to purchase in larger volume than normal or to agree to stock a new product the wholesaler is handling. In other cases, especially for wholesalers selling products for business use, promotional activities may be more extensive and include advertising and other promotional methods.

Distribution Method

Wholesalers have distribution methods similar to those of retailers in that customers may or may not be able to physically visit the wholesaler's location to acquire their purchases. For the purposes of our discussion of wholesaling, this category is separated based on whether or not a stationary location exists from which the wholesaler conducts the physical movement of products.

Stationary Location

In most common wholesaler arrangements the wholesaler has one or more fixed facilities where product handling operations take place. However, while stationary wholesalers share the characteristic of a permanent location, they often differ on whether customers can visit these facilities:

• Customer Accessible – At certain wholesaler locations buyers can shop at the facility. In fact, retail warehouse clubs, such as Costco and Sam's Club, also function as wholesalers for qualifying businesses. In addition to selecting their orders, buyers are responsible for making their own arrangements to transport their purchases.

- Not Customer Accessible – Most operations classified as wholesalers do not permit buyers to visit their facilities in order to select items, rather buyers place orders via phone, web or through person-to-person contact with wholesaler's representatives. Also, in most cases, the wholesaler takes responsibility for product delivery.

Non-Stationary Location

Not all wholesalers carry inventory at a stationary location. In fact, some do not carry inventory at all.

- Mobile – Several specialized wholesalers transport products to the customer's location using vans or trucks. Buyers then have the ability to purchase product by either walking through the mobile facility or ordering from the wholesaler who then selects the items from the vehicle.

- No Facilities – Some wholesalers do not have physical locations that store products. Instead, these operations rely on others, such as delivery companies, to ship products from one location (e.g., manufacturer) to the buyer's place of business.

Service Level

Wholesalers can be distinguished by the number and depth of services they provide to their customers.

- Full-Service – Wholesalers in this category mainly sell to the retail industry, and in most cases, require a strong, long-term retailer-wholesaler relationship. In addition to basic distribution services, such as providing access to an assortment of products and furnishing delivery, these wholesalers also offer customers additional services that aid retail store operations including offering assistance with: in-store merchandising, retail site location decisions (e.g., find best geographic location for a new store), store design and construction, back-end operations (e.g., payroll services), financial support, and many more.

- Limited Service – Compared to full-service wholesalers, buyers dealing with limited service firms receive far fewer services. Most offer basic services, such as shipping and allow credit purchasing, but few offer the number of service options found with full-service wholesalers.

- No Service – Some wholesalers follow a business model whose only service is to make products available for sale and only on a cash basis. In these instances, the buyer handles transportation of the product.

Product Ownership

Wholesalers can be classified based on whether they do or do not become the owners of the products they sell. By ownership we mean that **title** (i.e., legal ownership) has passed from the party from whom the wholesaler purchased the product (e.g., manufacturer) to the wholesaler. It also means the wholesaler assumes any risk that may arise with handling the product.

♦ <u>Do Take Title</u> – Wholesalers taking title own the products they purchase.

♦ <u>Do Not Take Title</u> – Wholesalers who do not take title are focused on activities that bring buyers and sellers together. Often these wholesalers never physically handle products.

WHOLESALE FORMATS

Considering the criteria by which wholesalers can be categorized, it is not surprising many different wholesale formats exist. Below we discuss ten wholesale formats. While many of these wholesalers also have an online presence, we do not distinguish an "e-wholesaler" as a separate format the way we did with "e-tailers" or online retailers. The reason? While most wholesalers do operate from a brick-and-mortar facility, only a small fraction of wholesale operations permit customer shopping at their facilities. Consequently, the nature of this industry for many years has been to have customers use communication tools (e.g., phone, fax) to place orders. With the wholesale industry, the Internet simply serves as another communication option rather than a significantly different distribution channel.

General Merchandise

These wholesalers offer broad but shallow product lines that are mostly of interest to retailers carrying a wide assortment of products, such as convenience stores, and smaller general merchandise stores, such as those offering closeout or novelty products. Since these wholesalers offer such a wide range of products, their knowledge of individual products may not be strong.

Specialty Merchandise

Many wholesalers focus on specific product lines or industries and in doing so supply a narrow assortment of products but within the product lines offered there is great depth. Additionally, these wholesalers tend to be highly knowledgeable of the markets they serve.

Contractual

In Chapter 8 we introduced the concept of wholesaler-sponsored channel arrangements where a wholesaler brings together and manages many independent retailers. The services of these wholesalers are supplied only to the retailers involved in the contractual arrangement.

Industrial Distributors

The industrial distributor mainly directs its operations to the business customer rather than to other resellers. Depending on the distributor, they can carry either broad or narrow product lines.

Cash-and-Carry

A wholesale operation common to the food industry is the cash-and-carry where buyers visit the wholesaler's facility, select their orders pay in cash (i.e., credit purchases not permitted), and then handle their own deliveries (i.e., carry) to their place of business. This form of wholesaling has begun to expand outside of the food industry as large wholesale clubs, such as Costco and Sam's Club, allow qualified businesses to purchase products intended for retail sale.

Truck

As the name suggests, truck wholesaling operations are primarily run out of a truck that is stocked with products. These wholesalers often have assigned geographic territories where they regularly visit buyer's locations. In most cases these wholesalers offer specialty product lines with many being found in the retail food industry and industrial markets.

Rack Jobber

Similar to truck wholesalers, the rack jobber also sells from a truck. However, the main difference is rack jobbers are assigned and manage space (i.e., racks) within a retailer's store. The rack jobber is then responsible for maintaining inventory and may even handle other marketing duties such as setting product price. This form of wholesaling is most prominent with magazines, candy, bakery, and health-and-beauty products. In some trades the name rack jobber is being replaced by the name **service merchandiser**.

Drop Shipper

Wholesalers in this category never take physical possession of products, though they do take ownership. Essentially they are shipping coordinators who receive orders from customers and then place the order with a product supplier. Shipping is then arranged so the supplier ships directly to the drop shipper's customer. Drop shipping is often most useful when very large orders are placed so that transportation and product handling costs can be spread over many items (see Box 10-2).

• •

Online sellers may see several advantages to having customers receive their orders from drop shippers. These advantages include: lower overhead due to less need for storage space, lower inventory investment since payment to the drop shipper may not have to occur until the customer pays, and gives the perception of offering a broader product selection by advertising products that normally would be too difficult to carry such as furniture. (4)

• •

Broker

A far less obvious type of wholesaler is the broker, who is responsible for bringing buyers and sellers together. However, brokers do not take ownership of products and often never handle the product. Brokers are paid based on a pre-negotiated percentage of the sale (i.e., commission) by the side that hires their services. In most cases the relationship that develops between the broker and the buyer and seller is short-term and only lasts through the purchase. Brokers can be found in the food industry, importing/exporting, and real estate.

Agent

Similar to brokers, agents also bring buyers and sellers together, though they tend to work for clients for an extended period of time. As with brokers, agents generally are paid on commission. A common type of agent is the **manufacturers' representative** who essentially assumes the role of a salesperson for a client. Manufacturers' representatives may handle several non-competing product lines at the same time and during a single meeting with a perspective buyer may discuss many products from several different companies.

Wholesaling Format Summary

Below in Table 10-1 we summarize each wholesale format by using the five categorization characteristics. The characteristics identified for each format should be viewed as the "most likely" case for that format and are not necessarily representative of all wholesalers that fall into this format.

Table 10-1: Wholesaling Format Summary

Format	Products Carried	Promotional Activities	Distribution Method	Service Level	Product Ownership
General Merchandise	general	limited	stationary not accessible	limited	take title
Specialty Merchandise	specialty	limited	stationary may be accessible	full or limited	take title
Contractual	general or specialty	extensive	stationary not accessible	full	take title
Industrial Distributor	general or specialty	limited	stationary may be accessible	limited	take title
Cash-and-Carry	specialty	limited	stationary accessible	no	take title
Truck	specialty	limited	non-stationary mobile	limited	take title
Rack Jobber	specialty	limited	non-stationary mobile	limited	take title
Drop Shipper	specialty	limited	non-stationary no facilities	limited	take title
Broker	specialty	extensive	non-stationary no facilities	limited	do not take title
Agent	specialty	extensive	non-stationary no facilities	limited	do not take title

MANAGING PRODUCT MOVEMENT

In addition to enlisting the assistance of retailers and wholesalers to make products available to customers, marketers also face additional concerns when trying to meet distribution objectives. In this section we examine the tasks that must be carried out in order to physically move products to customers. These tasks include:

♦ Ordering and Inventory Management

♦ Transportation

♦ Product Storage

In some cases the marketer will take on the responsibility of carrying out some functions, while other tasks may be assigned to distribution service providers. Whether handled by the marketer or contracted to others, these functions are crucial to having a cost-effective and efficient distribution system.

ORDERING AND INVENTORY MANAGEMENT

Having products available when customers want to make purchases may seem like a relatively straightforward process. All a seller needs to do is make sure there is product (i.e., inventory) in its possession and ready for the customer to purchase. Unfortunately, being prepared for customer purchasing is not always easy. Having the right product available when the customer is ready to buy requires a highly coordinated effort involving order entry and processing systems, forecasting techniques, customer knowledge, strong channel relationships, and skill at physically handling products.

ORDER ENTRY AND PROCESSING SYSTEMS

The marketer must have a system allowing customers to easily place orders. This system can be as simple as a consumer walking to the counter of a small food stand to purchase a few vegetables or as complicated as automated computer systems where an **electronic order** is triggered from a retailer to a manufacturer each time a consumer purchases a product at the retailer's store. In either case, the order processing system must be able to meet the purchasing needs of the customer. In some circumstances an efficient ordering system can be turned into a competitive advantage. Amazon turned its order handling system into a product feature with the patented "1-click" ordering option that streamlines online ordering by reducing the number of clicks needed to make purchases. (5)

• •

Amazon has unveiled an ordering system in which customers can text a book order through their cellphones. By sending a text message containing the book title or other identifier customers can receive a message back indicating whether Amazon carries the book and its price. A few extra entries on the cellphone lead to the purchase. (6)

• •

FORECASTING

Inventory management is often an exercise in predicting how customers will respond in the future. By predicting purchase behavior the marketer can respond by making sure the right amount of product is available. For most large-scale resellers effective inventory forecasting requires the use of sophisticated statistical tools that look at many variables, such as past purchase history, amount of promotional effort that triggers an increase in customer ordering, and other market criteria, to determine how much of the product will be needed to meet customer demand.

CUSTOMER KNOWLEDGE

Inventory management can be fine-tuned to respond to customers' needs. As a marketer learns more about a customer they begin to observe trends in how and when purchases are made. Combining customer knowledge with forecasting techniques allows the marketer to better estimate product demand and inventory requirements. As we discussed in Chapter 3, the key to understanding customers is having in place a customer relationship management (CRM) system for tracking and analyzing customer activity.

CHANNEL RELATIONSHIPS

While the marketer who uses channel members to sell consumer products has access to information for their immediate customers (e.g., resellers) they often do not have access to sales and customer behavior information controlled by the party selling to the final consumer (e.g., retailer). Knowing the demand patterns at the final consumer level can give marketers good insight into how the reseller may order. Developing strong relationships with the holder of consumer information can result in the reseller sharing this information with the marketer. In fact, as we noted in Chapter 8, some retailers allow marketers direct access to real-time, store-level inventory information so the marketer can monitor how products are selling in stores and be in a position to respond quickly if inventory needs change.

175

PHYSICAL HANDLING

An often overlooked area of inventory management involves the actions and skills needed to prepare a product to move from one point to another. Some products require special attention be given to ensure the product is not damaged during shipment. Such efforts must be carefully balanced against increased costs that arise (e.g., stronger packaging) in order to provide greater protection to products. Because of this, many marketers will accept the fact that some small level of damage occurs during the distribution process.

TRANSPORTATION

A key objective of product distribution is to get products into customers' hands in a timely manner. While delivery of digital products can be handled in a fairly smooth way by allowing customers to access their purchase over the Internet (e.g., download software, gain access to online subscription material), tangible products require a more careful analysis of delivery options in order to provide an optimal level of customer service. But as we noted earlier, "optimal" does not always translate into what a customer may consider is the best method (i.e., may not ship in fastest way possible).

Transportation Features

In terms of delivering products to customers, there are six distinct modes of transportation: air, digital, pipeline, rail, truck, and water. However, not all modes are an option for all marketers. Each mode offers advantages and disadvantages on key transportation features that include:

♦ Product Options – This feature is concerned with the number of different products realistically shipped using a certain mode. Some modes, such as pipeline, are very limited in the type of products that can be shipped while others, such as truck, can handle a wide-range of products.

♦ Speed of Delivery – This refers to how quickly it takes products to move from the shipper's location to the buyer's location.

♦ Accessibility – This transportation feature refers to whether the use of a mode can allow final delivery to occur at the buyer's desired location or whether the mode requires delivery to be off-loaded onto other modes before arriving at the buyer's destination. For example, most deliveries made via air must be loaded onto other transportation modes, often trucks, before they can be delivered to the final customer.

- Cost – The cost of shipment is evaluated in terms of the cost per item to cover some distance (e.g., mile, kilometer). Often for large shipments of tangible products cost is measured in terms of tons-per-mile or metric-tons-per-kilometer.

- Capacity – Refers to the amount of product shipped at one time within one transportation unit. The higher the capacity the more likely transportation cost can be spread over more individual products leading to lower transportation cost per-item shipped (see Box 10-2).

Box 10-2

THE COST ADVANTAGE OF BULK SHIPPING

As was noted in Box 10-1, transportation expense often represents a major portion of the final product cost. Because of the high cost of shipping product, suppliers often find it in the best interest of the distribution channel and the final customer to ship products in bulk quantities. In general, bulk shipping reduces the per-item transportation cost.

For instance, consider what it costs to operate a delivery truck with a shipping capacity of 1,000 boxes. In terms of operational expenses for the truck (e.g., fuel, truck driver's costs, other operational costs), let's assume it costs (US) $1,000 to go from point A to point B. In most cases, with the exception of a little decrease in fuel efficiency, it does not cost that much more to drive the truck whether it is filled with 1,000 boxes of a supplier's product or it only has 100 boxes.

Using this information it is easy to calculate the transportation-cost-per-item:

For the shipment of 100 boxes the transportation cost is:

$$\frac{\$1,000}{100} = \$10 \text{ per item}$$

For the shipment of 1,000 boxes the transportation cost is:

$$\frac{\$1,000}{1,000} = \$1 \text{ per item}$$

As this example illustrates, per-item transportation expense can be significantly reduced when marketers use bulk shipping. As we will see in Chapter 18, such advantages are a key reason suppliers offer quantity discounts to encourage large volume orders.

◆ <u>Intermodal Capable</u> – Intermodal shipping occurs when two or more modes can be combined in order to gain advantages offered by each mode. For instance, in an intermodal method called **piggybacking** truck trailers are loaded onto railroad cars without the need to un-load the trailer. When the railroad car has reached a certain destina-tion the truck trailers are off-loaded onto trucks for delivery to the customer's location.

Modes of Transportation Comparison

Shown in Figure 10-1 are the estimated percentages of product movement (i.e., freight traffic) that occurs within the United States for the five modes of trans-portation that handle tangible products for 2005. Also Table 10-2 presents a summary of the six modes compared on each of the key transportation features.

Figure 10-1: U.S. Domestic Freight Market Share

(percent of ton-miles in 1996 and 2005)

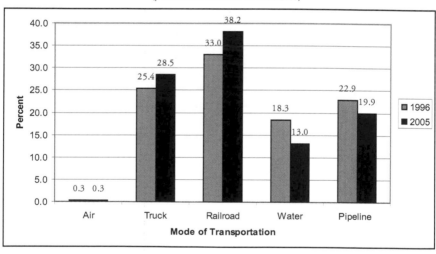

SOURCE: U.S. Department of Transportation, Bureau of Transportation Statistics. (7)

Table 10-2: Modes of Transportation Summary

Mode	Product Options	Speed	Accessibility	Cost	Capacity	Intermodal Capability
Truck	Very Broad	Moderate	High	Moderate	Low	Very High
Railroad	Broad	Slow	Moderate	Low	Moderate	Very High
Air	Narrow	Fast	Low	Very High	Very Low	Moderate
Water	Broad	Very Slow	Moderate	Very Low	Very High	Very High
Pipeline	Very Narrow	Very Slow	Low	Low	Very High	Very Low
Digital	Very Narrow	Very Fast	Very High	Very Low	Moderate	Very Low

PRODUCT STORAGE

The third important element in product movement concerns storing products for future delivery. Marketers of tangible products, and even digital products, may have storage concerns. Storage facilities, such as warehouses, play an important role in the distribution process for a number of reasons including:

- Hold Wide Assortment – As noted in Chapter 8, many resellers allow customers to purchase small quantities of many different products. Yet as we saw in Box 10-2 to obtain the best prices from suppliers, resellers must purchase in large quantities. In these situations the need exists for storage facilities that not only hold a large volume of product, but also hold a wide variety of inventory. Additionally, these facilities must be organized in a way permitting sellers to easily fill orders for its customers.

- Meet Unanticipated Demand – Holding products in storage offers a safeguard in cases of unexpected increases in demand for products.

- Needed for Large Shipping Quantities – As we noted in our discussion of transportation, manufacturers generally prefer to ship in large product quantities in order to more effectively spread transportation costs. This often means manufacturers must create storage areas in which the manufactured goods can build up in the quantities needed for such shipments to occur.

- Offer Faster Response – Additional storage facilities, strategically located in different geographical areas, allow a marketing organization to respond quickly to customers' needs. The ability to respond with quick delivery can be a major value-added feature since it reduces the buyer's need to maintain large inventory at its own locations.

- Security and Backup – For digital products, additional storage facilities are not only needed to offer customers faster access to products (e.g., online content and software) but are also needed to protect against technical glitches and security threats.

Types of Warehouses

The warehouse is the most common type of storage though other forms do exist (e.g., storage tanks, computer server farms). Some warehouses are massive structures that simultaneously support the unloading of numerous inbound trucks and railroad cars containing suppliers' products while at the same time loading multiple trucks for shipment to customers.

Below we discuss five types of warehouses:

Private Warehouse

This type of warehouse is owned and operated by channel suppliers and resellers and is used in their own distribution activity. For instance, a major retail chain may have several regional warehouses supplying its stores or a wholesaler will operate a warehouse at which it receives and distributes products.

Public Warehouse

The public warehouse is essentially space that can be leased to solve short-term distribution needs. Retailers operating their own private warehouses may occasionally seek additional storage space if their facilities have reached capacity or if they are making a special, large purchase of products. For example, retailers may order extra merchandise to prepare for in-store sales or order a large volume of a product offered at a low promotional price by a supplier.

Automated Warehouse

With advances in computer and robotics technology many warehouses now have automated capabilities. The level of automation ranges from a small conveyor belt transporting products in a small area all the way up to a fully automated facility where only a few people are needed to handle storage activity for thousands of pounds/kilograms of product. In fact, many warehouses use machines to handle nearly all physical distribution activities, such as moving product-filled **pallets** (i.e., platforms that hold large amounts of product) around buildings that may be several stories tall and the length of two or more football fields.

• •

Staples, a large office supply distributor with hundreds of stores, has a unique automated warehouse in which small robots are used to speed up order processing. The 3-foot long box-shaped robots are programmed to find and move racks of product to workers who then fill a customer's order. Once the order is filled the robots return the racks to a storage area. (8)

• •

Climate-Controlled Warehouse

Warehouses handle storage of many types of products including those that needing special handling conditions, such as freezers for storing frozen products, humidity-controlled environments for delicate products, including produce or flowers, and dirt-free facilities for handling highly sensitive computer products.

Distribution Center

There are some warehouses where product storage is considered a very temporary activity. These warehouses serve as points in the distribution system at which products are received from many suppliers and quickly shipped out to many customers. In some cases, such as with distribution centers handling perishable food (e.g., produce), most of the product enters in the early morning and is distributed by the end of the day.

REFERENCES

1. "2002 Census of Wholesale Trade," *United States Census Bureau.*

2. Lawrence, C., "Hawaiians Hit by Skyrocketing Shipping Costs," *CNN*, June 18, 2008.

3. *Wholesale Central* website.

4. Malta, C. and R. Cowie, "Drop Shipping Pros and Cons: The Cost of Convenience," *Worldwide Brands.*

5. Christ, P., "Patenting Marketing Methods: A Missing Topic in the Classroom," *Journal of Marketing Education*, 27 (1), 2005.

6. Mintz, J., "Amazon unveils TextBuyIt," *USA Today*, April 2, 2008.

7. "U.S. Domestic Freight Market Share," *Bureau of Transportation Statistics - U.S. Department of Transportation.*

8. West, E., "These Robots Play Fetch," *Fast Company*, July 2007.

Full text of many of the references can be accessed via links on the support website.

Chapter 11:

Promotion Decisions

Those unfamiliar with marketing often assume it is the same thing as advertising. Certainly our coverage so far in *KnowThis: Marketing Basics* has suggested this is not the case. Marketing encompasses many tasks and decisions, of which advertising may only be a small portion. Likewise, when non-marketers hear someone talk about "promotion" they frequently believe the person is talking about advertising. While advertising is the most visible and best understood method of promotion, it is only one of several approaches a marketer can choose.

In this chapter we begin our discussion of the promotion component of the Marketer's Toolkit. We start by defining promotion and we show how promotion is used to meet different objectives. Because communication is a key element of promotion we take an extended look at the communication process. Next, we explore different characteristics of promotion and how different promotional methods stack up to the characteristics. Finally, we discuss factors affecting the choice of promotional methods.

WHAT IS PROMOTION?

Promotion is the general name given to forms of corporate communication designed to reach a targeted audience with a certain message in order to achieve specific organizational objectives. Nearly all organizations, whether for-profit or not-for-profit, in all types of industries, must engage in some form of promotion. Such efforts may range from multinational firms spending large sums securing high-profile celebrities to serve as corporate spokespersons to the owner of a one-person enterprise passing out business cards at a local businesspersons' meeting.

Like most marketing decisions, an effective promotional strategy requires the marketer understand how promotion fits with other pieces of the marketing puzzle (e.g., product, distribution, pricing, target markets). Consequently, promotion decisions should be made with an appreciation for how it affects other areas of the company. For instance, running a major advertising campaign for a new product without first assuring there will be enough inventory to meet potential demand generated by the advertising would certainly not go over well with the company's production department (not to mention other key company executives). Thus, marketers should not work in a vacuum when making promotion decisions. Rather, the overall success of a promotional strategy requires input from other functional areas.

• •

A good example of how marketing works with other parts of the organization occurs in the car industry. For instance, in 2008 when faced with high fuel prices and an economic slowdown, most car manufacturers found their dealers were severely overstocked with less fuel efficient trucks and SUVs. In response automotive companies instituted major promotions that included low cost financing. Such promotional techniques must require the assistance and possible approval of the company's financial staff as such incentives can erode profit margins. (1)

• •

In addition to coordinating general promotion decisions with other business areas, individual promotions must also work together. Under the concept of **integrated marketing communication** marketers attempt to develop a unified and highly coordinated promotional strategy in which a consistent message is presented across many different types of promotional techniques. For instance, salespeople will discuss the same benefits of a product as mentioned in television advertisements. In this way no matter how customers are exposed to a marketer's promotional efforts they all receive the same information.

Finally, as discussed in Box 11-1, promotion is not limited to the communication of product information to customers. Marketers also use promotional methods to communicate with others who are outside their target market.

Box 11-1

COMMUNICATING BEYOND THE TARGET MARKET

The audience for an organization's marketing communication efforts is not limited to the marketer's target market. While the bulk of a marketer's promotional budget may be directed at the target market, there are many other groups that could also serve as useful targets of a marketing message including:

Influencers of the Organization's Target Market
There exists a large group of people and organizations with the potential to affect how a company's target market is exposed to and perceives a company's products. These influencing groups have their own communication mechanisms that reach the target market. With the right strategy the marketer may be able to utilize these influencers to its benefit. Influencers include the news media (e.g., offer company stories), special interest groups, opinion leaders (e.g., doctors directing patients), and industry trade associations.

Participants in the Distribution Process
Distribution channel members provide services to help the marketer gain access to final customers. Yet in many ways channel members, and particularly resellers, are also target markets. While their needs are different than those of the final customer, channel members must make purchase decisions when agreeing to handle a marketer's product (see Chapters 9 and 10). Aiming promotions at distribution partners (e.g., retailers, wholesalers, distributors) and other channel members is extremely important and, in some industries, represents a higher portion of a marketer's promotional budget than promotional spending directed at the final customer.

Other Companies
The most likely scenario in which a company will communicate with another company occurs when the marketer is probing to see if the company would have an interest in a joint venture such as a co-marketing arrangement where two firms share marketing costs. Using promotions, such as ads targeted to potential partners, could help create interest in discussing such a relationship.

Other Organizational Stakeholders
Marketers may also be involved with communication activities directed at other stakeholders. This group consists of those who provide services, support or in other ways impact the company. For example, an industry group that sets industry standards can affect company products through the issuance of recommended compliance standards for product development or other marketing activities. Communicating with this group is important to ensure the marketer's views of any changes in standards are known.

OBJECTIVES OF MARKETING PROMOTIONS

Many view promotional activities as the most glamorous part of marketing. This may have to do with the fact that promotion is often associated with creative activity undertaken to help distinguish a company's products from competitors' offerings. While creativity is an important element in promotion decisions, many times marketers are consumed with developing a highly creative promotion (e.g., humorous advertisement featuring a top Hollywood star) only to see it fail to change a company's situation (i.e., sales do not increase).

While creativity is certainly a major concern, marketers must first have a deep understanding of how marketing promotions help the organization achieve its objectives before embarking on the creative side of promotion. The most obvious objective marketers have for promotional activities is to convince customers to make a decision benefiting the marketer (of course the marketer believes the decision will also benefit the customer). For most for-profit marketers this means getting customers to buy an organization's product and, in most cases, to remain a loyal long-term customer. For other marketers, such as not-for-profits, it means getting customers to increase donations, utilize more services, change attitudes or change behavior (e.g., stop smoking campaigns).

However, marketers must understand getting customers to commit to a decision, such as deciding to make a purchase, is only achievable when a customer is ready to make the decision. As we saw in Chapter 4, customers often move through several stages before a purchase decision is made.

Additionally before turning into a repeat customer, purchasers analyze their initial purchase to see whether they received a good value, and then often repeat the purchase process again before deciding to make the same choice.

The type of customer the marketer is attempting to attract and which stage of the purchase process a customer is in will affect the objectives of a particular marketing communication effort. And since a marketer often has multiple simultaneous promotional campaigns, the objective of each could be different.

Types of Promotion Objectives

The possible objectives for marketing promotions may include the following:

♦ <u>Build Awareness</u> – New products and new companies are often un-known to a market, which means initial promotional efforts must focus on establishing an identity. In this situation the marketer's promotional objectives are to: 1) ensure the message reaches custom-ers, and 2) tell the market who they are and what they have to offer.

♦ <u>Create Interest</u> – Moving a customer from awareness of a product to making a purchase can present a significant challenge. As we saw in Chapter 4, customers must first recognize they have a need before they actively start to consider a purchase. The focus on creating messages convincing customers a need exists has been the hallmark of marketing for a long time with promotional appeals targeted at basic human characteristics such as emotions, fears, sex, and humor.

♦ <u>Provide Information</u> – Some promotion is designed to assist custom-ers in the search stage of the purchasing process. In some cases, such as when a product is so novel it creates a new category of product and has few competitors, the information is simply intended to ex-plain what the product is and may not mention any competitors. In other situations, where the product competes in an existing market, informational promotion may be used to help with a product posi-tioning strategy. As we discussed in Chapter 5, marketers may use promotional means, including direct comparisons with competitor's products, in an effort to get customers to mentally distinguish (i.e., position) the marketer's product from those of competitors.

♦ <u>Stimulate Demand</u> – The right promotion can drive customers to make a purchase. In the case of products a customer has not previ-ously purchased or has not purchased in a long time, the promotion-al efforts may be directed at getting the customer to try the product. This is often seen on the Internet where software companies allow for free demonstrations or even free downloadable trials of their prod-ucts. For products with an established customer base promotion can encourage customers to increase their purchasing by providing a reason to purchase products sooner or purchase in greater quanti-ties than they normally do. For example, a pre-holiday newspaper advertisement may remind customers to stock up on beverages for the holiday by purchasing more than they typically purchase during non-holiday periods.

- ◆ Reinforce the Brand – Once a purchase is made, a marketer can use promotion to help build a strong relationship that can lead to the purchaser becoming a loyal customer. For instance, many retail stores now ask for a customer's email address so follow-up emails containing additional product information or even an incentive to purchase other products from the retailer can be sent in order to strengthen the customer-marketer relationship.

In some cases, the marketer looks to achieve several objectives within a single promotional campaign. For example, when telecommunication's company AT&T bought out the wireless firm Cingular they needed to not only build awareness and provide information explaining the merger to potentially new customers, but also reinforce the brand among existing customers by explaining how the combined companies will benefit them. (2)

THE COMMUNICATION PROCESS

Before we venture into in-depth analysis of promotion, it is important to lay some additional groundwork by examining how communication works. By understanding the basic concepts of communication the marketer will have a better idea of what actions should be pursued or avoided in order to get its message out to its customers.

The act of communicating has been evaluated extensively for many, many years. One of the classic analyses of communication took place in the 1940s and 1950s when researchers, including Claude Shannon and Warren Weaver (3), Wilbur Schramm (4), and others, offered models describing how communication takes place. In general, communication is how people exchange meaningful information.

Models that reflect how communication occurs often include the elements shown on Figure 11-1:

Figure 11-1: The Communication Process

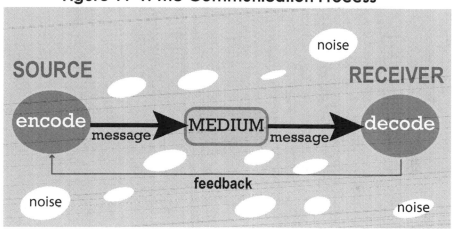

On the next few pages we further discuss the elements of the communication process shown in Figure 11-1.

COMMUNICATION PARTICIPANTS:

For communication to occur there must be at least two participants:

- Message Source – The source of communication is the party intending to convey information to another party. The message source can be an individual (e.g., salesperson) or an organization (e.g., through advertising). In order to convey a message, the source must engage in **message encoding**, which involves mental and physical processes necessary to construct a message in order to reach a desired goal (i.e., convey meaningful information). This undertaking consists of using sensory stimuli, such as visuals (e.g., words, symbols, images), sounds (e.g., spoken word), and scents (e.g., fragrance) to convey a message.

- Message Receiver – The receiver of communication is the intended target of a message source's efforts. For a message to be understood the receiver must engage in **message decoding** by undertaking mental and physical processes necessary to give meaning to the message. Clearly, a message can only be decoded if the receiver is actually exposed to the message.

COMMUNICATION DELIVERY:

Communication takes place in the form of a **message** exchanged between a source and receiver. A message can be shaped using one or a combination of sensory stimuli working together to convey meaning that meets the objectives of the sender. The sender uses a **transmission medium** to send the message. In marketing the medium may include the use of different media outlets (e.g., Internet, television, radio, print), promotion-only outlets (e.g., postal mail, billboards), and person-to-person contact (e.g., salespeople).

Additionally, communication can be improved if there is a two-way flow of information in the form of a **feedback channel**. This occurs if the message receiver is able to respond, often quickly, to the message source. In this way, the original message receiver now becomes the message source and the communication process begins again.

OBSTACLES TO EFFECTIVE COMMUNICATION

While a message source may be able to deliver a message through a transmission medium, there are many potential obstacles to the message successfully reaching the receiver the way the sender intends. The potential obstacles affecting good communication include:

- Poor Encoding – This occurs when the message source fails to create the right sensory stimuli to meet the objectives of the message. For instance, in person-to-person communication, verbally phrasing words poorly so the intended communication is not what is actually meant is the result of poor encoding. Poor encoding is also seen in advertisements that are difficult for the intended audience to understand, such as words or symbols lacking meaning or worse, have totally different meaning within a certain cultural groups. This often occurs when marketers use the same advertising message across many different countries. Differences due to translation or cultural understanding can result in the message receiver having a different frame of reference for how to interpret words, symbols, sounds, etc. This may lead the message receiver to decode the meaning of the message in a different way than was intended by the message sender.

. . . .

Companies seeking to sell internationally often must have their promotional material translated into the local language. For companies that do not possess the capability to handle translations, assistance will be needed. There are several options available ranging from low-cost software programs to high-cost language vendors. While software programs may seem an attractive option, the results are often inconsistent and could present encoding problems. Instead, marketers are advised to hire professional qualified translation firms. (5)

. . . .

- Poor Decoding – This refers to a message receiver's error in processing the message so that the meaning given to the received message is not what the source intended. This differs from poor encoding when it is clear, through comparative analysis with other receivers, that a particular receiver perceived a message differently than others. Clearly, as we noted above, if the receiver's frame of reference is different (e.g., meaning of words are different) then decoding problems can occur. More likely, when it comes to marketing promotions, decoding errors occur due to personal or psychological factors, such as not paying attention to a full television advertisement, driving too quickly past a billboard, or allowing one's mind to wander while talking to a salesperson.

- Medium Failure – Sometimes communication channels break down and end up sending out weak or faltering signals. Other times the wrong medium is used to communicate the message. For instance, trying to educate doctors about a new treatment for heart disease using television commercials that quickly flash highly detailed information is not going to be as effective as presenting this information in a print ad where doctors can take their time evaluating the information.

- Communication Noise – Noise in communication occurs when an outside force in someway affects delivery of the message. The most obvious example is when loud sounds block the receiver's ability to hear a message. Nearly any distraction to the sender or the receiver can lead to communication noise. In advertising, many customers are overwhelmed (i.e., distracted) by the large number of advertisements they encounter each day. Such **advertising clutter** (i.e., noise) makes it difficult for advertisers to get their message through to desired customers.

• •

To break through noise some television marketers look for innovative techniques intended to keep their audience watching the screen during commercial breaks. Methods with such names as mini-sodes, micro-series, bitcoms, and clips are being tested as promotion vehicles. Each offers a non-traditional, entertainment-driven method for promoting products. (6)

• •

As discussed in Box 11-2, knowledge of the communication process can help marketers avoid these obstacles.

Box 11-2

IMPROVING COMMUNICATION

For marketers understanding how the communication process works can improve the delivery of their message. Marketers should focus on the following to improve communication with their targeted audience:

Carefully Encode

Marketers should make sure the message they send is crafted in a way that will be interpreted by message receivers as intended. This means having a good understanding of how their audience interprets words, symbols, sounds, and other stimuli used by marketers. This is particularly important when communicating to target markets that are beyond the marketer's own experiences. For instance, marketers targeting sub-cultures that are significantly different than their own (e.g., age group difference) or marketing outside their native country may encounter cultural differences that can lead to misinterpretation.

Allow Feedback

Encouraging the message receiver to provide feedback can greatly improve communication and help determine if a marketer's message was decoded and interpreted properly. Feedback can be improved by providing easy-to-use options for responding such as phone numbers and email. Additionally, the creation of online forums and corporate blogs containing comment boxes may also enhance feedback.

Reduce Noise

In many promotional situations the marketer has little control over interference with its message. However, there are a few instances where the marketer can proactively lower the noise level. For instance, salespeople can be trained to reduce noise by employing techniques limiting customer distractions, such as scheduling meetings during non-busy times, or by inviting potential customers to an environment offering fewer distractions such as a conference facility. Additionally, advertising can be developed in ways that separate the marketer's ad from others, including the use of whitespace in magazine ads.

Choose Right Audience

Targeting the right message receiver will go a long way to improving a marketer's ability to promote its products. Messages are much more likely to be received and appropriately decoded by those who have an interest (see *Involvement* discussion in Chapter 4) in the content of the message.

CHARACTERISTICS OF PROMOTIONS

Before we discuss the different types of promotion options available to a marketer, it is useful to gain an understanding of the features that set different options apart. For our discussion we isolate eight characteristics on which each promotional option can be judged. While these characteristics are widely understood as being important in evaluating the effectiveness of each type of promotion, they are by no means the only criteria used for evaluation. In fact, as new promotional methods emerge the criteria for evaluating promotional methods will likely change.

For our discussion we will look at the following characteristics of a promotional method:

1. Intended Coverage: Mass vs. Targeted
2. Payment Model: Paid vs. Non-Paid
3. Message Flow: One-Way vs. Two-Way
4. Interaction Type: Personal vs. Non-Personal
5. Demand Creation: Quick vs. Lagging
6. Message Control: Total vs. Minimal
7. Message Credibility: High vs. Low
8. Cost Assessment: Exposure vs. Action

1. INTENDED COVERAGE: MASS VS. TARGETED

Promotions can be categorized based on the intended coverage of a single promotional message. For instance, a single television advertisement for a major sporting event, such as the Olympics, Super Bowl or World Cup, could be seen by millions of viewers at the same time. Such mass promotion, intended to reach as many people as possible, has been a mainstay of marketers' promotional efforts for a long time.

Unfortunately, while mass promotions are delivered to a large number of people, the actual number experiencing the promotion that fall within the marketer's target market may be small. Because of this, many who use mass promotion techniques find it to be an inefficient way to reach desired customers. Instead, today's marketers are turning to newer techniques designed to focus promotional delivery to only those with a high probability of being in the marketer's target market. For example, Google, Microsoft, Yahoo, and other Internet search engines employ methods for delivering highly targeted ads to customers as they enter search terms. The assumption made by advertisers is that customers who enter search terms are interested in the information they have entered, especially if they are searching by entering detailed search strings (e.g., phrases rather than a single word). Following this logic, advertisers are much more likely to have their ads displayed to customers within their target market leading to a potentially higher return on their promotional investment. The movement to highly targeted promotions has gained tremendous traction in recent years and, as new and improved targeting methods are introduced, its importance will continue to grow.

• •

Pepsi-Cola is often considered a mass promoter that uses promotion to reach a large audience. However, it also uses a more narrowly targeted approach with selected products. One new product, Tava, is a no-calorie, carbonated drink targeted to men and women ages 34-49. To reach this group the company uses promotional methods that include product samples made available at company office buildings and event locations. (7)

• •

2. PAYMENT MODEL: PAID VS. NON-PAID

Most efforts to promote products require marketers to make direct payment to the medium delivering the message. For instance, a company must pay a magazine publisher to advertise in the magazine. However, there are several forms of promotion that do not involve direct payment in order to distribute a promotional message. While not necessarily "free" since there may be indirect costs involved, the ability to have a product promoted without making direct payment to the medium can be a viable alternative to expensive promotion options.

3. MESSAGE FLOW: ONE-WAY VS. TWO-WAY

Promotions can be classified based on whether the message source enables the message receiver to respond with immediate feedback. Such feedback can then be followed with further information exchange between both parties. Most efforts at mass promotion, such as television advertising, offer only a one-way information flow that does not allow for easy response by the message receiver. However, many targeted promotions, such as using a sales force to promote products, enable message recipients to respond immediately to information from the message sender.

4. INTERACTION TYPE: PERSONAL VS. NON-PERSONAL

Promotions involving real people communicating with other people is considered personal promotion. While salespeople are a common and well understood type of personal promotion, another type of promotion, called **controlled word-of-mouth promotion** (also called **buzz marketing**) is emerging as a form of personal promotion. This type of promotion uses real people to spread information about a product, however, it is not intended to get a buyer to buy directly from the person who is doing the promoting (see *Controlled Word-of-Mouth* discussion in Chapter 16).

One key advantage personal promotions have is the ability for the message sender to adjust the message as they gain feedback from message receivers (i.e., two-way communication). So if a customer does not understand something in the initial message (e.g., doesn't fully understand how the product works) the person delivering the message can adjust the promotion to address questions or concerns. Many non-personal forms of promotion, such as radio advertisements, are inflexible, at least in the short-term, and cannot be easily adjusted to address questions raised by the audience experiencing the ad.

5. DEMAND CREATION: QUICK VS. LAGGING

As we discussed earlier, the success of promotional activity may not always be measured by comparing spending to an increase in product sales since marketers may use promotion to achieve other objectives. However, when a marketer is looking to increase demand, certain promotional activities offer advantages in turning exposure to promotion into a quick increase in demand. In general, these activities are most effective when customers are offered an incentive to make the purchase either in a monetary way (e.g., save money) or in psychological way (e.g., improves customer's perceived group role or status level).

6. MESSAGE CONTROL: TOTAL VS. MINIMAL

Most promotions are controlled by the marketer who encodes the message (or hires specialists such as advertising agencies to create the promotion) and then pays to have the message delivered. However, no marketer can totally control how the news media, customers or others talk about a company or its products. Reporters for magazines, newspaper, and websites, as well as posters to Internet forums may discuss a company's products in ways that can benefit or hinder a company's marketing efforts. This is particularly true with non-paid promotions where a marketer is looking to obtain a free "mention" by an influential message medium (e.g., newspaper article).

7. Message Credibility: High vs. Low

The perceived control of the message can influence the target market's perception of message credibility. For example, many customers viewing a comparative advertisement, where one product is shown to be superior to a competitor's product, may be skeptical about the claims since the company with the superior product is paying for the advertisement. Yet, if the same comparison is mentioned in a newspaper article it may be more favorably viewed since readers may perceive the author of the story (e.g., reporter) has an unbiased point-of-view.

8. Cost Assessment: Exposure vs. Action

The final characteristic classifies promotions based on the method by which costs are determined for running a promotion. For instance, as we will see in Chapter 12, when it comes to advertising marketers face numerous costs ranging from promotion creation to message delivery. Costs can be assessed in two main ways: 1) based on general exposure to the promotion, and 2) based on action taken. Box 11-3 provides further insight on these options.

Box 11-3

Measures of Promotional Effectiveness

Whether a promotion is working or not is primarily determined by analyzing the cost of running a particular promotion versus the results obtained. In general, there are two main methods available for assessing promotional effectiveness:

- Measurement Based on Exposure
- Measurement Based on Action

Effectiveness Based on Exposure

With the exposure method, marketers make promotional decisions based on how many people will be exposed to the promotion in relation to the cost of running the promotion. This method has been a mainstay for assessing promotion for a long time primarily because it is easy to calculate. However, the presumption of marketers using this approach is that exposure leads customers to do something, such as make a product purchase.

Yet tying exposure to a customer action is not always possible (see *Effectiveness Based on Action* discussion below) and, consequently, the exposure option may be all that is available.

Within the exposure method are two options:

1. Cost-per-Mille (CPM)

The CPM option relates to how many people are exposed to a promotion in relation to the cost of the promotion. CPM (also called **cost-per-thousand** as mille means thousand) is a commonly used promotional measurement for mass media outlets, such as print and broadcast industries, although in the online advertising industry it is also used though it is sometimes referred to as **cost-per-impression (CPI)**. CPM calculates how much promotion costs for each 1,000 exposures. For example, if an advertisement costs (US) $10,000 in a city newspaper having a circulation of 500,000 then the CPM for that advertisement is calculated as follows:

$$\text{CPM} = \frac{\$10,000}{500,000 \,/\, 1,000} = \$20$$

A national or international television advertisement, while expensive to create and broadcast, actually produces a very low CPM given how many people are exposed to the ad.

2. Cost-per-Targeted Exposure (CPTE)

A low CPM can be misleading if a large percentage of the promotion's audience is not within the marketer's target market, in which case the CPTE may be a better metric for gauging promotion effectiveness. The CPTE approach looks at what percentage of an audience is within the marketer's customer group and, thus, legitimate targets for the promotion. Clearly, CPTE is higher than CPM, but it offers a better indication of how much promotion is reaching targeted customers.

Effectiveness Based on Action
An even more effective way to evaluate promotional costs is through the **cost-per-action (CPA)** metric. With CPA the marketer evaluates how many people actually respond to a promotion. Response may be measured by examining purchase activity, number of phone inquiries, website traffic, clicks on advertisements, and other means within a short time after the promotional message was delivered.

Unfortunately, measuring CPA is not always easy and tying it directly to a specific promotion can also be difficult. For example, a customer who purchases a snack product may have first learned about the snack product several weeks before from a television advertisement. The fact that it took the customer some time to make the purchase does not mean the advertisement was not effective in generating sales, though if the CPA was measured within a day or two after the ad was broadcast this person's action would not have been counted. With the growing trend to more targeted promotions, especially those delivered through the Internet, combined with the development of sophisticated customer tracking techniques, the ability to compare promotion to actual customer activity is bound to one day be the dominant method for measuring promotional effectiveness.

THE PROMOTION MIX

Marketers have at their disposal four major methods of promotion. Taken together these comprise the promotion mix. In this section a basic definition of each method is offered while in the next section a comparison of each method based on the characteristics of promotion is presented.

ADVERTISING

Involves non-personal paid promotions often using mass media outlets to deliver the marketer's message. While historically advertising has involved one-way communication with little feedback opportunity for the customer experiencing the advertisement, the advent of computer technology and, in particular the Internet, has increased the options allowing customers to provide quick feedback.

SALES PROMOTION

Involves the use of special short-term techniques, often in the form of incentives, to encourage customers to respond to or undertake some activity. For instance, the use of retail coupons with expiration dates requires customers to act while the incentive is still valid.

PUBLIC RELATIONS

Also referred to as publicity, this type of promotion uses third-party sources, and particularly the news media, to offer a favorable mention of the marketer's company or product without direct payment to the publisher of the information.

PERSONAL SELLING

As the name implies, this form of promotion involves personal contact between company representatives and those who have a role in purchase decisions (e.g., make the decision, such as consumers or have an influence on a decision, such as members of a company buying center). Often this occurs face-to-face or via telephone, though newer technologies allow this to occur online via video conferencing or text chat.

Each of these methods will be covered in much greater detail in later chapters.

Promotion Mix Summary

Table 11-1 below compares each of the promotion mix options on the eight key promotional characteristics. The summary should be viewed only as a general guide since promotion techniques are continually evolving and how each technique is compared on a characteristic is subject to change.

Table 11-1: Promotion Mix Summary

Characteristics	Advertising	Sales Promotion	Public Relations	Personal Selling
Intended Coverage	mass targeted	mass targeted	mass	targeted
Payment Model	paid limited non-paid	paid	non-paid	paid
Message Flow	one-way two-way	one-way two-way	one-way	two-way
Interaction Type	non-personal	personal non-personal	non-personal	personal
Demand Creation	lagging	quick	lagging	quick
Message Control	good	good	poor	very good
Message Credibility	low-medium	low-medium	high	medium-high
Cost Assessment	CPM – low CPTE – varies CPA – varies	CPM – medium CPTE – varies CPA – varies	CPM – none CPTE – none CPA – none	CPM – high CPTE – high CPA – high

Factors Affecting Promotion Choice

With four promotional methods to choose from how does the marketer determine which ones to use? The selection can be complicated by corporate and marketing decision issues.

CORPORATE ISSUES

- Promotional Objective – As we discussed, there are several different objectives a marketer may pursue with its promotional strategy. Each type of promotion offers different advantages in terms of helping the marketer reach its objectives. For instance, if the objective of a software manufacturer is to get customers to try a product, the use of sales promotion, such as offering the software in a free downloadable form, may yield better results than promoting through a general Internet advertisement.

- Availability of Resources – The amount of money and other resources that can be directed to promotion affects the marketer's choice of promotional methods. Marketers with large promotional budgets may be able to spread spending among all promotion options while marketers with limited funds must be more selective on the promotion techniques they use.

- Company Philosophy – Some companies follow a philosophy dictating where most promotional spending occurs. For instance, some companies follow the approach that all promotion should be done through salespeople while other companies prefer to focus marketing funds on product development and hope word-of-mouth communication by satisfied customers helps to create interest in their products.

. . . .

Whole Foods Market, a leading organic and natural food retailer with over 270 stores in the North America and the United Kingdom, is an example of a company whose philosophy is to limit spending on advertising. Instead, it relies heavily on word-of-mouth recommendations to drive customers to its stores. Overall the company spends less than 0.5% of total sales on advertising. (8)

. . . .

MARKETING DECISION ISSUES

- Target Market – As one might expect, customer characteristics dictate how promotion is determined. Characteristics such as size, location, and type of target markets affect how the marketer communicates with customers. For instance, for a small marketer serving business markets with customers widely dispersed, it may be very expensive to utilize a sales force versus using advertising.

- Product – Different products require different promotional approaches. For the consumer market, products falling into the convenience and shopping goods categories are likely to use mass market promotional approaches while higher-end specialty goods are likely to use personalized selling. Therefore, products that are complex and take customers extended time to make a purchase decision may require personal selling rather than advertising. This is often the case with products targeted to the business market. Additionally, as we discussed in Chapter 7, products pass through different stages in the Product Life Cycle. As a product moves through these stages the product itself may evolve and also promotional objectives will change. This leads to different promotional mix decisions from one stage to the next. (See more detailed discussion on the marketing strategies and the PLC in Chapter 20.)

- Distribution – Marketing organizations selling through channel partners can reach the final customer either directly using a **pull promotion strategy** or indirectly using a **push promotional strategy**. The pull strategy is so named since it creates demand for a product by promoting directly to the final customers in the hopes their interest in the product will help "pull" more product through the distribution channel. This approach can be used when channel partners are hesitant about stocking a product unless they are assured of sufficient customer interest. The push strategy uses promotion to encourage channel partners to stock and promote the product to their customers. The idea is that by offering incentives to channel members the marketer is encouraging its partners (e.g., wholesalers, retailers) to "push" the product down the channel and into customers' hands. Most large consumer products companies will use both approaches while smaller firms may find one approach works better.

- Price – The higher the price of a product the more likely a marketer will need to engage in personalized promotion compared to lower priced products that can be marketed using mass promotion.

REFERENCES

1. Bennett, J., N.E. Boudette, and S. Ng, "GM Slates Sweeping Rebates As Toyota Closes In on No. 1," *Wall Street Journal*, June 24, 2008.

2. Vella, M., "AT&T Rebrands. Again," *BusinessWeek*, September 11, 2007.

3. Shannon, C.E. and W. Weaver, <u>The Mathematical Theory of Communication</u>, University of Illinois Press, 1949.

4. Schramm, W., <u>The Process and Effects of Mass Communication</u>, University of Illinois Press, 1960.

5. "The Global Market: Translating and Localizing," *Sales & Marketing Management*, October 29, 2007.

6. Elliott, S., " New Efforts to Make Long Commercial Breaks Sizzle," *New York Times*, July 7, 2008.

7. Elliott, S., "For a New Brand, Pepsi Starts the Buzz Online," *New York Times*, March 14, 2008.

8. *Whole Foods Market 2007 Annual Report.*

Full text of many of the references can be accessed via links on the support website.

Chapter 12:

Advertising

Spending on advertising is huge. One often quoted statistic by marketing research firm ZenithOptimedia estimates that yearly worldwide spending on advertising exceeds (US) $400 billion. (1) This level of spending supports thousands of companies and millions of jobs. In fact, in many countries most media outlets, such as television, radio, and newspapers, would not be in business without revenue generated through the sale of advertising.

In this chapter we present the first of a two-part examination of advertising with a discussion of advertising basics. We begin by covering several fundamental issues in advertising including examining what advertising is and why it is important to the marketing organization. We also look at managing the advertising effort by comparing in-house management to that offered by advertising professionals, such as advertising agencies. Finally, we identify different types of advertising and address trends facing the advertising industry.

WHAT IS ADVERTISING?

Advertising is a non-personal form of promotion delivered through selected media outlets that, under most circumstances, requires the marketer to pay for message placement. Advertising has long been viewed as a method of mass promotion in that a single message can reach a large number of people. But this mass promotion approach presents problems since many exposed to an advertising message may not be within the marketer's target market. Because of this some marketers view it as an inefficient use of promotional funds. However, this is changing as new advertising technologies and the emergence of new media outlets offer more options for targeted advertising.

Advertising also has a history of being considered a one-way form of marketing communication where the message receiver (i.e., target market) is not in position to immediately respond to the message (e.g., can not immediately seek more information). This too is changing. For example, in the next few years technologies will be readily available to enable a television viewer to click a button to request more details on a product seen on their favorite TV program. In fact, it is expected over the next 10-20 years advertising will move away from a one-way communication model and become one that is highly interactive.

. . . .

Microsoft is actively pursuing the interactive advertising market including purchasing Navic Network, which offers services enabling customers to respond to on-screen activities including taking part in polls and trivia questions using their remote controls. The hope is if viewers are comfortable interacting in these ways they will also become comfortable interacting with ads. (2)

. . . .

Another characteristic that may change as advertising evolves is the view advertising does not stimulate immediate demand for the product advertised. That is, customers cannot quickly purchase a product they see advertised. But as more media outlets allow customers to interact with the messages being delivered the ability of advertising to quickly stimulate demand will improve.

OBJECTIVES OF ADVERTISING

In Chapter 11 we explained five objectives that may be achieved using promotion. Advertising can address all of these, though at different levels of effectiveness.

♦ Building Product Awareness – Advertising has the potential to reach a large number of people in a short period of time. The mass communication nature of advertising makes it a particularly attractive promotional option for marketers who are introducing new products and looking to quickly build market awareness. Additionally, advertising can be used to help support a strategy to reposition a product (see *Product Positioning* discussion in Chapter 5) by creating awareness among a target market to benefits offered by the product that are new or that may not have been previously known.

♦ Creating Interest – Advertisements are creative productions with the power to capture customers' attention. As we will see in Chapter 13, the large number of methods for advertising presents marketers with ample ways to create interesting ads to excite customer interest.

♦ Providing Information – Many forms of advertising expose a targeted market to a message in a brief way and are often not suitable for providing extensive information. However, there are some forms of advertising that can convey a great deal of information. For instance, advertisements sent by direct mail can offer extensive information such as the inclusion of detailed booklets and even DVD videos.

♦ Stimulating Demand – Advertising is often used as part of a campaign to encourage a target market to make a purchase. While this certainly seems an obvious usage of advertising, in fact, by itself advertising is not the most effective promotional tool to achieve this objective. Advertisements that on the surface appear to have the objective of stimulating demand are generally also associated with other forms of promotion, most notably sales promotion (see Chapter 14).

♦ Reinforcing the Brand – Repeated use of advertising is often required to support a product. Given the number of ads a target market is exposed to on a regular basis, it almost has become a necessity for marketers to consistently advertise as they fear customers will forget about their product if competitors advertise more frequently. Marketers operating in markets where competitors spend heavily on advertising must also spend in order to maintain a consistent **share-of-voice** (i.e., percentage of one marketer's spending on advertising in relation to total spending) within the market.

MANAGING ADVERTISING DECISIONS

Delivering an effective marketing message through advertising requires many different decisions as the marketer develops its advertising campaign. For small campaigns involving little creative effort, one or a few people may handle the bulk of the work. In fact, the Internet has made do-it-yourself advertising an easy to manage process and has especially empowered small businesses to manage their advertising decisions. As we will see, not only can small firms handle the creation and placement of advertisements appearing on the Internet, new services have even made it possible for a single person to create advertisements that run on local radio and television.

For larger campaigns the skills needed to make sound advertising decisions can be quite varied and may not be easily handled by a single person. While larger companies manage some advertising activities within the company, they are more likely to rely on the assistance of advertising professionals, such as those found at advertising agencies (see Box 12-1), to help bring their advertising campaign to market.

TYPES OF ADVERTISING

If you ask most people what is meant by "type" of advertising, invariably they will respond by defining it in terms of how it is delivered (e.g., television ad, radio ad, etc.). But in marketing, type of advertising refers to the primary "focus" of the message being sent and falls into one of the following categories:

PRODUCT-ORIENTED ADVERTISING

Most advertising spending is directed toward the promotion of a specific good, service or idea, what we have collectively labeled as an organization's product. In most cases the goal of product advertising is to clearly promote a specific product to a targeted audience. Marketers can accomplish this in several ways from a low-key approach that simply provides basic information about a product (**informative advertising**) to blatant appeals that try to convince customers to purchase a product (**persuasive advertising**) including using direct comparisons between the marketer's product and its competitor's offerings (**comparative advertising**).

Box 12-1

ADVERTISING AGENCY FUNCTIONS

When marketers look for advertising help they often turn to advertising agencies. The services offered by an ad agency will vary depending on the size and expertise of the agency, though for most major ad agencies it is becoming a necessity for the agency and its personnel to have expertise in offline and online methods. (3) For full-service agencies service offerings will often include:

Account Management

Within an advertising agency the account manager or account executive handles all major decisions related to a specific client. These responsibilities include locating and negotiating to acquire clients. Once the client has agreed to work with the agency, the account manager works closely with the client to develop an advertising strategy. For very large clients an advertising agency may assign an account manager to work full-time with only one client and possibly with only one of the client's product lines. For smaller accounts an account manager may manage several different, non-competing accounts.

Creative Team

Agency account managers delegate creative tasks, such as generating ideas, designing concepts, and creating the final advertisements, to the agency's creative team. An agency's creative team consists of specialists in graphic design, film and audio production, copywriting, computer programming, and much more.

Researchers

Full-service advertising agencies employ marketing researchers who assess a client's market situation, including understanding customers and competitors, and also test creative ideas. For instance, in the early stages of an advertising campaign researchers may run focus group sessions with selected members of the client's target market in order to get their reaction to several advertising concepts. Following the completion of an advertising campaign they may use research to measure whether the campaign reached its objectives.

Media Planners

Once an advertisement is created it must be placed in appropriate advertising media outlets. Each advertising media has its own unique methods for accepting advertisements, such as different advertising cost structures (i.e., what it costs marketers to place an ad), different requirements for accepting ad designs (e.g., size of ad), different ways placements can be purchased (e.g., direct contact with media or through third-party seller), and different time schedules (i.e., when ad will run). Understanding the nuances of different media is the role of media planners, specialists who assist with the development of media strategies including looking for the best media match and negotiating promotional deals with media outlets.

However, sometimes marketers intentionally produce product advertising where the target audience cannot readily see a connection to a specific product. Marketers of new products may follow this **teaser advertising** approach in advance of a new product introduction to prepare the market for the product. For instance, one week before the launch of a new product a marketer may air a television advertisement proclaiming *"After next week the world will never be the same"* but do so without any mention of a product or even the company behind the ad. The goal is to create curiosity in the market and interest when the product is launched.

IMAGE ADVERTISING

Image advertising is undertaken primarily to enhance an organization's perceived importance to a target market. Image advertising does not focus on specific products as much as it presents what an organization has to offer. In these types of ads, if products are mentioned it is within the context of "what we do" rather than a message touting the benefits of a specific product. Image advertising is often used in situations where an organization needs to educate the targeted audience on some issue. For instance, image advertising may be used in situations where a merger has occurred between two companies and the newly formed company has taken on a new name or if a company has received recent negative publicity and the company wants to let the market know they are about much more than this one issue.

• •

Xerox is most famous as a photocopier manufacturer, but in the digital age this image is too narrow as potential customers are more interested in products that can solve broader "document management" problems. To help reposition the company, Xerox launched a multimillion dollar image advertising campaign designed to re-position the company. The campaign included the development of a new corporate logo. (4)

• •

ADVOCACY ADVERTISING

Organizations also use advertising to send a message intended to influence a targeted audience. In most cases there is an underlying benefit sought by an organization when they engage in advocacy advertising. For instance, an organization may take a stand on a political issue which they feel could negatively impact the organization and will target advertisements to voice its position on the issue.

PUBLIC SERVICE ADVERTISING

In some countries, not-for-profit organizations are permitted to run advertisements through certain media outlets free of charge if the message contained in the ad concerns an issue viewed as for the "greater good" of society. For instance, ads directed at social causes, such as teen-age smoking, illegal drug use, and mental illness, may run on television, radio, and other media without cost to organizations sponsoring the advertisement.

TRENDS IN ADVERTISING

Like most areas of marketing, advertising is changing rapidly. Some argue that change has affected advertising more than any other marketing function. The more important trends in advertising include:

DIGITAL CONVERGENCE

While many different media outlets are available for communicating with customers, the ability to distinguish between outlets is becoming more difficult due to the convergence of different media types. Advertising convergence, and more appropriately digital convergence, refers to a growing trend for using computer technology to deliver media programming and information. Convergence allows one media outlet to take advantage of features and benefits offered through other media outlets. For instance, in many areas around the world television programming is now delivered digitally via cable, telephone or satellite hookup. This delivery method uses the same principles of information delivery that are used to allow someone to connect the Internet.

The convergence of television and Internet opens many potential opportunities for marketers to target customers in ways not available with traditional television advertising. For example, technology may allow ads delivered to one household to be different than ads delivered to a neighbor's television even though both households are watching the same program. But convergence is not limited to just television. Many media outlets are experiencing convergence as can be seen with print publications that now have a strong web presence. The future holds even more convergence opportunities. These include outdoor billboards that alter displays as cars containing global positioning systems (GPS) and other recognizable factors (e.g., GPS tied to satellite radio) pass by or direct mail postcards that carry a different message based on data that matches a household's address with television viewing habits.

FOCUS ON AUDIENCE TRACKING

The movement to digital convergence provides marketers with the basic resources needed to monitor users' activity, namely, digital data. Any media outlet relying on computer technology to manage the flow of information does so using electronic signals that eventually form computer data. In simple form, electronic data is represented by either an "on" or "off" electronic signal. In computer language this is further represented by two numbers "0" and "1" and, consequently, is known as **digital data**. All digital information can be stored and later evaluated.

For media outlets delivering information in digital form, the potential exists for greater tracking and matching this with information about the person receiving the digital data. And tracking does not stop with what is delivered, it also works with information being sent from the customer. For instance, as we noted earlier, by clicking on their television screen viewers will soon be able to instantly receive information about products they saw while watching a television show. This activity can be tracked then used in future marketing efforts. Yet while tracking provides marketers with potentially useful information, this research method has raised many concerns as discussed in Box 12-2.

AD SKIPPING AND BLOCKING

As noted in Box 12-2, television recording devices offer marketers tremendous insight into viewers' habits and behavior. Yet from the consumer side, the DVR is changing how people view television programs by allowing them to watch programming at a time that is most convenient for them.

Viewer convenience is not the only advantage of the DVR. The other main reason consumers are attracted to the DVR is their ability to quickly skip over commercials. Of course this presents major issues for advertisers who are paying for advertisements. As more DVR devices with ad skipping or even ad blocking features are adopted by mainstream consumers the advertiser's concern with whether they are getting the best value for the advertising money becomes a bigger issue. Advertisers who feel frustrated with television ad-skipping may opt to invest their promotional funds in other media outlets where consumers are more likely to be exposed to an advertisement.

Box 12-2

AUDIENCE CONCERN WITH TRACKING

While media convergence offers marketers more options for tracking response to advertisements, as discussed in Box 1-2 in Chapter 1, such activity also raises ethical and legal concerns. Many consumers are not pleased to learn their activities are being monitored when they engage a media outlet. Some examples of how marketers track customers include:

Television Viewing

The advent of digitally delivered television allows cable, telephone, and satellite providers to track user activity through the set-top boxes connected to a subscriber's television. Future innovation will make the user television experience even more interactive and, consequently, open to even more tracking.

Television Recording

The days of television videotape recording are quickly coming to an end, replaced by recording using computer technology. **Digital video recorder (DVR)**, such as TiVo, can track users recording habits and, based on a viewers' past activity, make suggestions for programs they may want to record. Additionally, advertising services can program the DVR to insert special advertisements within a program targeted to a particular viewer.

Website Visits

Each time a visitor accesses a website they leave an information trail that includes how they got to the site, how they navigated through the site, what they clicked on, what was purchased, and loads of other information. When matched to a method for customer identification, such as website login information, the marketer has the ability to track a customer's activity over repeated visits to the site.

Internet Spyware

Downloading entertainment from the Internet, such as games, video, and software, may contain a hidden surprise – spyware. Spyware is a special program that runs in the background of a user's computer and regularly forwards information over the Internet to the spyware's company. In some cases spyware keeps track of websites the user has visited. The information is then used to gain an understanding of the user's interests. One form of spyware, called adware, may use the information obtained to deliver ads based on what is learned about a user's website activity.

Cellphone Usage

A new frontier for user tracking is the cellphone. Tracking companies, such as Nielsen, are moving aggressively into this area. Research includes tracking of websites visits, videos viewed, and other activity undertaken while using the cellphone. (5)

· ·

*Research conducted by the NBC Universal television network suggests that fast forwarding through ads does not automatically mean viewers do not see and remember the ad. Using **biometric measurements**, researchers found ads with certain elements could still be effective even if viewers play it up to six times faster. In particular, viewers were more likely to recall ads in which the product logo was in the middle of the screen, the ads showed recognizable characters, and scenes did not change rapidly. (6)*

· ·

CHANGING MEDIA CHOICES

There is a major cultural shift occurring in how people use media for entertainment, news, and information. Many traditional media outlets, such as newspapers and major commercial television networks, are seeing their customer base eroded by the emergence of new media outlets. The Internet has become the major driver of this change. In particular, a number of important applications tied to the Internet are creating new media outlets and drawing the attention of many, mostly younger, consumers. Examples include:

- Podcasting – This involves delivering programming via downloadable online audio and video files that can be experienced on players such as Apple's iPod. Many news websites and even other information sites, such as blogs, offer free downloadable programming.

- Small Screen Video – While the downloading of audio and video files as been available for some time, the streaming of live video over high speed wireless networks to small, handheld devices, including cellphones, is in its infancy. Many television networks are now experimenting with making its programming available in this format including offering advertising opportunities.

- RSS Feeds – This is an Internet information distribution technology allowing for news and content to be delivered instantly to anyone who has signed up for delivery. Clearly those registering for RSS feeds represent a highly targeted market since they requested the content.

- Networked Gaming – While gaming systems have been around for some time, gaming systems attached to the Internet for group play is relatively new and becoming more practical as more people move to faster Internet connections. This type of setup will soon enable marketers to insert special content, such as advertising, within game play.

• •

Electronic gaming, such as Playstation, Xbox and Wii, along with fantasy world websites, such as Second Life, provide in-game advertising opportunities. For instance, games whose visuals contain billboards, such as sports and racing games, can have ads updated automatically. (7)

• •

For marketers these new technologies should be monitored closely as they become accepted alternatives to traditional media outlets. While these technologies are currently not major outlets for advertising, they may soon offer such opportunity. As these technologies gain momentum and move into mainstream acceptance marketers may need to consider shifting advertising spending.

Marketers should also be aware that new media outlets will continue to emerge as new applications are developed. The bottom line for marketers is they must stay informed of new developments and understand how their customers are using these in ways that may offer advertising opportunities.

• •

Information from leading media ratings researcher Nielsen indicates the number of people in the U.S. watching video online is growing rapidly. For May 2008, Nielsen estimates that over 119 million people watched video programming over the Internet. While the time per month spent watching online video is still low compared to television (2 hours for Internet and 127 hours for TV) the trend is decidedly upwards and should be of interest to advertisers. (8)

• •

REFERENCES

1. *ZenithOptimedia* Press Release, March 31, 2008.

2. Johnson, C.Y., "Microsoft Acquires Interactive TV Firm," *Boston Globe*, June 18, 2008.

3. "Ad Agencies' Most Wanted: Integrated-Marketing Pros," *Wall Street Journal*.

4. Paul, R., "Xerox Softens Image in Brand Overhaul," *Reuters*, January 7, 2008.

5. Story, L., "Nielsen Adds to Cellphone Tracking," *New York Times*, June 28, 2007.

6. Kang, S., "Why DVR Viewers Recall Some TV Spots," *Wall Street Journal*, February 26, 2008.

7. Gaudiosi, J., "Games Advertisers Love Most," *Business 2.0*, July 10 2007.

8. Stetler, B., "Whichever Screen, People Are Watching," *New York Times*, July 8, 2008.

Full text of many of the references can be accessed via links on the support website.

Chapter 13:

Managing the Advertising Campaign

Most organizations, large and small, rely on marketing to create customer interest by engaging in consistent use of advertising. This includes regularly developing advertising campaigns, which involve a series of decisions for planning, creating, delivering, and evaluating an advertising effort.

In this chapter we continue our discussion of advertising by taking a closer look at the decisions involved in creating an advertising campaign. Whether a marketer employs a professional advertising agency to handle its advertising campaign or chooses to undertake all advertising tasks on its own, a successful campaign requires a number of important decisions including: 1) setting the advertising objective; 2) setting the advertising budget; 3) selecting media for message delivery; 4) creating a message; and 5) evaluating campaign results. For major consumer products companies that spend large sums to promote their products each of these decisions is intensely evaluated. Smaller companies with limited budgets may focus what little money they have on fewer decisions, such as message development and selecting media, and give less attention to other areas. No matter the organization's size, knowledge of all advertising campaign decisions is important and should be well understood by all marketers.

SETTING THE ADVERTISING OBJECTIVE

As we noted in Chapter 12, marketing promotion, which includes advertising, can be used to address several broad objectives including building product awareness, creating interest, providing information, stimulating demand, and reinforcing the brand. To achieve one or more of these objectives, advertising is used to send a message containing information about some element of the marketer's offerings. For example:

♦ Message About Product – Details about the product play a prominent role in advertising for new and existing products. In fact, a very large percentage of product-oriented advertising includes some mention of features and benefits offered by the marketer's product. Advertising can be used to inform customers of changes taking place in existing products. For instance, if a beverage company has purchased the brands of another company resulting in a brand name change, an advertising message may stress *"New Name but Same Great Taste."*

♦ Message About Price – Companies that regularly engage in price adjustments, such as running short term sales (i.e., price markdown), can use advertising to let the market know of price reductions. Alternatively, advertising can be used to encourage customers to purchase now before a scheduled price increase takes place.

♦ Message About Other Promotions – Advertising often works hand-in-hand with other promotional mix items. For instance, special sales promotions, such as contests, may be announced within an advertisement. Also, advertising can help salespeople gain access to new accounts if the advertising precedes the salesperson's attempt to gain an appointment with a prospective buyer. This may be especially effective for a company entering a new market where advertising may help reduce the uncertainty a buyer may have with setting up an appointment with a salesperson from a new company.

♦ Message About Distribution – Within distribution channels, advertising can help expand channel options for a marketer by making distributors aware of the marketer's offerings. Also, advertising can be used to let customers know locations where a product can be purchased.

SETTING THE ADVERTISING BUDGET

Setting an advertising objective is easy, but achieving the objective requires a well thought out strategy. One key factor affecting the strategy used to achieve advertising objectives is how much money an organization has to spend. The funds designated for advertising make up the advertising budget and reflect the amount an organization is willing to commit to achieve its advertising objectives.

Organizations use several methods for determining advertising budgets including:

♦ Percentage of Sales – Under this approach advertising spending is set based on either a percentage of previous sales or a percentage of forecasted sales. For example, an organization may set next year's advertising budget at 10 percent of this year's sales level. One problem with this approach is that the budget is based on what has already happened and not what is expected to occur. If the overall market grows rapidly in the following year, the 10 percent level from the previous year may be well below what is necessary for the company to maintain or increase its sales. Alternatively, companies may consider allocating advertising funds based on a percentage of forecasted sales. In this way advertising is viewed as a driver of future sales and spending on advertising is linked directly to meeting future sales forecasts. However, since future sales are not guaranteed, the actual percentage spent may be considerably higher than expected if the sales forecast is greater than what actually occurs.

♦ What is Affordable – Many smaller companies find spending of any kind to be constraining. In this situation, advertising may be just one of several tightly allocated spending areas with the level spent on advertising varying over time. For these companies, advertising may only occur when extra funds are available.

♦ Best Guess – Companies entering new markets often lack knowledge of how much advertising is needed to achieve their objectives. In cases where the market is not well understood, marketers may rely on their best judgment (i.e., executive's experience) of what the advertising budget should be.

SELECTING MEDIA OUTLETS

With an objective and a budget in place, the advertising campaign next focuses on developing the message. However, before effort is placed in developing a message the marketer must first determine which media outlets will be used to deliver its message since the choice of media outlets guides the type of message that can be created and how frequently the message will be delivered.

Characteristics of Media Outlets

An advertising message can be delivered via a large number of media outlets. These range from traditional outlets, such as print publications, radio, and television, to newly emerging outlets, such as the Internet and mobile devices. However, each media outlet possesses different characteristics and offers marketers different advantages and disadvantages.

The characteristics by which different media outlets can be assessed include the following seven factors:

1. Creative Options
2. Creative Cost
3. Media Market Reach
4. Message Placement Cost
5. Length of Exposure
6. Advertising Clutter
7. Response Tracking

1. CREATIVE OPTIONS

An advertisement has the potential to appeal to four senses – sight, sound, smell, and touch. (It should be noted that promotion can also appeal to the sense of taste but generally these efforts fall under the category of sales promotion which is discussed in Chapter 14.) However, not all advertising media have the ability to deliver multi-sensory messages. Traditional radio, for example, is limited to delivering audio messages while roadside billboards offer only visual appeal. Additionally, some media may place limits on when particular options can be used. For instance, some websites may only accept certain types of graphical-style ads if these conform to certain large dimensions and limit smaller size advertising to text-only ads (see *Internet Advertising* discussion below).

2. CREATIVE COST

The media type chosen to deliver a marketer's message also impacts the cost of creating the message. For media outlets that deliver a multi-sensory experience (e.g., television and Internet for sight and sound; print publications for sight, touch, and smell) creative cost can be significantly higher than for media targeting a single sensory experience. But creative costs are also affected by the expectation of quality of the media delivering the message. In fact, media outlets may set minimal production standards for advertisements and reject ads not meeting these standards. Television networks, for example, may set high production quality levels for advertisements they deliver. Achieving these standards requires expensive equipment and high cost labor, which may not be feasible for small businesses. Conversely, creating a simple text-only Internet advertisement requires very little cost that almost anyone is capable of creating.

3. MEDIA MARKET REACH

The number of customers exposed to a single promotional effort within a target market is considered the reach of a promotion. Some forms of advertising, such as television advertising, offer an extensive reach, while a single roadside billboard on a lightly traveled road offers very limited reach.

Market reach can be measured along two dimensions: 1) channels served, and 2) geographic scope of a media outlet.

Channels Served

This dimension relates to whether a media outlet is effective in reaching the members within the marketer's channel of distribution. Channels can be classified as:

- Consumer Channel – Does the media outlet reach the final consumer market targeted by the marketer?

- Trade Channel – Does the media outlet reach a marketer's channel partners who help distribute its product?

- Business-to-Business Channel – Does the media outlet reach customers in the business market targeted by the marketer?

Geographic Scope

This dimension defines the geographic breadth of the channels served and includes:

- <u>International</u> – Does the media outlet have multi-country distribution?

- <u>National</u> – Does the media outlet cover an entire country?

- <u>Regional</u> – Does the media outlet have distribution across multiple geographic regions such as counties, states, provinces, territories, etc.?

- <u>Local</u> – Does the media outlet primarily serve a limited geographic area?

- <u>Individual</u> – Does the media outlet offer individual customer targeting?

4. MESSAGE PLACEMENT COST

Creative development is one of two major spending considerations for advertising. The other cost is for media placement which is the purchase of ad time, space or location from media outlets that deliver the message. Advertising placement costs vary widely from very small amounts for certain online advertisements to highly expensive rates for advertising on major television programs (see Box 13-1). For example, in the United States the highest cost for advertising placement occurs with television ads shown during the National Football League's Super Bowl championship game where ad rates for a single 30-second advertisement are nearly (US) $3 million. (1) By contrast, ads placed through online search engines may cost less than (US) $5.

5. LENGTH OF EXPOSURE

Some products require customers be exposed to just a little bit of information in order to build customer interest. For example, the features and benefits of a new snack food can be explained in a short period of time using television or radio commercials. However, complicated products need to present more information for customers to fully understand the product. Consequently, advertisers of these products will seek media formats that allot more time to deliver the message.

Media outlets vary in how much exposure they offer to their audience. Magazines and other publications provide opportunities for longer exposure times since these media types can be retained by the audience (i.e., keep old magazines) while exposure on television and radio are generally limited to the length of time the ad is broadcast.

Box 13-1

DETERMINE ADVERTISING RATES

Media outlets set advertising rates using several factors though the most important are the following:

Audience Size

The first factor refers to the number of people who experience the media outlet during a particular time period. For example, for television outlets audience size is measured in terms of the number of program viewers, for print publications audience is measured by the number of readers, and for websites audience is measured by the number of visitors. In general, the more people who are reached through a media outlet, the more the outlet can charge for ads. However, actual measurement of the popularity of media outlets is complicated by many factors to the point where the media outlets are rarely trusted to give accurate figures reflecting their audience size. To help ensure the validity of **audience measurements**, nearly all media major outlets have agreed to be audited by third-party organizations and most marketers rely on these auditors to determine whether the cost of placement is justified given the audited audience size.

Audience Type

When choosing a media outlet, selection is evaluated based on the outlet's customer profile (i.e., viewers, readers, website visitors) and whether these match the characteristics of the marketer's desired target market. The more selectively targeted the audience, the more valuable this audience is to advertisers, since targeted advertising funds are being spent on those with the highest potential to respond to the advertiser's message. The result is that media outlets, whose audience shares very similar characteristics (e.g., age, education level, political views, etc.), are in a position to charge higher advertising rates than media outlets that do not appeal to such a targeted group.

Characteristics of the Advertisement

Media outlets also charge different rates based on creative characteristics of the message. Characteristics that create ad rate differences include:

- Run Time – such as 15-second versus a 30-second television advertisement

- Size – such as a small box versus a full size banner Internet advertisement

- Print Style – such as black-and-white versus color postcard

- Location in Media – such as placement on the back cover versus on an inside page of a magazine

6. Advertising Clutter

In order to increase revenue, media outlets often include a large number of ads within a certain time, space or location. For instance, television programs may contain many ads inserted during the scheduled run-time of a program. A large number of advertisements create an environment of advertising clutter, which makes it difficult for those in the targeted market to recognize and remember particular advertisements. And clutter is expected to increase with the advent of thin computer screens that enable advertising to appear in an almost unlimited number of locations (e.g., outdoor signage) and on millions of devices (e.g., cellphones). (2)

To break through the clutter advertisers may be required to increase the frequency of their advertising efforts (i.e., run more ads). Yet greater **advertising frequency** increases advertising expense. Alternatively, advertisers may seek opportunities offering less clutter where an ad has a better chance of standing out from others. This can be seen with online downloads (e.g., podcasts) of sports and news programming where a 5-10 minute story will be presented with a single 30-60 second ad.

7. Response Tracking

As we noted in Chapter 12, marketers are embracing new technologies making it easier to track audience response to advertisements. Newer media developed using Internet technology offers effective methods for tracking audience response compared to traditional media. But Internet-media are not alone in providing response tracking. Other advertising outlets, such as advertising by mail and **television infomercial** programming (i.e., long-form commercials), also provide useful measures of audience reaction.

Type of Media Outlets

While just a few years ago marketers needed to be aware of only a few advertising outlets, today's marketers must be well-versed in a wide range of media options. The reason for the growing number of media outlets lies with advances in communication technology, in particular the Internet. Below we discuss the leading media outlets used for advertising.

TELEVISION ADVERTISING

Television advertising offers the benefit of reaching large numbers in a single exposure. Yet because it is a mass medium capable of being seen by nearly anyone, television lacks the ability to deliver an advertisement to highly targeted customers compared to other media outlets. Television networks are attempting to improve their targeting efforts. In particular, networks operating in the pay-to-access arena, such as those with channels on cable and satellite television, are introducing more narrowly themed programming designed to appeal to selective audiences. However, television remains an option that is best for products targeted to a broad market.

The geographic scope of television advertising ranges from advertising within a localized geographic area using fee-based services, such as cable and fiber optic services, to national coverage using broadcast programming.

Television advertising, once viewed as the pillar of advertising media outlets, is facing numerous challenges from alternative media (e.g., Internet) and from the invasion of technology devices, such as digital video recorders, that have empowered customers to be more selective on the advertisements they view. Additionally, television lacks effective response tracking which has led many marketers to investigate other media offering stronger tracking options.

• •

Turner Broadcasting is now allowing marketers to pair advertisements with specific content appearing on network programs. The system will determine the best place within a show that matches the content of the ad. For instance, during the commercial break that follows a program in which a food allergy was mentioned an ad for a drug store chain may run. (3)

• •

RADIO ADVERTISING

Promotion through radio has been a viable advertising option for over 80 years. Radio advertising is mostly local to the broadcast range of a radio station, however, at least three options exist offering national and potentially international coverage. First, in many countries there are radio networks using many geographically distinct stations to broadcast simultaneously. In the United States such networks as Disney (children's programming) and ESPN (sports programming) broadcast nationally either through a group of company-owned stations or through a **syndication arrangement** (i.e., business agreement) with partner stations. Second, within the last few years the emergence of radio programming delivered via satellite has become an option for national advertising. Finally, the potential for national and international advertising may become more attractive as radio stations allow their signals to be broadcast over the Internet.

In many ways radio suffers the same problems as television, namely, its a mass medium that is not highly targeted and offers little opportunity to track responses. But unlike television, radio presents the additional disadvantage of limiting advertisers to audio-only advertising. For some products advertising without visual support is not effective.

PRINT PUBLICATION ADVERTISING

Print publications include magazines, newspapers, and special issue publications. The geographic scope of print publications varies from locally targeted community newspapers to internationally distributed magazines. Magazines, especially those targeting specific niches or specialized interest areas, are more narrowly targeted compared to broadcast media. Additionally, magazines offer the option of allowing marketers to present their message using high quality imagery (e.g., full color) and can also offer touch and scent experiences (e.g., perfume).

. . . .

The Los Angeles Times is offering advertisers the ability to produce "scratch-and-sniff" advertisements through the use of scented ink. In one movie advertisement the paper produced the smell of frosted cake. (4)

. . . .

Newspapers have also incorporated color advertisements, though their main advantage rests with their ability to target local markets. **Special issue publications** can offer very selective targeting since these often focus on extremely narrow topics (e.g., auto buying guide, tour guides, college and university ratings, etc.).

The downside of print publications is that readership has dropped consistently over the last few decades. Again, the emergence of the Internet is a key reason for the decline. Newspapers are particularly vulnerable and there are many who question the future viability of printed news as an important media outlet.

INTERNET ADVERTISING

The fastest growing media outlet for advertising is the Internet. Compared to spending in other media, the rate of spending for Internet advertising is experiencing tremendous growth and in the U.S. for 2007 trails only newspaper and television advertising in terms of total spending. (5) Internet advertising's influence continues to expand and each year more major marketers shift a larger portion of their promotional budget to this medium. Two key reasons for this shift rest with the Internet's ability to: 1) narrowly target an advertising message, and 2) track user response to the advertiser's message.

The Internet offers several advertising options including.

- Website Advertising – Advertising tied to a user's visit to a website accounts for the largest spending on Internet advertising. Today marketers have a large number of website advertising options available as discussed in Box 13-2.

- Email Advertising – Using email to deliver an advertisement affords marketers the advantage of low distribution cost and potentially high reach. In situations where the marketer has a highly targeted list, response rates to email advertisements may be quite high. This is especially true if those on the list have agreed to receive email, a process known as **opt-in marketing**. Email advertisement can take the form of a regular email message or be presented within the context of more detailed content such as an electronic newsletter. Delivery to a user's email address can be viewed as either plain text or can look more like a website using web coding (i.e., **HTML**). However, as most people are aware, there is significant downside to email advertising due to highly publicized issues related to abuse (i.e., spam).

- RSS Feed Advertising – Recently advertising began through RSS feeds used by marketers to communicate website updates (see Chapter 3). Advertisements are embedded in the feeds sent automatically to subscribers who then view these when accessing the feed through a feed reader.

- In-Text Advertising – Another recently developed online advertising method ties ads to words found on the webpage, such as within articles or other content. In most cases, the words are formatted to be distinct from other words (e.g., underline) and an ad will be triggered in the form of a pop-up box when the website visitor moves her/his cursor over the word. (6)

Box 13-2

OPTIONS FOR WEBSITE ADVERTISING

Website advertising offers a host of options for marketers to consider. Among the options are:

Creative Types
Internet advertising allows for a large variety of creative types including text-only, image-only, video, and advanced interactive, including advertising in the form of online games.

Size
In addition to a large number of creative types, Internet advertisements can be delivered in a number of different sizes (measured in screen pixels) ranging from full screen to small square ads that are only a few pixels in size. The most popular Internet ad sizes include standard banner ads (468 x 60 pixels), leaderboard (728 x 90 pixels), and skyscraper (160 x 600 pixels).

Targeting
The leading locations for placing ads are on high traffic websites, such as major search engines and other leading content sites, though advertisers can also choose to advertise on thousands of smaller, specialized websites. Ads placed on websites can be targeted by demographics, such as ads appearing on sites more likely viewed by a certain age group, geographics where ads only appear to visitors who access a website from a certain location, and timing such as limiting the display of ads to certain times of day.

Placement
The delivery of an Internet advertisement can occur in many ways including fixed placement in a certain website location, such as at the top of the page, processed placement where the ad is delivered based on user characteristics, such as in response to the entry of certain words in a search engine query, or on a separate web-page in the form of a pop-under where the user may not see the ad until they leave a site or close his/her browser. Advertisements may also appear within live chat areas of a site. For example, during the 2008 Apple Worldwide Developer Conference website MacRumorsLive.com had a reporter submit updates on the Keynote address given by Apple CEO Steve Jobs. The text appeared automatically on the website with ads displayed several times in between the reporter's posts. (7)

Delivery
When it comes to placing advertisements on websites marketers can, in some cases, negotiate with websites directly to place an ad on the site or marketers can place ads via a third-party advertising network, which has agreements to place ads on a large number of partner websites.

DIRECT MAIL

This method of advertising uses postal and other delivery services to ship advertising materials, including postcards, letters, brochures, catalogs, and flyers, to a physical address of targeted customers. Direct mail is most effective when it is designed in a way that makes it appear to be special to the customer. For instance, a marketer using direct mail can personalize mailings by including message recipients' names on the address label or by inserting their names within the content of marketer's message.

Direct mail can be a very cost-effective method of advertising, especially if mailings contain printed material. This is due to cost advantages obtained by printing in high volume since the majority of printing costs are realized when a printing machine is initially setup to run a print job and not because of the quantity of material printed. Consequently, the total cost of printing 50,000 postcards is only slightly higher than printing 20,000 postcards, but when the total cost is divided by the number of cards printed the cost per-card drops dramatically as more pieces are printed. Obviously there are other costs involved in direct mail, primarily postage expense.

While direct mail offers the benefit of low cost for each distributed piece, the actual cost-per-exposure can be quite high as large numbers of customers may discard the mailing before reading. This has led many to refer to direct mail as **junk mail** and, due to the name, some marketers view the approach as ineffective. However, direct mail, when well-targeted, can be an extremely effective promotional tool.

• •

In addition to some marketers questioning the effectiveness of junk mail, environmentalists have raised concerns about its impact on the environment. A recent study appears to offer some support by suggesting that only a small percentage of direct mailers regularly incorporate into their mailings such environmentally aware products as biodegradable envelopes, environmentally friendly inks, and recycled paper. (8)

• •

227

SIGNAGE

The use of signs to communicate a marketer's message places advertising in geographically identified areas in order to capture customer attention. The most obvious method of using signs is through **billboards**, which are generally located in high traffic areas. Outdoor billboards come in many sizes, though the most well-known are large structures located near transportation points intending to attract the interest of people traveling on roads or public transportation. Indoor billboards are often smaller than outdoor billboards and are designed to attract the attention of foot traffic (i.e., those moving past the sign). For example, smaller signage in airports, train terminals, and large commercial office space fit this category.

While billboards are the most obvious example, there are many other forms of signage advertising including:

- Sky writing where airplanes use special chemicals to form words

- Plane banners where large signs are pulled behind an airplane

- Mobile billboards where signs are placed on vehicles, such as buses and cars, or even carried by people

- Plastic bags such as those used to protect newspapers delivered to homes

- Advertisements attached to grocery carts

As creative people, marketers are continually looking for new outlets for placing advertisements. For example, a promotion company hired by the Turner Broadcasting's Cartoon Network came up with a unique way to promote one of the network's programs. The idea was to place box-shaped blinking electronic signs in various public locations in several major U.S. cities. However, this scheme backfired badly when it triggered several bomb scares. The stunt resulted in the arrest of two promotion company associates and the firing of the head of the Cartoon Network. (9)

PRODUCT PLACEMENT ADVERTISING

Product placement is an advertising approach that intentionally inserts products into entertainment programs such as movies, TV programs, and video games. Placement can take several forms including:

- visual imagery in which the product appears within the entertainment program

- actual product use by an actor in the program

- words spoken by an actor that include the product name

Product placement is gaining acceptance among a growing number of marketers for two main reasons. First, in most cases the placement is subtle so as not to divert significant attention from the main content of the program or media outlet. This approach may lead the audience to believe the product was selected for inclusion by program producers and not by the marketer. This may heighten the credibility of the product in the minds of the audience since their perception, whether accurate or not, is that the product was selected by an unbiased third-party. Second, as we discussed in Chapter 12, entertainment programming, such as television, is converging with other media, particularly the Internet. In the future a viewer of a television program may be able to easily request information and purchase products that appear in a program by simply pointing to the product on the screen. As this technology emerges and as marketers explore other options (see Box 13-3) it is expected product placement opportunities will become a powerful promotional option for many marketers.

• •

When it comes to product placement in movies and television programs, automobile companies are among the most aggressive. As evidence of their push for placement nearly all auto companies have their own product placement promotional firms, have set aside hundreds of cars for use, and spend time with directors and producers in an effort to encourage them to include their products. (10)

• •

Box 13-3

OTHER SENSORY PRODUCT PLACEMENT

Product placement is not limited to movies and television. Other options are currently in use and more are being actively explored. Some additional product placement options include:

Musical Product Placement

Electronic games have become wildly popular and are often on par with television for attracting the entertainment attention of many teens and young adults, in particular, those in the important 18-25 year-old demographic. For many of today's gamers, their gaming system includes not only the gaming machine attached to a television but also includes connections to an advanced audio system. Game developers have taken advantage of the enhanced gaming environment by populating their software with numerous songs from genres aimed at younger players. Most songs are up-tempo tunes that help create an atmosphere of excitement while players battle on the screen. After playing a game for many weeks, the gamer may be exposed to a song well over 100 times. In fact, for avid gamers, they will hear the song much more playing video games than they will through local radio outlets. The result is that many new artists have benefited from this intense exposure, and the placement of their songs within an electronic game can be a key factor in helping to launch a successful musical career.

Scent Product Placement

The intentional inclusion of scent as a promotional aid has garnered much attention and could lead to a number of product placement opportunities. Olfactory elements have been used for several years to enhance customers' experience at amusement parks' shows and rides. A broader consumer market will almost certainly develop with gaming most likely being the first to seriously explore this sensory product placement option. As scent becomes a recognized sensory experience for media programming, there is little doubt scent-related product placements will follow. For instance, a bathroom scene in a movie may one day result in the smell of brand name room deodorizer wafting through the theatre.

Tactile Product Placement

Touch or feel sensations may also be a product placement opportunity. Today's gamers use feel devices to heighten the experience by way of such items as vibrating controllers and motion chairs. Some time soon a television viewer may experience a program from several sensory angles including a tactile one. For example, a television show may not only show the visual product placement of a certain brand of automobile, the inclusion of tactile placement could suggest the smooth ride one might get from being in the real thing.

SPONSORSHIPS

A subtle method of advertising is an approach in which marketers pay or offer resources and services, for the purpose of being seen as a supporter of an organization's event, program or product offering (e.g., section of a website). Sponsorships are not viewed as blatant advertisements and in this way may be appealing for marketers looking to establish credibility with a particular target market.

There are numerous local, regional, national, and international sponsorship opportunities ranging from a local art center to the Olympics. Exposure opportunities include signage, printed

handouts, free gifts, sponsored receptions, and much more. However, many sponsorship options lack the ability to tie spending directly to customer response. Additionally, the visibility of the sponsorship may be limited to relatively small mentions especially if the marketer is sharing sponsorship with many other organizations.

OTHERS

While the nine advertising outlets discussed above represent the overwhelming majority of advertising methods, there are several more including:

- advertising using telephone recordings (e.g., political candidate's messages)

- advertising via fax machine (though such methods may be legally prohibited in some areas)

- advertising through inserted material in product packaging (e.g., inside credit card bill)

- advertising imprinted on retail receipts (e.g., grocery store, cash machine)

• •

*Some have termed the placement of ads on non-conventional media as **ad creep**. Recent examples have included placements on school buses, on students' report cards, and within phone conversations. (11)*

• •

CREATING A MESSAGE

In our discussion of the communication process in Chapter 11, we saw that effective communication requires the message source create (encoding) a message that can be interpreted (decoding) by the intended message receiver. In advertising, the act of creating a message is often considered the creative aspect of carrying out an advertising campaign. And because it is a creative process, the number of different ways a message can be generated is limited only by the imagination of those responsible for developing the message.

When creating an advertising message the marketer must consider such issues as:

GENERAL MESSAGE CREATION FACTORS

When developing the message the marketer must take into consideration several factors that affect how it is created including:

- Characteristics of the Target Audience – The makeup of the target audience (e.g., age, location, attitudes, etc.) impacts what is conveyed in the message.

- Type of Media Used – The media outlet (e.g., television, print, Internet, etc.) used to deliver the message impacts the way a message will be created.

- Product Factors – Products that are highly complex require a different message than simpler products. Additionally, the target market's familiarity with a product affects what is contained in a message. For instance, a new product attempting to gain awareness in the market will have a message that is much different than a product that is well known.

- Overall Advertising Objective – As mentioned, the objective of the advertising campaign can affect the type of ad that is designed. For example, an advertisement with the objective of stimulating immediate sales for an existing product will have a different message than an advertisement seeking to build initial awareness of a new product.

MESSAGE ELEMENTS

Most advertising messages share common elements within the message including:

- The Appeal – This refers to the underlying idea that captures the attention of a message receiver. Appeals can fall into such categories as emotional, fearful, humorous, and sexual.

- <u>Value Proposition</u> – The advertising message often contains a reason for customers to be interested in the product which often means the ad will emphasize the benefits obtained from using the product.

- <u>Slogan</u> – To help position the product in a customer's mind and distinguish it from competitors' offerings, advertisements will contain a word or phrase that is repeated across several different messages and different media outlets.

MESSAGE TESTING

Before choosing a specific message marketers running large advertising campaigns will want to have confidence in their message by having potential members of the targeted audience provide feedback. The most popular method of testing advertising for the marketer (or its ad agency) is to conduct focus groups where several advertising messages are presented. On the Internet, advertising delivery technology allows for testing of ads by randomly exposing website visitors to different ads and then measuring their response.

EVALUATING CAMPAIGN RESULTS

The final step in an advertising campaign is to measure the results of carrying out the campaign. In most cases the results measured relate directly to the objectives the marketer is seeking to achieve with the campaign. Consequently, whether a campaign is judged successful is not always tied to whether product sales have increased since the beginning of the campaign. In some cases, such as when the objective is to build awareness, a successful campaign may be measured in terms of how many people are now aware of the product.

In order to evaluate an advertising campaign it is necessary for two measures to take place. First, there must be a pre-campaign or **pre-test measure** that evaluates conditions prior to campaign implementation. For instance, prior to an advertising campaign for Product X a random survey may be undertaken of customers within a target market to see what percentage are aware of Product X. Once the campaign has run, a second, post-campaign or **post-test measure** is undertaken to see if there is an increase in awareness. Such pre- and post-testing can be done no matter what the objective.

REFERENCES

1. Silverstein, B., "Brands Line Up for Super Bowl XLII," *brandchannel*, January 28, 2008.

2. Schlender, B., "Advertising Everywhere," *Fortune*, January 28, 2008.

3. Elliott, S., "Turner to Offer Marketers Way to Link Ads to Content," *New York Times*, May 15, 2008.

4. Elliott, S., "Movies Soon Really Will Smell; This One, in an Ad, Like a Cake," *New York Times*, September 3, 2007.

5. "IAB Internet Advertising Revenue Report," *Interactive Advertising Bureau*, May 2008.

6. Kesmodel, D. and J. Angwin, "Is It News...or Is It an Ad?" *Wall Street Journal*, November 27, 2006.

7. "Worldwide Developer Conference 2008 Keynote Live Coverage," *MacRumorsLIve.com*, June 9th, 2008.

8. Krol, C., "Direct Marketers Not Feeling Green," *B to B*, May 5, 2008.

9. "Head of Cartoon Network Resigns Over Marketing Stunt," *USA Today*, February 9, 2007.

10. Bensinger, K., "Carmakers are Kings of Product Placement Deals," *Los Angeles Times*, June 14, 2008.

11. Remson, A., "School Buses Latest Victim of Ad Creep," *Brandweek*, February 4, 2008.

Full text of many of the references can be accessed via links on the support website.

Chapter 14:

Sales Promotion

In a time when customers are exposed daily to a nearly infinite number of promotional messages, many marketers are discovering advertising alone is not enough to move members of a target market to take action, such as getting them to try a new product. In addition, some marketers are finding certain characteristics of their target market (e.g., small but geographically dispersed) or characteristics of their product (e.g., highly complex) make advertising a less attractive option. Still for other marketers, the high cost of advertising may drive many to seek alternative, lower cost promotional techniques to meet their promotion goals. For these marketers better results may be obtained using other promotional approaches and may lead to directing all their promotional spending to non-advertising promotions.

In this chapter we continue our discussion of promotion decisions by looking at a second promotional mix item: sales promotion. Sales promotions are used widely in many industries and especially by marketers selling to consumers. We show that the objectives of sales promotion are quite different than advertising and are specifically designed to encourage customer response. Coverage includes a detailed looked at promotions aimed at consumers, channel partners, and business-to-business markets. Finally, we will look at the trends shaping the sales promotion field.

WHAT IS SALES PROMOTION?

Sales promotion describes promotional methods using special short-term techniques to persuade members of a target market to respond or undertake certain activity. As a reward, marketers offer something of value to those responding generally in the form of lower cost of ownership for a purchased product (e.g., lower purchase price, money back) or the inclusion of additional value-added material (e.g., something more for the same price).

Sales promotions are used by a wide range of organizations in both the consumer and business markets, though the frequency and spending levels are much greater for consumer products marketers. By some estimates spending on sales promotion in the U.S. exceeds that of advertising. (1) Additional comparison to advertising is discussed in Box 14-1.

Box 14-1

SALES PROMOTION VS. ADVERTISING

Sales promotion is often confused with advertising. For instance, a television advertisement mentioning a contest awarding winners with a free trip to a Caribbean island may give the contest the appearance of advertising. While the delivery of the marketer's message through television media is certainly labeled as advertising, what is contained in the message, namely the contest, is considered a sales promotion. The factors that distinguish between the two promotional approaches are:

Evidence of Time Constraint
Sales promotions involve a short-term value proposition where an advertisement does not. In general, if there is a limited time period within which action must be taken then it most likely qualifies as a sales promotion. In the contest example, a stated entry deadline would indicate a time constraint.

Customer Action Required
Sales promotions require customers to perform some activity in order to be eligible to receive the value proposition. For instance, in our Caribbean trip example, customers may need to complete a form to make them eligible to be entered in the contest.

The inclusion of BOTH, a timing constraint and an activity requirement are hallmarks of sales promotion. While an advertisement may be used to communicate the elements of the sales promotion, the promotional method that rewards the customer is considered a sales promotion.

OBJECTIVES OF SALES PROMOTION

Sales promotion is a tool used to achieve most of the five major promotional objectives discussed in Chapter 11:

- ◆ <u>Building Product Awareness</u> – Several sales promotion techniques are highly effective in exposing customers to products for the first time and can serve as key promotional components in the early stages of new product introduction. Additionally, as part of the effort to build product awareness, several sales promotion techniques have the added advantage of capturing customer information at the time of exposure to the promotion. In this way sales promotion can act as an effective customer information gathering tool (i.e., sales lead generation), which can then be used as part of follow-up marketing efforts.

- ◆ <u>Creating Interest</u> – Marketers find that sales promotions are very effective in creating interest in a product. In fact, creating interest is often considered the most important use of sales promotion. In the retail industry an appealing sales promotion can significantly increase customer traffic to retail outlets. Internet marketers can use similar approaches to bolster the number of website visitors. Another important way to create interest is to move customers to experience a product. Several sales promotion techniques offer the opportunity for customers to try products for free or at low cost.

- ◆ <u>Providing Information</u> – Generally sales promotion techniques are designed to move customers to some action and are rarely simply informational in nature. However, some sales promotions do offer customers access to product information. For instance, a promotion may allow customers to try a fee-based online service for free for several days. This free access may include receiving product information via email.

- ◆ <u>Stimulating Demand</u> – Next to building initial product awareness, the most important use of sales promotion is to build demand by convincing customers to make a purchase. Special promotions, especially those that lower the cost of ownership to the customer (e.g., price reduction), can be employed to stimulate sales.

- ◆ <u>Reinforcing the Brand</u> – Once customers have made a purchase sales promotion can be used to both encourage additional purchasing and also as a reward for purchase loyalty (see *Loyalty Programs* discussion below). Many companies, including airlines and retail stores, reward good or "preferred" customers with special promotions such as email "special deals" and surprise price reductions at the cash register.

CLASSIFICATION OF SALES PROMOTION

Sales promotion can be classified based on the primary target audience to whom the promotion is directed. These include:

♦ Consumer Market Directed – Possibly the most well-known methods of sales promotion are those intended to appeal to the final consumer. Consumers are exposed to sales promotions nearly every day and, as discussed later, many buyers are conditioned to look for sales promotions prior to making purchase decisions.

♦ Trade Market Directed – Marketers use sales promotions to target all customers including partners within their channel of distribution. Resellers, who are often referred to as trade partners, are targets for the majority of such spending. Trade promotions are initially used to entice channel members to carry a marketer's products and, once products are stocked, marketers utilize promotions to strengthen the channel relationship.

♦ Business-to-Business Market Directed – A small but important subset of sales promotions are targeted to the business-to-business market. While these promotions may not carry the glamour associated with consumer or trade promotions, B-to-B promotions are used in many industries.

In the next few sections we discuss each classification in more detail.

CONSUMER SALES PROMOTION

Consumer sales promotions encompass a variety of short-term promotional techniques designed to induce customers to respond in some way. The most popular consumer sales promotions are directly associated with product purchasing. These promotions are intended to enhance the value of a product purchase by either reducing the overall cost of the product (i.e., get same product but for less money) or by adding more benefit to the regular purchase price (i.e., get more for the money).

While tying a promotion to an immediate purchase is a major use of consumer sales promotion, it is not the only one. As we noted above, promotion techniques can be used to achieve other objectives such as building brand loyalty or creating product awareness. Consequently, marketers have available a wide assortment of consumer promotions as discussed below:

PROMOTIONAL PRICING

One of the most powerful sales promotion techniques is the short-term price reduction or, as known in some areas, "on sale" pricing. Lowering a product's selling price can have an immediate impact on demand, though marketers must exercise caution since the frequent use of this technique can lead customers to anticipate the reduction and, consequently, withhold purchase until the price reduction occurs again.

As we will see in our discussion in Chapter 18, promotional pricing is also considered within the framework of price setting. More on of this technique will be provided in that discussion.

LOYALTY PROGRAMS

Promotions offering customers a reward, such as price discounts and free products, for frequent purchasing or other activity are called loyalty programs. These promotions have been around for many years but grew rapidly in popularity when introduced in the airline industry as part of frequent-flier programs. Loyalty programs are also found in numerous other industries, including grocery, pizza purchasing, and online book purchases, where they may also be known as **club card** programs since members often must use a verification card as evidence of enrollment in the program.

Many loyalty programs have become ingrained as part of the value offered by a marketer. That is, a retailer or marketing organization may offer loyalty programs as general business practice. Under this condition the loyalty program does not qualify as a sales promotion since it does not fit the requirement of offering a short-term value since it is always offered. However, even within a loyalty program that is part of a general business practice, a sales promotion can be offered such as a special short-term offer that lowers the number of points needed to acquire a free product.

COUPONS

Most consumers are quite familiar with this form of sales promotion, which offers purchasers price savings or other incentives when the coupon is redeemed at the time of purchase. Coupons are short-term in nature since most (but not all) carry an expiration date. Also, coupons require consumer involvement in order for value to be realized. In most cases involvement consists of the consumer making an effort to obtain the coupon (e.g., clip from newspaper) and then presenting it at the time of purchase. Customers are exposed to coupons in many different ways as explained in Box 14-2.

Box 14-2
How Coupons Are Obtained

Coupons are used widely by marketers across many retail industries and reach consumers in a number of different delivery formats including:

Free-Standing Inserts (FSI)
The traditional approach to distributing coupons is to insert these within media, such as newspapers and direct mail. This method may require the customer to remove the coupon from surrounding material (e.g., clip from newspaper) in order to use.

Printout
A delivery method that is common in many food stores is to present coupons to a customer at the conclusion of the purchasing process. These coupons, which are often printed on the spot, are intended to be used for a future purchase and not for the current purchase which triggered the printing.

Cross-Product
These consist of coupons placed within or on other products. Often a marketer uses this method to promote one product by placing the coupon inside another major selling product. For example, a sports drink marketer may imprint a coupon for its product on the package of a high-energy snack. Also, this delivery approach is used when two marketers have struck a **cross promotion** arrangement where each agrees to undertake certain marketing activity for the other.

Product Display
Some coupons are nearly impossible for customers to miss as they are located in close proximity to the product. In some instances coupons may be contained within a coupon dispenser fastened to the shelf holding the product while in other cases coupons may be attached to a special display (see *Point-of-Purchase Displays* discussion below) where customers can remove them (e.g., tear off).

Internet
Several specialized websites and even some manufacturers' sites, allow customers to print out coupons. (2) These coupons are often the same ones appearing in other media such as newspapers or direct mail. In other cases, coupons may be sent via email, though to be effective the customer's email program must be able to receive HTML email (and not text only) in order to maintain required design elements (e.g., bar code).

Electronic
The Internet is also seeing the emergence of new non-printable coupons redeemable through website purchases. These electronic coupons are redeemed when the customer enters a designated **coupon code** during the purchase process.

Cellphone
The newest method for delivering coupons is via messages sent to customers' cellphones. (3) The coupon may appear along with a barcode image. The customer then flashes the cellphone screen containing the image to the retailer or in front of an electronic reader that will then process the coupon.

REBATES

Rebates, like coupons, offer value to purchasers typically by lowering the customer's final cost for acquiring the product. While rebates share some similarities with coupons, they differ in several keys aspects. First, rebates are generally handed or offered (e.g., accessible on the Internet) to customers after a purchase is made and cannot be used to obtain immediate savings in the way coupons are used. (So called **instant rebates**, where customers receive price reductions at the time of purchase, have elements of both coupons and rebates, but for our purposes we will classify these as coupons based on the timing of the reward to the customer.)

Second, rebates often request the purchaser to submit personal data in order to obtain the rebate. For instance, customer identification, including name, address, and phone or email contact information, is generally required to obtain a rebate. Also, the marketer may ask those seeking a rebate to provide additional data, such as indicating the reason for making the purchase.

Third, unlike coupons that always offer value when used in a purchase (assuming it is accepted by the retailer), receiving a rebate only guarantees value if the customer takes actions. Marketers know that not all customers will respond to a rebate. Some will misplace or forget to submit the rebate while others may submit after a required deadline. Marketers factor in the **non-redemption rate** as they attempt to calculate the cost of the rebate promotion.

Finally, rebates tend to be used as a value enhancement in higher priced products compared to coupons. For instance, rebates are a popular promotion for automobiles and computer software where large amounts of money may be returned to the customer.

SAMPLES AND FREE TRIALS

Enticing members of a target market to try a product is often easy when the trial comes at little or no cost to the customer. The use of samples and free trials may be the oldest of all sales promotion techniques dating back to when society advanced from a culture of self-subsistence to a culture of trade.

Samples and free trials give customers the opportunity to experience products, often in small quantities or for a short duration, without purchasing the product. Today, these methods are used in almost all industries and are especially useful for getting customers to try a product for the first time. Sampling can take place at a person's home (e.g., through the mail, included with newspaper), in-store (e.g., attach to the packaging of another product, demonstrations), and out-of-home (e.g., at sporting events). (4)

FREE PRODUCT

Some promotional methods offer free products but with the condition that a purchase be made. The free product may be in the form of additional quantities of the same purchased product (e.g., buy one, get one free) or specialty packages (e.g., value pack) that offer more quantity for the same price as regular packaging.

PREMIUMS

Another form of sales promotion involving free merchandise is premium or "give-away" items. Premiums differ from samples and free product in that these often do not consist of the actual product, though there is often some connection. For example, a cellphone manufacturer may offer access to free downloadable ringtones for those purchasing a cellphone.

TRADE-IN

Trade-in promotions allow consumers to obtain lower prices by exchanging something the customer possesses such as an older product that the new purchase will replace. While the idea of gaining price breaks for trading in another product is most frequently seen with automobile sales, these promotions are used in other industries, such golf equipment, where the customer's exchanged product can be resold by the marketer in order to extract value.

CONTESTS AND SWEEPSTAKES

Consumers are often attracted to promotions where the potential value obtained is very high. In these promotions only a few lucky consumers receive the value offered in the promotion. Two types of promotions offering high value are contests and sweepstakes.

Contests are special promotions awarding value to winners based on skills they demonstrate compared to others. For instance, a baking company may offer free vacations to winners of a baking contest. Contest award winners are often determined by a panel of judges.

Sweepstakes or drawings are not skill based but rather based on luck. Winners are determined by random selection. In some cases the chances of winning may be higher for those who make a purchase if entry into the sweepstake occurs automatically when a purchase is made. But in most cases, anyone is free to enter without the requirement to make a purchase.

A sub-set of both contests and sweepstakes are **games**, which come in a variety of formats, such as scratch-off cards and collection of game pieces. Unlike contests and sweepstakes, which may not require purchase, to participate in a game customers may be required to make a purchase. In the United States and other countries, where eligibility is based on purchase, games may be subjected to rigid legal controls and may actually fall under the category of lotteries. In the U.S. a promotion is considered to be a **lottery** if it contains three elements: an award or prize, won by chance, and the requirement that those entering must pay for the chance. Such promotional methods are tightly controlled and may be illegal in several states.

- -

A California court ruled that payment for the chance to win a promotion can extend to the cost associated with a free entry. The promotion in question had participants enter by text messaging to a certain number. While the entry in the promotion itself was free the participants were charged for the text message. The court ruled the cost of texting may be considered a form of payment for a chance, thereby, making it an illegal lottery. (5)

- -

DEMONSTRATIONS

Many products benefit from customers being shown how products are used through a demonstration. Whether the demonstration is experienced in-person or via video form, such as over the Internet, this promotional technique can produce highly effective results. Unfortunately, demonstrations are often very expensive to arrange. Costs involved in demonstrations include paying the expense of the demonstrator, which can be high if the demonstrator is well-known (e.g., nationally known chef), setup costs, and also paying for the space where the demonstration is given.

PERSONAL APPEARANCES

An in-person appearance by someone of interest to the target market, such as an author, sports figure or celebrity, is another form of sales promotion capable of generating customer traffic to a physical location. However, as with demonstrations, personal appearance promotion can be expensive since the marketer normally must pay a fee for the person to appear.

TRADE SALES PROMOTIONS

As note in Chapter 11, certain promotions can help "push" a product through the channel by encouraging channel members to purchase and also promote the product to their customers. For instance, a trade promotion aimed at retailers may encourage them to instruct their employees to promote a marketer's brand over competitors' offerings. With thousands of products competing for limited shelf space, spending on trade promotion is nearly equal that spent on consumer promotions.

Many sales promotions aimed at building relationships with channel partners follow similar designs as those directed to consumers, including promotional pricing, contests, and free product. In addition to these, several other promotional approaches are specifically designed to appeal to trade partners including:

POINT-OF-PURCHASE DISPLAYS

Point-of-purchase (POP) displays are specially designed materials intended for placement in retail stores. These displays allow products to be prominently presented, often in high traffic areas, and thereby increase the probability the product will stand out. POP displays come in many styles, though the most popular are ones allowing a product to stand alone, such as in the middle of a store aisle or sit at the end of an aisle (i.e., **end-cap promotion**) where it will be exposed to heavy customer traffic.

For channel partners, POP displays can result in significant sales increases compared to sales levels experienced at the product's normal shelf position. Also, many marketers will lower the per-unit cost of products in the POP display as an incentive for retailers to agree to include the display in their stores.

· ·

An emerging technology containing certain elements of POP displays is the computerized shopping cart. These carts, which have a small computer and monitor, offer shoppers several features including the ability to scan products to determine pricing and product information, and also keep a running count of total cost of products added to the cart. Additionally, using an in-store tracking system the cart will alert the customer to special bargains as he/she approaches the product. (6)

· ·

ADVERTISING SUPPORT PROGRAMS

In addition to offering promotional support in the form of physical displays, marketers can attract channel members' interest by offering financial assistance in the form of advertising money. These funds are often directed to retailers who then include the company's products in their advertising. In certain cases the marketer will offer to pay the entire cost of advertising, but more often the marketer offers partial support known as **co-op advertising** funds.

PROMOTIONAL PRODUCTS

Among the most widely used methods of sales promotions is the promotional product, products labeled with the brand or company name that serve as reminders of the actual product. For instance, companies often hand out free calendars, coffee cups, and pens that contain the product logo. Table 14-1 presents a breakdown of the top 10 categories marketers use for promotional products. (7)

Table 14-1: Top 10 Promotional Products

Product	Percentage
Wearable Clothing	30.7
Writing Instruments	10.4
Bags	7.1
Drinkware	6.3
Desk/Office/Business Accessories	6.2
Calendars	5.5
Recognition Awards/Trophies/Jewelry	3.6
Computers	3.1
Sporting Goods	2.6
Automotive	2.5

Short Term Trade Allowances

This promotion offers channel partners price breaks for agreeing to stock the product. In most cases the allowance is not only given as encouragement to purchase the product but also as an inducement to promote the product in other ways, such as offering attractive shelf space or store location, highlighting the product in company-produced advertising or website display, or by agreeing to have the retailer's sales personnel "talk-up" the product to customers.

Allowances can be in the form of price reductions, also called **off-invoice promotion**, and **buy-back guarantees** if the product does not sell in a certain period of time.

Sales Incentives or Push Money

Since sales promotions are intended to stimulate activity that leads to meeting promotional objectives, it makes sense these can also apply to those in a channel member's organization who also affect sales. Thus, a marketer may offer sales promotions to its resellers' sales force and customer service staff where they are used as incentives to help sell more of the marketer's product. Sometimes called push money, these promotions typically offer employees cash or prizes, such as trips, for those that meet sales requirements.

Trade Shows

One final type of trade promotion is the industry trade show. Trade shows are organized events bringing industry buyers and sellers together in one central location. Spending on trade shows is one of the highest of all sales promotions.

Marketers are attracted to trade shows since these offer the opportunity to reach a large number of potential buyers in one convenient setting. At these events most sellers attempt to capture the attention of buyers by setting up a display area to present their product offerings and meet with potential customers. These displays can range from a single table covering a small area to erecting specially built display booths that dominate the trade show floor.

. . . .

*Because of the cost and time commitment required to participate in trade shows, several companies are experimenting with shows that are held online. These **virtual trade shows** allow presenters to build 3-D exhibits where potential customers can view products and interact with company representatives. (8)*

. . . .

BUSINESS-TO-BUSINESS SALES PROMOTIONS

The use of sales promotion is not limited to consumer products marketing. In business markets sales promotions are also used as a means of moving customers to action. However, the promotional choices available to the B-to-B marketer are not as extensive as those found in the consumer or trade markets. For example, most B-to-B marketers do not use coupons as a vehicle for sales promotion with the exception of companies that sell to both consumer and business customers (e.g., products sold through office supply retailers). Rather, the techniques more likely to be utilized include:

- price-reductions
- free product
- trade-in
- promotional products
- trade shows

Of the promotions listed, trade shows are by far the mostly widely used sales promotion within the business-to-business market.

TRENDS IN SALES PROMOTION

Marketers who employ sales promotion as a key component in their promotional strategy should be aware of how the climate for these types of promotions is changing. The important trends in sales promotion include:

CUSTOMERS EXPECTATIONS

The onslaught of sales promotion activity over the last several decades has eroded the value of the short-term requirement to act on sales promotions. Many customers are conditioned to expect a promotion at the time of purchase otherwise they may withhold or even alter their purchase if a promotion is not present. For instance, food shoppers are inundated on a weekly basis with such a wide variety of sales promotions that their loyalty to certain products has been replaced by their loyalty to current value items (i.e., products with a sales promotion). For marketers the challenge is to balance the advantages offered by short-term promotions versus the potential of eroding loyalty to the product.

ELECTRONIC DELIVERY

Sales promotions are delivered to customers in many ways such as by mail, in-person or within print media. However, the Internet and mobile technologies, such as cellphones, present marketers with a number of new delivery options. For example, the combination of mobile devices and geographic positioning technology will soon permit marketers to target promotions to a customer's physical location. This will allow retailers and other businesses to issue sales promotions, such as electronic coupons, to a customer's mobile device when they are near the location where the coupon can be used.

. . . .

Grocery stores are experimenting with digital coupons pre-loaded on customer loyalty cards. To load the coupons customers must first visit the grocer's website and select the desired coupons. The coupon is then added to the customer's loyalty card account and is redeemed at checkout. (9)

. . . .

TRACKING

As we discussed in our coverage of advertising, tracking customer response to marketers' promotional activity is critical for measuring the success of an advertisement. In sales promotion, tracking is also used. For instance, grocery retailers, whose customers are in possession of loyalty cards, have the ability to match customer sales data to coupon use. This information can then be sold to coupon marketers who may use the information to get a better picture of the buying patterns of those responding to the coupon, including using the information to generate instant coupons at the checkout counter.

INTERNET COMMUNICATION

For many years consumers typically became aware of sales promotions in passive ways. That is, most customers obtained promotions not through an active search but by being a recipient of a marketer's promotion activity (e.g., received coupons in the mail). The Internet is changing how customers obtain promotions. In addition to websites offering access to coupons, there are a large number of community forum sites where members share details about how to obtain good deals which often include information on how or where to find a sales promotion. Monitoring these sites may offer marketers insight into how customers feel about certain promotions and may even suggest ideas for future sales promotions.

• •

*Several websites make it easy for customers to locate coupon codes that shoppers can enter in a **promotion code** box when making an online purchase. Sites, such as Currentcodes, RetailMeNot, BradsDeals, and CouponCabin, scour the Internet using special software as well as human researchers to locate current codes. (10)*

• •

CLUTTER AND NEED FOR CREATIVITY

In the same way an advertisement competes with other ads for customers' attention, so too do sales promotions. This is particularly an issue with inserted coupon promotions that may be included in mailing or printed media along with numerous other offerings. The challenge facing marketers is to find creative ways to separate their promotions from those offered by their competitors.

REFERENCES

1. Myers, J., "JackMyers Media Spending 2006-2009 Estimates," *JackMyers.com*, September 15, 2007.

2. Holahan, C., "Cutting Costs with Online Coupon Sites," *BusinessWeek*, May 6, 2008.

3. Quinton, B., "Mobile Couponing on the Grow," *Promo Magazine*, July 1, 2008.

4. Averbook, A., "Nothing Like Free," *Promo Magazine*, July 1, 2007.

5. "Text Message Sweepstakes: What Game Are You Playing?" *AdLaw by Request*, December 14, 2007.

6. *MediaCart* website.

7. "The 2007 Estimate of Promotional Products Distributor Sales," *Promotional Products Association International*.

8. Clancy, H., "Cyberspace Trade Shows Bring Action to the Desktop," *New York Times*, September 12, 2007.

9. "From Clipping Coupons to Clicking on Them," *MSNBC*, January 13, 2008.

10. O'Donnell, J., "Online Buyers Crack the Code on Deals," *USA Today*, April 4, 2008.

Full text of many of the references can be accessed via links on the support website.

Chapter 15:

Public Relations

Of the four promotional mix options available to marketers public relations (PR) is probably the least understood and, consequently, often receives the least amount of attention. Many marketers see public relations as only handling rudimentary communication activities, such as issuing press releases and responding to questions from the news media. But in reality, in a time when customers are inundated with thousands of promotional messages everyday, public relations offers powerful methods for cutting through the clutter.

In this chapter we investigate how public relations is growing in importance as a marketing tool and is now a critical component in helping marketers reach their objectives. We look at both the advantages and disadvantages of using PR for promotion. We see that PR uses a variety of tools to enhance the relationship between an organization and its target audience. And we show how when handled correctly, PR can allow a marketer's message to rise above other promotional methods.

WHAT IS PUBLIC RELATIONS?

Public relations involves the cultivation of favorable relations for organizations and products with their key publics through the use of a variety of communications channels and tools. Traditionally, this meant public relations professionals would work with members of the news media to build a favorable image by publicizing the organization or product through stories in print and broadcast media. But today the role of public relations is much broader and includes:

♦ Building awareness and a favorable image for a company and/or product within stories and articles found in relevant media outlets.

♦ Closely monitoring numerous media channels for public comment about a company and its products.

♦ Managing crises that threaten company or product image.

♦ Building goodwill among an organization's target market through community, philanthropic, and special programs and events.

In this chapter most of our focus is on how public relations supports marketing by building product and company image (sometimes referred to as **publicity**). Yet, it should be noted that there are other stakeholders companies reach via the public relations function such as employees and non-target market groups (see Box 11-1 in Chapter 11). Favorable media coverage about a company or product often reaches these audiences as well and may offer potential benefit to the marketer.

Finally, in most large companies, **investor relations (IR)** or **financial public relations** is a specialty in itself guided by specific disclosure regulations. However, coverage of this type of PR will not be provided here.

Advantages of PR

Public relations offers several advantages not found with other promotional options. First, PR is often considered a highly credible form of promotion. One of PR's key points of power rests with helping to establish credibility for a product, company or person (e.g., CEO) in the minds of targeted customer groups by capitalizing on the influence of a third-party — the media. Audiences view many media outlets as independent sources that are unbiased in their coverage, meaning the decision to include the name of the company and the views expressed about the company is not based on payment (i.e., advertisement) but on the media outlet's judgment of what is important. For example, a positive story about a new product in the business section of a local newspaper may have greater impact on readers than a full-page advertisement for the product since readers perceive the news media as presenting an impartial perspective of the product.

Second, a well-structured PR campaign can provide the target market with more detailed information than they receive with other forms of promotion. That is, media sources often have more space and time for explanation of a product.

Third, depending on the media outlet, a story mentioning a company may be picked up by a large number of additional media resulting in a single story spreading to many locations.

. . . .

The New Oxford American Dictionary saw the benefits of having a story spread to other media outlets when it promoted its word of the year. The PR effort for the word "locavore", which means someone who eats locally grown food, netted the company's executives appearances on national radio shows and the story was mentioned in over 25 newspapers. (1)

. . . .

Finally, in many cases public relations objectives can be achieved at very low cost when compared to other promotional efforts. This is not to suggest public relations is not costly, it may be especially when a marketer hires PR professionals to handle the work. But when compared to the direct cost of other promotions, in particular advertising, the return on promotional expense can be quite high.

Disadvantages of PR

While public relations holds many advantages for marketers, there are also concerns when using this promotional technique. First, while public relations uses many of the same channels as advertising, such as newspapers, magazines, radio, TV, and Internet, it differs significantly from advertising in that marketers do not have direct control over whether a message is delivered and where it is placed for delivery. For instance, a marketer may spend many hours talking with a magazine writer who is preparing an industry story only to find that her company is never mentioned in the article.

Second, while other promotional messages are carefully crafted and appear as written in pre-determined a media vehicle (e.g., advertisements in newspapers), public relations generally conveys information to a member of the news media (e.g., reporter) who then recrafts the information as part of a news story or feature. Consequently, the final message may not be precisely what the marketer planned.

Third, while a PR campaign has the potential to yield a high return on promotional expense, it also has the potential to produce the opposite if the news media feels there is little value in running a story **pitched** (i.e., suggested via communication with the news outlet) by the marketer.

Fourth, with PR there is always a chance a well devised PR story will get "bumped" from planned media coverage because of a more critical breaking news story, such as wars, severe weather or serious crime.

Fifth, in some areas of the world the impact of traditional news outlets is fading forcing public relations professionals to scramble to find and understand new ways to reach their target markets.

Finally, marketers accustom to handling many of their own tasks may find that public relations requires a different skill set than other types of promotion. As explained in Box 15-1, for many marketers PR functions are better left to professionals.

Box 15-1

THE BENEFITS OF PR PROFESSIONALS

While do-it-yourself public relations is certainly undertaken by many marketers, gaining satisfactory results can often prove difficult for those who have little experience in this promotional area. Instead, most marketers are better served by seeking the assistance of PR professionals who understand all aspects of this diverse field. Skilled PR professionals offer many advantages for marketers with the two most important being:

Understand the Story
An important tool for PR is the development of media relations (see *Media Relations* discussion below). Public relations professionals are trained to unearth good stories about a company and its products that can then be presented to the media in the form of a story idea. Just like selling products, selling story ideas requires those pitching the story to present it in terms that will benefit the media outlet. PR professionals are skilled at presenting stories in ways that capture the interest of members of the media.

Know the Media
Knowledge of the media market may place PR professionals in a better position to match stories to the news angles sought by specific media members. Their skill at targeting the right media may prove to be a more efficient use of promotional resources than would occur if a marketer, who has little understanding of media needs, attempted to handle this on his/her own.

OBJECTIVES OF PUBLIC RELATIONS

Like other aspects of marketing promotion, public relations is used to address several broad objectives including:

♦ <u>Building Product Awareness</u> – When introducing a new product or relaunching an existing product, marketers can use a PR element to generate consumer attention and awareness through media placements and special events.

♦ <u>Creating Interest</u> – Whether a PR placement is a short product article or is included with other products in "round up" article, stories in the media can help entice a targeted audience to try the product. For example, around the holiday season, a special holiday food may be promoted with PR through promotional releases sent to the food media or through special events that sample the product.

♦ <u>Providing Information</u> – PR can be used to provide customers with more in depth information about products and services. Through articles, collateral materials, newsletters, and websites, PR delivers information to customers that can help them gain understanding of the product.

♦ <u>Stimulating Demand</u> – While not as effective as sales promotion for moving customers to make a purchase, PR can still be a useful technique for building demand. For example, a positive article in a newspaper, TV news show or mentioned on the Internet, can lead to a discernable increase in product sales.

♦ <u>Reinforcing the Brand</u> – In many companies the public relations function is also involved with brand reinforcement by maintaining positive relationships with key audiences and thereby aiding in building a strong image. Today it is ever more important for companies and brands to build a good image. A strong image helps the company build its business and it can help the company in times of crises as well.

PUBLIC RELATIONS TOOLS

Whether handling PR internally or hiring professionals (see Box 15-1), marketers should be familiar with the tools available for public relations. The key tools available for PR are discussed in detail below.

MEDIA RELATIONS

Historically the core of public relations has been media relations, which includes all efforts to publicize products or the company to members of the press — TV, radio, newspaper, magazine, newsletter, and Internet. In garnering media coverage, PR professionals work with the media to place stories about products, companies, and company spokespeople. This is done by developing interesting and relevant story angles that are pitched to the media. It is important to remember that media placements come with good stories and no payment is made to the media for placements. In fact, in order to maintain the highest level of credibility, many news organizations bar reporters from accepting even the smallest gifts (e.g., free pencils with product logo) from companies.

As PR people know, many story ideas for newspapers, magazines, and television news often start with a suggestion from a PR person. This may occur through one of the media building techniques discussed in Box 15-2 or through direct conversations with journalists, which may involve visiting reporters and editors at their offices. (2) If things work out, a journalist will, at best, write a positive story with the company as a key feature or, at minimum, include the company's name somewhere within an industry-focused article.

MEDIA TOUR

Some new products can be successfully publicized when launched with a media tour. On a media tour a company **spokesperson** travels to key cities to introduce a new product by being booked on TV and radio talk shows and conducting interviews with print and Internet reporters or influencers (e.g., bloggers). The spokesperson can be a company employee or someone hired by the company, perhaps a celebrity or "expert" who has credibility with the target audience. One common use of the media tour is the book tour, where an author travels the country to promote a newly released book. A media tour may include other kinds of personal appearances in conjunction with special events, such as public appearances, speaking engagements or autograph signing opportunities.

Box 15-2

TECHNIQUES FOR BUILDING MEDIA RELATIONS

While the objective of media relations is to obtain favorable mentions for a company or product without direct payment to a media outlet, the process of building strong media relations is by no means free. Public relations professionals pitch stories to reporters and news editors with the assistance of a variety of techniques that are often expensive to produce. These techniques include:

Press Kits

This is the name given to prepared materials, such as a news release, organization background, key spokesperson biographies, and other supporting materials, that provide information useful to reporters. Such kits can be sent to reporters via delivery services or accessible on a company's website. As more companies utilize press kits, the design and content have changed with many now packaged in uniquely detailed containers such as bags, pouches, plastic cases, and cardboard tubes. (3)

Audio or Video News Releases

These are prerecorded features distributed to news media that may be included within media programming. For instance, a local news report about amusement parks may include portions of a video news release from a national amusement park company.

Matte Release

Some media, especially small local newspapers, may accept articles written by companies as filler material when their publications lack sufficient content. PR professionals submit matte releases through **syndicated news services** (i.e., services that supply content to many media outlets) or directly to targeted media via email, fax or postal mail.

Industry Articles

Many industry websites and print publications allow companies to submit articles authored by company personnel such as a CEO or Marketing Manager. Depending on the media outlet the articles can cover specific happenings at a company or may be written with the intention of addressing a business issue. In either case, PR professionals may have significant input into the creation of the article even though they are not identified as the author.

Website Press Room

While hard copies of materials are used and preferred by some media, marketers are well served to establish an online press room catering to media needs (e.g., press kits) and providing company contact information.

NEWSLETTERS

Marketers who have captured names and addresses of customers and potential customers can use a newsletter for regular contact with their targeted audience. Newsletters can be directed at trade customers, final consumers or business buyers and can be distributed either by regular mail or via electronic means (i.e., newsletters delivered via email or RSS feed). Marketers using newsletters strive to provide content of interest to customers as well as information on products and promotions. For instance, a bookstore may include reviews of new books, information on online book chats, and information on in-store or online promotions. A food manufacturer may include seasonal recipes, information on new products, and coupons. Online newsletters also offer the opportunity to include hyperlinks to stores carrying the marketer's product.

SPECIAL EVENTS

These run the gamut from receptions to elegant dinners to stunts. Special events can be designed to reach a specific narrow target audience, such as individuals interested in college savings plans to major events like a strawberry festival designed to promote tourism and regional agriculture. Stunts, such as building the world's largest ice cream sundae during National Ice Cream month, capture the attention of an audience in the immediate area, but also attract the attention of mass media, such as TV news and major newspapers, which provide broad reach. In the U.S., the Oscar Mayer Wienermobile is a classic example, providing a recognizable icon that travels the country garnering attention wherever it visits. (4) As with all PR programs, special event planners must work hard to ensure the program planned conveys the correct message and image to the target audience.

SPEAKING ENGAGEMENTS

Speaking before industry conventions, trade association meetings, and other groups provides an opportunity for company experts to demonstrate their expertise to potential clients and customers. Generally these opportunities are not explicitly for company or product promotion, rather they are a chance to talk on a topic of interest to potential customers and serve to highlight the speaker's expertise in a field. Often the only mention of the company or its products is in the speaker biography. Nevertheless, the right speaking engagement puts the company in front of a good target audience and offers networking opportunities for generating customer leads.

EMPLOYEE COMMUNICATIONS

For many companies communicating regularly with employees is important in keeping employees informed of corporate programs, sales incentives, personnel issues, as well as keeping them updated on new products and programs. Companies use a variety of means to communicate with employees, including Intranet, email, and newsletters. In larger firms an in-house PR department often works in conjunction with the Human Resources Department to develop employee communications.

COMMUNITY RELATIONS AND PHILANTHROPY

For many companies fostering good relations with key audiences includes building strong relationships with their regional community. Companies implement programs supportive of the community ranging from supporting local organizations and institutions (e.g., arts organizations, community activities, parks) to conducting educational workshops (e.g., for teachers, parents) to donating product or money in support of community events. The goal is generally to develop a positive relationship with members of the community (i.e., be known as a good neighbor). Effective community relations can help a company weather bad publicity or a crisis situation that can unexpectedly arise due to a problem with a product, unethical behavior by management, or even by false rumors. Some companies also make an effort to contribute to charitable organizations, often organizations that have some relationship to the company's mission or to a key principal of the company.

ADDITIONAL PUBLIC RELATIONS ACTIVITIES

In addition to serving as means to help achieve marketing objectives, PR professionals may undertake additional activities aimed at maintaining a positive image for an organization. These activities include:

MARKET MONITORING

Monitoring public comment about a company and its products is becoming increasingly important especially with the explosion of information channels on the Internet. Today monitoring includes watching what is written and reported in traditional print and broadcast media and also keeping an eye on discussions occurring through various Internet outlets, such as forums, chatrooms, blogs, and other public messaging areas (see Box 15-3). Marketers must be prepared to respond quickly to erroneous information and negative opinions about products as it can spin out of control very quickly through the new technology channels. Failure to correct misinformation can be devastating to a product or a company's reputation. It should be noted that specialized monitoring services can be contracted to help companies keep track of "buzz" about the company and its products.

Box 15-3

MONITORING WHERE CUSTOMERS VOICE THEIR OPINIONS

The web has evolved from a platform whose main purpose was to provide information to one that now embraces the development of communities where members interact. In particular, several web applications serve as platforms for people to voice their opinions, and from a public relations point of view, require close monitoring. These applications include:

Blogs

Blogs, short for weblogs, are a phenomenon that shows just how powerful and influential the Internet has become as a communication medium. The initial blog posting is often controlled by those responsible for managing the blog, but follow-up comments may be open to nearly anyone, though some blogs will filter responses to reduce the risk of undesirable posts (e.g., spam). The topics covered by blogs are endless and literally hundreds of thousands now exist. Fortunately, for monitoring purposes a number of specialized search engines have been developed to search millions of postings.

Web Forums

Web forums are the child of the old Internet bulletin board services where people can post their opinions often anonymously. Forums pose both opportunities and threats for those involved in PR. A presence in an influential forum helps build credibility for an organization as forum members recognize a company's effort to reach out to the public. On the other hand, forums can cause major problems as breeding grounds for rumor and accusation. Public relations personnel must continually monitor forums and respond to misguided comments posted on a web discussion board to help squelch rumors before they can catch fire.

Social Network Sites

Social network sites combine elements of blogs and forums by allowing the creation of individual pages and encouraging others to post comments. The two most popular social networks are MySpace and Facebook, but there are others including photo sharing (e.g., Flickr), video sharing (e.g., YouTube), and business contact sharing (e.g., Linkedin). When possible monitoring social networks offers the same advantages as found with blogs and forums. However, doing so may prove more difficult since access to the full contents of an individual page within most social networks requires approval by the owner of the page.

Social Bookmarking Sites

In addition to the general social networking sites listed above, several specialized websites have emerged allowing users to share links they have found to news items, blog postings, and other websites. On bookmarking sites, such as Digg, Delicious, and StumbleUpon, users can bookmark (also called **tagging**) sites and then provide the opportunity for others to see how many people are also bookmarking the same links.

News Sites
Many news publications allow readers to post comments to articles appearing on their websites. Though as we discussed with blogs, comments may be moderated by the administrators of the news site.

Dell is an example of a company that aggressively responds to Internet postings. The company has taken the position that it will respond to complaints and criticism in a direct manner by posting its own comments. (5)

CRISIS MANAGEMENT

Marketers need to be prepared to respond quickly to negative information about the company. When a problem with a product arises—in fact or substantiated only by rumor—a marketer's investment in a product can be in serious jeopardy. Today, with the prevalence of the Internet and wireless communications, negative information can spread rapidly. Through techniques monitoring marketers can track the issues and respond in a timely fashion.

To manage response effectively, many companies have crises management plans in place that outline steps to take and the company spokespeople authorized to speak on behalf of the company should an event occur.

Mattel faced a public relations crisis when it was forced to recall more than 20 million toys due to potential lead paint contamination. The company's PR strategy was to react quickly by apologizing for the recall and presenting the company's CEO to the news media. (6)

TRENDS IN PUBLIC RELATIONS

Until recently most public relations activity involved person-to-person contact between PR professionals and members of the media such as journalists and television news reporters. However, several trends are developing that alter the tasks performed by PR people. In most cases these changes are the result of new Internet technologies that are quickly gaining widespread acceptance among Internet users and are becoming new media outlets in their own right.

The important trends in public relations include:

UPDATING CORPORATE NEWS

Developing websites has long been a time-consuming and often overly technical undertaking for the vast majority of marketers. But this changed with the evolution of easier to use site development applications, called **content management systems (CMS)**, which allow for quick creation and convenient updating of site information. With CMS those with access, including public relations personnel, can add information on a regular basis. In addition, posting company news to websites can be tied to RSS feeds (see Chapter 3), thereby allowing for automatic notification to those who have subscribed to the feed. Many journalists and other media members are finding RSS feeds to be a more convenient way to acquire information, particularly if they follow a specific industry and can identify specific information websites to monitor. By subscribing to relevant RSS feeds they have information delivered rather than spending time searching.

* *

PR professionals will find that, in addition to using RSS feeds, corporate news can also be spread using social bookmarking links such as Digg and Delicious (see Box 15-3). These services allow for tracking of the news items in order to gauge popularity and, in some cases, to see reaction to the news. (7)

* *

CORPORATE BLOGGING

Blogs may be most famous as a tool for political discussion and used as a personal journal for individuals, but they are also becoming an important communication tool for public relations. Many companies in high-tech fields, such as eBay, Google, and Microsoft, and traditionally low-tech fields, such as General Motors, McDonalds, and Well Fargo Bank, now produce in-house blogs that report on happenings at the company. These blogs enable company employees, including CEOs and marketers, to post messages updating company developments and, consequently, serve as useful PR tool. As with corporate news, blog postings can also be quickly communicated to news media and others via RSS feeds.

PODCASTING

The emergence of the Apple iPod and other digital audio players has significantly altered how people listen to music. It has also opened the door for PR professionals to distribute audio programming such as audio news releases. But newer digital players have gone beyond audio downloads and now offer access to other content including video programming. Public relations may soon find podcasting to be a quick and easy way to send out video news releases and other visual promotional material.

SEARCH ENGINE OPTIMIZATION

Publicity is about getting media outlets to mention the name of a product, company, or person. For several years Internet marketers have recognized the importance of getting their companies and products listed in the top rankings in search engines. So called efforts at Search Engine Optimization (SEO) involve concerted efforts and specific techniques to attain higher rankings.

While at first glance SEO may not seem like a responsibility of public relations, it would appear to contain the main characteristics for making it so, namely getting a third-party media outlet (i.e., search engine) to mention the company (i.e., search rankings) at no direct cost the company (i.e., no payment for ranking). And, just as PR people can use methods to affect coverage within traditional media, optimizing a website can work to influence results in search engines by using techniques that allow a website to fit within ever-changing search engine ranking criteria. In this way SEO does what PR professionals do, namely obtain good placement in third-party media outlet. Consequently, SEO may soon become an important PR function. (8)

* *

*When writing news releases or posting other material to a company website, PR professionals should include the right **keywords** in an effort to maximize the chance that the information will appear in response to a user's search engine query. In particular, important keywords should appear in the title of the release and in the first few sentences. (9)*

* *

REFERENCES

1. Newman, A.A., "How Dictionaries Define Publicity: The Word of the Year," *New York Times*, December 10, 2007.

2. Tiku, N., "Deskside Story," *Inc*, December 2007.

3. Armstrong, L., "Trash Proof Press Kits," *Exhibitor Magazine*, April 2008.

4. *Oscar Mayer Wienermobile* website.

5. Worthen, B., "Dell Incites Internet Buzz," *Wall Street Journal*, June 3, 2008.

6. Quinton, B., "Sticky Situations," *Promo Magazine*, Oct 1, 2007.

7. Meranus, R., "Public Relations 2.0," *Entrepreneur Magazine*, June 27, 2007.

8. Christ, P., "Internet Technologies and Trends Transforming Public Relations," *Journal of Website Promotion*, 1 (4), 2007.

9. Meranus, R., "Become the Key(word) Master," *Entrepreneur Magazine*, March 14, 2008.

Full text of many of the references can be accessed via links on the support website.

Chapter 16:

Personal Selling

In the past few chapters we saw how marketers can use advertising, sales promotion, and public relations to reach a large number of customers. While these methods of promotion offer many advantages, they each share one major disadvantage: they are a non-personal form of communication. And whether a company is in retailing or manufacturing, sells goods or services, is a large multi-national or a local startup, is out to make a profit or is a non-profit, in all probability at some point they will need to rely on personal contact with customers. In other words, they will need to promote using personal selling.

In this chapter, we define personal selling, look at the advantages and disadvantages, and see how it fits within an organization's promotional strategy. We also see there are a variety of different selling roles available to the marketing organization, including some whose objectives are not tied to getting customers to buy. Finally, we examine several trends facing the personal selling field.

WHAT IS PERSONAL SELLING?

Personal selling is a promotional method in which one party (e.g., salesperson) uses skills and techniques for building personal relationships with another party (e.g., those involved in a purchase decision) resulting in both parties obtaining value. In most cases the "value" for the salesperson is realized through the financial rewards of the sale while the customer's "value" is realized from the benefits obtained from consuming the product. However, as we will discuss, getting a customer to purchase a product is not always the objective of personal selling. For instance, selling may be used for the purpose of simply delivering information.

Because selling involves personal contact, this promotional method often occurs through face-to-face meetings or via telephone conversation, though newer technologies allow contact to take place over the Internet, including using video conferencing or text messaging (e.g., online chat).

Among marketing jobs, more are employed in sales positions than any other marketing-related occupation. In the United States alone, the *U.S. Department of Labor* estimates that over 14 million or about 11% of the overall labor force is directly involved in selling and sales-related positions. (1) Worldwide this figure may be closer to 100 million. Yet these figures vastly underestimate the number of people who are actively engaged in some aspect of selling as part of their normal job responsibilities. While millions of people can easily be seen as holding sales jobs, the promotional techniques used in selling are also part of the day-to-day activities of many who are usually not associated with selling. For instance, top corporate executives, whose job titles are CEO or COO, are continually selling their companies to major customers, stock investors, government officials, and many other stakeholders. The techniques they employ to gain benefits for their companies are the same used by the front-line salesperson to sell to a small customer. Consequently, our discussion of the promotional value of personal selling has implications beyond marketing and sales departments.

• •

Creative artists often find they must convince dealers to stock their work in stores and galleries. In doing so many feel their work alone is enough to convince someone to buy. Yet to be successful many artists are now finding that the product alone is not enough to get a buyer to buy and, instead, are applying basic selling skills when interacting with dealers. (2)

• •

Advantages of Personal Selling

One key advantage personal selling has over other promotional methods is that it is a two-way form of communication. In selling situations the message sender (e.g., salesperson) can adjust the message as they gain feedback from message receivers (e.g., customer). So if a customer does not understand the initial message (e.g., doesn't fully understand how the product works) the salesperson can make adjustments to address questions or concerns. Many non-personal forms of promotion, such as a radio advertisement, are inflexible, at least in the short-term, and cannot be easily adjusted to address questions that arise by the audience experiencing the ad.

The interactive nature of personal selling also makes it the most effective promotional method for building relationships with customers, particularly in the business-to-business market. This is especially important for companies that either sell expensive products or sell lower cost but high volume products (i.e., buyer must purchase in large quantities) that rely heavily on customers making repeat purchases. Because such purchases may take a considerable amount of time to complete and may involve the input of many people at the purchasing company (i.e., buying center), sales success often requires the marketer develop and maintain strong relationships with members of the purchasing company.

Finally, personal selling is the most practical promotional option for reaching customers who are not easily reached through other methods. The best example lies in selling to the business market where, compared to the consumer market, advertising, public relations, and sales promotions are often not well received.

Disadvantages of Personal Selling

Possibly the biggest disadvantage of personal selling is the degree to which this promotional method is misunderstood. Most people have had some bad experiences with salespeople who, in their view, were overly aggressive or even downright annoying.

But as we discuss in Box 16-1, while there are certainly many salespeople that fall into this category, the truth is salespeople are most successful if they focus their efforts on satisfying customers over the long term and not focusing on their own selfish interests.

Box 16-1

A MISUNDERSTOOD FIELD

Here's a quick question: Which of the following mental images comes closest to what you think about when you hear that someone's job involves "selling"?

1. Someone who is highly extroverted and quick with stories that keep everyone laughing.

2. Someone on a used car lot who makes every car sound like a gem.

3. Someone in a clothing store who corrals customers when they first enter and then won't leave them alone.

4. Someone calling at dinner time trying to get the "head of the household" to buy a vacation timeshare.

5. A knowledgeable, hard-working, and highly trained professional who uses finely honed communication techniques to fully understand and satisfy the needs of his/her customers.

If you chose one of the first four options, don't feel bad, you're in tremendous company. Lots of people share the view that selling is something done by people who are manipulative, arrogant, aggressive, greedy, and only concerned about getting the sale. While there certainly are some salespeople that fit these descriptions, today the most successful salespeople are ones who work hard to understand their customers' needs with the ultimate goal of ensuring the customer is satisfied at a high level. Additionally, to fully understand customers, the most important characteristic of a good salesperson is not their ability to carry on a conversation, but their ability to listen to the customer. (3)

Also, personal selling holds a key role in the promotional activities of a large number of organizations. In fact, in the business market, where one company sells products to another company, money spent to support the selling function far exceeds spending on advertising. Thus, while many people have had poor experiences with salespeople, the truth is selling is one of the most important methods for building customer relationships and those successful at selling are much more likely to reflect the description presented in #5. (4)

A second disadvantage of personal selling is the high cost of maintaining this type of promotional effort. Costs incurred in personal selling include:

♦ High cost-per-action (CPA) – As noted in Chapter 11, CPA can be an important measure of the success of promotion spending. Since personal selling involves person-to-person contact, the money spent to support a sales staff can be steep. For instance, in some industries it costs well over (US) $300 each time a salesperson contacts a potential customer regardless of whether a sale is made. These costs include compensation (e.g., salary, commission, bonus), providing support materials, allowances for entertainment spending, office supplies, telecommunication, and much more. With such high costs for maintaining a sales force, this is often not a practical option for selling products that do not generate a large amount of revenue.

♦ Training Costs – Most forms of personal selling require the sales staff be extensively trained on product knowledge, industry information, and selling skills. For companies that require their salespeople to attend formal training programs, the cost of training can be quite high and include such expenses as travel, hotel, meals, and training equipment, while also paying the trainees salary while they attend.

A third disadvantage is that personal promotion is not for everyone. Job turnover in sales is much higher than other marketing positions. For companies that assign salespeople to handle certain customer groups (e.g., geographic territory), turnover may leave a company without representation in a customer group for an extended period of time while the company recruits and trains a replacement.

OBJECTIVES OF PERSONAL SELLING

Personal selling is used to meet the five objectives of promotion in the following ways:

♦ Building Product Awareness – A common task of salespeople, especially when selling in the business markets, is to educate customers on new product offerings. In fact, salespeople serve a major role at industry trade shows where they discuss products with show attendees. But building awareness using personal selling is also important in consumer markets. The advent of controlled word-of-mouth promotion (see Box 16-2) is leading to personal selling becoming a useful mechanism for introducing consumers to new products.

- ◆ <u>Creating Interest</u> – The fact personal selling involves person-to-person communication makes it a natural method for getting customers to experience a product for the first time. In fact, creating interest goes hand-in-hand with building product awareness as sales professionals can often accomplish both objectives during the first encounter with a potential customer.

- ◆ <u>Providing Information</u> – When salespeople engage customers a large part of the conversation focuses on product information. Marketing organizations provide their sales staff with large amounts of sales support, including brochures, research reports, computer programs, and many other forms of informational material.

- ◆ <u>Stimulating Demand</u> – The most important objective of personal selling is to convince customers to make a purchase. As we will see below in our discussion of selling roles, getting customers to buy is the major function of a large segment of selling jobs.

- ◆ <u>Reinforcing the Brand</u> – Most personal selling is intended to build long-term relationships with customers. A strong relationship can only be built over time and requires regular communication with a customer. Meeting with customers on a regular basis allows salespeople to repeatedly discuss their company's products and by doing so helps strengthen customers' knowledge of what the company has to offer.

CLASSIFYING SELLING ROLES

Worldwide millions of people have careers that fit in the personal selling category. However, the actual functions carried out by someone in sales may be quite different. Below we discuss the four major types of selling roles: order getters, order takers, order supporters, and sales supporters. It should be noted that these roles are not mutually exclusive and that a salesperson can perform more than one and possibly all activities.

Order Getters

The role most synonymous with selling is a position in which the salesperson is actively engaged in using his/her skills to obtain orders from customers. Such roles can be further divided into:

New Business Development

A highly challenging yet potentially lucrative sales position is one where the main objective is to find new customers. Sales jobs in this category are often in fields that are very competitive, but offer high rewards for those that are successful. The key distinguishing factor of these positions is that once a sale is made new business salespeople pass customers on to others in their organization who handle account maintenance. These positions include:

- Business Equipment Sales – These salespeople are often found in industries where a company's main profits come from the sale of supplies and services that come after an initial equipment purchase. The key objective of business equipment salespeople is to get buyers to purchase the main piece of equipment for which supplies and services are needed in order for the equipment to function. For instance, traditionally in the photocopier industry business equipment salespeople focus on locating new accounts and once a photocopier sale is made they pass along the account to other sales personnel who handle sales of maintenance and supplies.

- Telemarketing – This category includes product sales over the phone, whether aimed at business or consumer. While in the U.S. laws restrict unsolicited phone selling in the consumer market, the practice is still widely used in the business market.

- Consumer Selling – Certain companies are very aggressive in their use of salespeople to build new consumer business. These include: retailers selling certain high priced consumer products, including furniture, electronics, and clothing; housing products, including real estate, security services, and building replacement products (e.g., windows); and in-home product sellers, including those selling door-to-door, and products sold at "home party" events, such as cosmetics, kitchenware, and decorative products.

Account Management

Most people engaged in sales are not only involved in gaining the initial order, but work to build and maintain relationships with their clients that will hopefully last a long time. Salespeople involved in account management are found across a broad range of industries. Their responsibilities involve all aspects of building customer relationships from initial sale to follow-up account servicing. These include:

- Business-to-Business – These salespeople sell products for business use with an emphasis on follow-up sales. In many cases, business-to-business salespeople have many different items available for sale (i.e., broad and/or deep product line) rather than a single product. So while the initial sale may only result in the buyer purchasing a few products, the potential exists for the buyer to purchase many other products as the buyer-seller relationship grows.

271

- Trade Selling – Sales professionals working for consumer products companies normally do not sell to the final user (i.e., consumer). Instead their role is focused on first getting distributors, such wholesalers and retailers, to handle their products and once this is accomplished, helping distributors sell their product by offering ideas for product advertising, in-store display, and sales promotions.

• •

The boom in Internet marketing has created high demand for salespeople who specialize in selling online advertising. Job recruitment firms report that bidding wars have often occurred between companies trying to lure top salespeople. While demand is strong, companies are being selective preferring salespeople who are at least conversant in the technology side of the Internet. (5)

• •

Order Takers

Selling does not always require a salesperson use methods designed to encourage customers to make a purchase. In fact, the greatest number of people engaged in selling are not order getters, rather they are considered order takers. In this role, salespeople primarily assist customers with a purchase in ways that are much less assertive than how order getters handle their role. As might be expected, compensation for order takers is generally lower than order getters. Among those serving an order taker role are:

♦ Retail Clerks – While some retail salespeople are involved in new business selling, the vast majority of retail employees handle order taking tasks, which range from directing customers to products to handling customer checkout.

♦ Industrial Distributor Clerks – Industrial purchase situations, such as distributors of building products, also have clerks to handle customer purchases.

♦ Customer Service – Order taking is also handled in non face-to-face ways through customer service personnel. Usually this occurs via phone conversation, though newer technologies are allowing for these tasks to be handled through electronic means such as online chat.

Order Supporters

Some salespeople are not engaged in direct selling activity at all. That is, they do not actively sell to the person who is the ultimate customer for their product. Examples of order support salespeople include:

♦ Missionary – These salespeople are used in industries where customers make purchases based on the advice or requirements of others. In this role the salesperson concentrates on selling activities that target those who influence purchases made by the final customer. Two industries in which missionary selling is commonly found are pharmaceuticals, where salespeople, known as **product detailers**, discuss products with doctors (influencers) who then write prescriptions for their patients (final customer) and higher education, where college professors (influencers) select textbooks students (final customer) must use.

> *The relationship between pharmaceutical sales representatives and doctors has been criticized for contributing to the escalating cost of health care. Some critics say that doctors are more likely to prescribe more expensive, though not necessarily more effective, medications when they allow pharmaceutical detailers to talk with them. To educate doctors on the sales practices of medical representatives some medical schools are incorporating role-playing, videos, and other exercises to teach medical students how to deal with such sales situations. (6)*

♦ Controlled Word-of-Mouth Promotion – As discussed in Box 16-2, marketers are experimenting with another type of order supporter who specializes in word-of-mouth promotion. This type of promotion, which also is known by such terms as **buzz marketing** and **advocacy marketing**, is similar to missionary selling in that salespeople do not actively look to make a sale. However, it differs from missionary selling in that salespeople will talk to the eventual purchaser of the product. While still a fairly new approach to personal selling, marketers may one day view this as a standard personal selling option.

Box 16-2

CONTROLLED WORD-OF-MOUTH PROMOTION

One of the most influential forms of promotion occurs when one person speaks highly of a product to someone else, particularly if the message sender is considered an unbiased source of information. (7) Until recently, marketers have had little control over person-to-person promotion that did not involve salespeople (i.e., biased source). However, marketers are beginning to experiment with new methods of promotion that strategically take advantage of the benefits offered by word-of-mouth promotion. Unlike salespeople who often attempt to obtain an order from customers, controlled word-of-mouth promotion uses real people to help spread information about a product but do not directly elicit customer orders. (8)

With controlled word-of-mouth promotion a marketer hires individuals to spread positive information about a product but in a way that does not make it obvious that they are being paid to do so. This technique is especially useful when building awareness of new products and this approach has been dubbed "buzz" marketing as a way to describe its objective of building a high level of awareness for a product. For example, a brewer may form a team of word-of-mouth marketers who visit local taverns and night spots. As part of their job these marketers may "talk up" a new beer sold by the brewer and even purchase the product for some customers. But in the course of doing so some promoters may not directly disclose that they are being compensated by the brewer for their efforts.

Controlled word-of-mouth has received a great deal of publicity though much of it has focused on potential ethical issues. Some have expressed concern that paying people to "act" as if they are interested in a product without any indication of their relationship with the product breaches ethical standards.

As more companies explore controlled word-of-mouth marketing it is expected to become an even more scrutinized form of personal selling.

Sales Supporters

A final group involved in selling assist mostly with the selling activities of other sales professionals. These include:

♦ Technical Specialists – When dealing with the sale of technical products, particularly in the business market, salespeople may need to draw on the expertise of others to help with the process. This is particularly the case when the buying party consists of a buying center. In Chapter 4 we indicated that in business selling many people from different functional areas are involved in the purchase decision. If this buying center includes technical people, such as scientists and engineers, a salesperson may seek assistance from members of her/his own technical staff to help address specific questions.

◆ Office Support – Salespeople also may receive assistance from their company's office staff in the form of promotional materials, setting up sales appointments, finding sales leads, arranging meeting space or organizing trade shows exhibits.

TRENDS IN PERSONAL SELLING

While the basic premise of personal selling, building relationships, has not changed much in the last 50 years, there are a number of developments impacting this method of promotion including:

CUSTOMER INFORMATION SHARING

Possibly the most dramatic change to occur in how salespeople function on a day-to-day basis involves the integration of customer relationship management (CRM) systems into the selling arena. As we discussed in Chapter 3, CRM is the name given to both the technology and the philosophy that drives companies to gain a better understanding of their customers with the goal of building stronger long-term relationships. The essential requirement for an effective CRM system is the need for all customer contact points (e.g., salespeople, customer service, websites) to gather information to share with others in the company.

But CRM has faced some rough times within the sales force for the exact reason it is important: salespeople must share their information. Salespeople historically have been very good at developing relationships and learning about customers, but often loath sharing this since, in effect, information is what makes them important. In the minds of some salespeople, letting go of the information reduces their importance to the company. For example, some salespeople feel sharing all they know about a customer will make them expendable since a company can simply insert someone new at anytime.

While the attitude toward CRM has made its implementation difficult in many companies, salespeople should understand that it is not going away. CRM and information sharing has proven to be critical in maintaining strong customer relations and salespeople must learn to adapt to it.

MOBILE TECHNOLOGY AND WEB-BASED COMPUTING

The move to an information sharing approach is most effective when salespeople have access to information sharing features when they need it most. Mobile technology, such as wireless (WiFi) and cellular Internet access, allows salespeople to retrieve needed information at any time. For example, if a salesperson takes a customer to lunch, she/he can quickly access company material to respond to questions such as how long it may take to receive product if an order is placed.

Additionally, there is a growing trend to make key business applications available through a browser rather than having programs loaded on a salesperson's computer. This enables software applications to be accessed from anywhere. For example, many companies have moved to web-based CRM systems where simply having Internet access allows salespeople to enter and retrieve information. Also, many new office productivity applications, such as word processing and spreadsheets, are now web-accessible.

New generation cellphones or **smartphones** along with other handheld devices, such as **personal digital assistants (PDA)**, lighten the burden of carrying laptop computers. But because these handheld devices are web-enabled they provide access to much of the same information as a standard computer. While the computing power of handheld devices is still underpowered compared to conventional computers, the move to web-based computing may some day make the handheld the main instrument for inputting and outputting information.

• •

Another technology area that has gained acceptance among some salespeople who seek new business is through online business social networks. Like their consumer counterparts, MySpace and Facebook, business social networks evolve based on relationships with others within the network, primarily by having one person invite others to join. For those involved in sales the most popular business social network is Linkedin. Since it is primarily of interest to business people the contacts found through business social networks have the potential to be high quality contacts. (9)

• •

ELECTRONIC SALES PRESENTATIONS

Technology also plays a major role in how sales professionals reach prospects and existing customers. While audio/video conferencing has been available for many years using high-end telecommunications hookups, recent improvements in Internet access speeds, computing power, and meeting software have made this method a practical alternative to face-to-face sales meetings. These options include:

- Online Video Conferencing – Online conferencing essentially acts in the same way as telecommunications videoconferencing, with one big exception, it is delivered over the Internet. Anyone who has an Internet connection knows that delivering video over the Internet can be a trying experience as video often appears to be slow, jittery, and sometimes not even recognizable. But these problems are quickly disappearing and while real time Internet video conferencing (i.e., television quality video and audio) is still not routinely accessible to most salespeople, this is expected to change.

- Web/Phone Conferencing – To offset the problems associated with Internet delivery of real time audio and video, many companies deliver sales presentations using a combination of web and telecommunications. The most widely used are services that use the Internet to deliver visual material (typically a slide presentation) and telecommunications to provide voice conversation. The process has a salesperson arrange a conference time with a prospect who enters the conference by: 1) using his/her web browser to gain access to the visual presentation, and 2) using his/her telephone to call into an audio conference. Splitting the visual and audio feeds allows for smoother presentations since the conference participants' computers need only process the visual material. It should be noted that while audio access is now being carried out over telephone connections, the emergence of telephone over the Internet (i.e., VOIP - voice of internet protocol) may soon help resolve some of the problems that have been encountered when delivering both.

- Online Text Chat – Online chat allows for real time communication between multiple participants using text messaging. While this form of buyer-seller communication may not be very effective at getting customers to make a purchase, it has proven very effective in building initial interest in products. For example, potential customers visiting a website may use the chat feature to ask a few questions about the company's products. Engaging customers this way can then lead to the customer agreeing to a phone call from a salesperson to further discuss the product.

277

· ·

Online chat is being combined with customer tracking software to enable salespeople to watch how a customer is maneuvering around a website. If tracking suggests the customer is showing interest in a product a salesperson can subtly ask if they can assist by sending a text message that appears in chat box visible to the customer. (10)

· ·

ELECTRONIC SALES TRAINING

Developing the skills and techniques needed to be successful at selling requires an extensive commitment by the individual seller and the seller's company to sales training. Sales training is the hallmark of professional selling. If there is one thing that separates the truly successful salesperson from those who are not successful it is the amount of training and preparation they have.

Most organizations employing a sales force offer new salespeople an extensive formal training program, often held at dedicated training facilities. These training programs range from a few days to many months depending on the industry. But once a salesperson has made the move to the field, training does not stop. Those involved in selling must continue to stay abreast of their products, customers, markets, and competitors. While many companies continue to employ the same methods used when they first trained their salespeople, a large number of firms are finding that ongoing training can be just as effective using electronic options, such as delivering training over the Internet, through downloadable computer programs or through interactive CDs or DVDs.

While feedback using electronic means is not as personal as in-person training, sophisticated electronic training programs are effective in educating and testing trainees' knowledge. Also, a real trainer can be contacted very quickly via e-mail, online chat,or by a phone call if a question does arise.

Using electronic delivery the cost to the company for adding or updating training material is inexpensive and quick compared to the cost and time need to produce and ship paper-based materials. Additionally, the use of RSS feeds or email enables salespeople to be immediately notified when new material is made available. This is useful when the sales force must be made aware of a recent change impacting how the product is promoted, such as a price change, new information to be used as comparison to competitor's products, a potential problem with a product or some other adjustment.

Use of Customer Sales Teams

As we noted in our discussion of technical specialists, salespeople may require the assistance of others in their organization in order to effectively deal with prospects. In fact, many companies are moving away from the traditional sales force arrangement where a single salesperson handles nearly all communication with an account in favor of a team approach where multiple people are involved.

Teams consist of individuals from several functional areas such as marketing, manufacturing, distribution, and customer service. In some configurations all members share bonuses if the team meets sales goals. Clearly to be effective a team approach will require the implementation of customer relationship management systems that we discussed earlier.

REFERENCES

1. "Occupational Employment and Wages," *Bureau of Labor Statistics - U.S. Department of Labor.*

2. Miller, K., "Creative Artists Confront Sales Anxiety," *BusinessWeek*, February 6, 2008.

3. Hunter, M., "Shut Up, Listen and Sell," *B to B*, October 8, 2007.

4. For more information on what it takes to be successful at selling see: Anderson, R., Dubinsky, A., and Mehta, R., *Personal Selling: Building Customer Relationships and Partnerships*, Houghton-Mifflin, 2007.

5. Hempel, J., "Hot Job: Selling Web Ads," *Forbes*, October 2 2007.

6. Weintraub, A., "Building Up Docs' Marketing Resistance," *BusinessWeek*, January 18, 2008.

7. Hollis, N., "What's the Word?" *MillwardBrown*, January 2008.

8. For more details on word-of-mouth marketing see *Word of Mouth Marketing Association* website.

9. Bruno, J.B., "New Networking Sites Mean Business," *USA Today*, July 17, 2007.

10. Sloan, P., "Live Chat: Your New Online Salesperson," *Business 2.0*, October 4, 2007.

Full text of many of the references can be accessed via links on the support website.

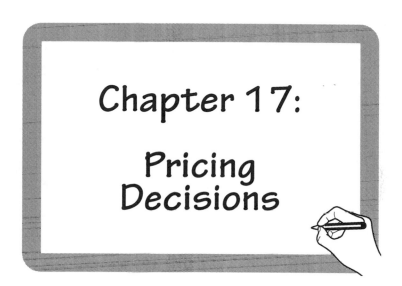

Chapter 17:

Pricing Decisions

What do the following words have in common? Fare, dues, tuition, interest, rent, and fee. The answer is that each of these is a term used to describe what one must pay to acquire benefits from another party. More commonly, most people simply use the word price to indicate what it costs to acquire a product. The pricing decision is a critical one and marketers must consider many factors when arriving at the selling price for their product.

In this chapter we begin a two-part discussion of the pricing component of the Marketer's Toolkit. We start by defining price and see how it has different meaning for different parties to a transaction. We next look at why price is important to marketing and to the organization. Finally, considerable attention is given to the internal and external factors that influence pricing decisions.

WHAT IS PRICE?

In general terms price is a component of an exchange or transaction that takes place between two parties and refers to what must be given up by one party (i.e., buyer) in order to obtain something offered by another party (i.e., seller). Yet this view of price provides a somewhat limited explanation of what price means to participants in the transaction. In fact, price means different things to different buyers and sellers in an exchange:

♦ Buyers' View – For those making a purchase, such as final customers, price refers to what must be given up to obtain benefits. In most cases what is given up is financial consideration (e.g., money) in exchange for acquiring access to a good or service. But financial consideration is not always what the buyer gives up. Sometimes in a **barter** situation a buyer acquires a product by giving up his/her own product. For instance, two farmers may exchange cattle for crops. Also, as we discuss in Box 17-1, buyers may also give up other things to acquire the benefits of a product that are not direct financial payments (e.g., time required to learn to use the product).

Box 17-1

PRICE VS. VALUE

For most customers price by itself is not the key factor when considering a purchase. This is because most customers compare the entire marketing offering and do not simply make purchase decisions based solely on a product's price. When a purchase situation arises price is one of several variables customers evaluate when they mentally assess a product's overall value.

As we discussed in Chapter 1, value refers to the perception of benefits received for what someone must give up. Since price often reflects an important part of what someone gives up, a customer's perceived value of a product will be affected by a marketer's pricing decision. An easy way to see this is to view value as a calculation:

$$\text{Value} \quad = \quad \frac{\text{perceived benefits received}}{\text{perceived price paid}}$$

For the buyer the value of a product changes as perceived price paid and/or perceived benefits received change. But the price paid in a transaction is not only financial it can also involve other things a buyer may be giving up. For example, in addition to paying money a customer may have to spend time learning to use a product, pay to have an old product removed, close down current operations while a product is installed or incur other expenses.

For marketers the **value equation** suggests that to improve customers' perception of value requires they either increase benefits offered, while maintaining price levels, or lower price for current benefits offered.

♦ <u>Sellers' View</u> – To the selling organization, price reflects the revenue generated for each product sold and is an important factor in determining profit. For those responsible for marketing decisions price serves as a marketing tool and is a key element in marketing promotions. For example, most retailers highlight product pricing in their advertising campaigns.

• •

For some customers price is the number one reason they purchase a product. Marketers targeting these customers are likely to promote their low pricing as the key marketing advantage. An example can be found with Charles Shaw that sells low-price wines nicknamed Two Buck Chuck. These wines sell for around (US) $2 a bottle and are only sold in California. The low price strategy has been very successful. In its first five years on the market over 300 million bottles were sold and in 2006 Two Buck Chuck accounted for 8 percent of all wine sales in California. (1)

• •

Price is commonly confused with the notion of **cost** as in "*I paid a high cost for buying my new cell phone.*" Technically these are different concepts. Price is what a buyer pays to acquire products from a seller. Cost concerns the seller's investment (e.g., manufacturing expense) in the product exchanged with a buyer. For marketing organizations seeking to make a profit the hope is price will exceed cost so the organization can see financial gain from the transaction.

Finally, while product pricing is a main topic for discussion when a company is examining its overall profitability, pricing decisions are not limited to for-profit companies. Not-for-profit organizations, such as charities, educational institutions, and industry trade groups, also set prices. For instance, charities seeking to raise money may set different "target" levels for donations that reward donors with increases in status (e.g., name in newsletter), gifts, or other benefits. While a charitable organization may not call it a "price" in their promotional material, in reality these donations are equivalent to price since donors are required to give a contribution in order to obtain something of value.

IMPORTANCE OF PRICING

When marketers talk about what they do as part of their responsibilities for marketing products, the tasks associated with setting price are often not at the top of the list. Marketers are much more likely to discuss activities related to promotion, product development, marketing research, and other tasks often considered the more interesting and exciting parts of the job.

One reason for the lack of attention paid to pricing is that many believe price setting is a mechanical process requiring the marketer to utilize financial tools, such as spreadsheets, to build their case for setting price levels. While pricing may not tap into a marketer's creative skills to the same degrees as other marketing tasks, pricing decisions can have important consequences for the marketing organization and the attention given by the marketer to pricing is just as important as the attention given to more recognizable marketing activities.

Some reasons pricing is important include:

Most Flexible Marketing Decision

For marketers price is the most adjustable of all marketing decisions. Unlike product and distribution decisions, which can take months or years to change, or some forms of promotion, which can be time consuming to alter (e.g., creating a new television advertisement), price can be changed very rapidly. The flexibility of pricing decisions is particularly important in times when the marketer seeks to quickly stimulate demand or respond to competitor price actions. For instance, a marketer can agree to a field salesperson's request to lower price for a potential prospect during a phone conversation. Likewise a marketer in charge of online operations can raise prices on hot selling products with the click of a few website buttons.

Need for Setting the Right Price

Pricing decisions made hastily without sufficient research, analysis, and strategic evaluation can lead the marketing organization to lose revenue. Prices set too low may mean the company is missing out on additional profits that could be earned if the target market is willing to spend more to acquire the product. Additionally, attempts to raise an initially low priced product to a higher price may be met by customer resistance if they feel the marketer is attempting to take advantage of its customers. Prices set too high can also impact revenue as it prevents interested customers from purchasing the product. Setting the right price level takes considerable market knowledge and, especially with new products, testing of different pricing options.

Trigger of Early Perception

Often times customers' perceptions of a product is formed as soon as they learn the price, such as when a product is first seen in a store. While the final decision to make a purchase may be based on the value offered by the entire marketing offering (i.e., actual and augmented product), it is possible the customer will not evaluate a marketer's product at all based on price alone. It is important for marketers to know if customers are more likely to dismiss a product when all they know is its price. If so, pricing may become the most important of all marketing decisions if it can be shown that customers are avoiding learning more about the product because of the price.

Important Part of Sales Promotion

Many times price adjustments are part of sales promotions that lower price for a short term to stimulate interest in the product. However, as we noted in our discussion of promotional pricing in Chapter 14, marketers must guard against the temptation to adjust prices too frequently since continually increasing and decreasing price can lead customers to be conditioned to anticipate price reductions and, consequently, withhold purchase until the price reduction occurs again.

Affects Demand of Other Products

How a company prices one product can affect the overall demand for other products. This is especially the case where the demand for other products is directly tied to the demand for a main product. This is a consideration for marketers making the bulk of their profits from the sale of goods and services used to support the main product. For example, operators of gambling casinos often entice customers by offering low hotel room rates knowing they can generate higher revenue when customers visit the casino. Even some airlines have experimented with very low cost rates hoping to make up the difference by charging for in-flight food and entertainment. (2)

• •

For digital goods, companies are finding that giving away products for free can pay big dividends. Yahoo, Google, and many other online companies offer a host of free services, including email, blogging software, online games, and photo storage space but make up for this through the sale of advertising. Providers of other types of digital products, such as books and music, may soon find that giving away some products at very low prices will enhance the sale of other offerings. For example, musical groups may find that allowing free downloads of their latest music will bolster the sales obtained through touring and selling group merchandise. (3)

• •

285

FACTORS AFFECTING PRICING DECISION

For the remainder of this chapter we look at factors that affect how marketers set price. The final price for a product may be influenced by many factors which can be categorized into two main groups:

♦ Internal Factors – When setting price, marketers must take into consideration several factors which are the result of company decisions and actions. To a large extent these factors are controlled by the company and, if necessary, can be altered. However, while the organization may have control over these factors making a quick change is not always realistic. For instance, product pricing may depend heavily on the productivity of a manufacturing facility (e.g., how much can be produced within a certain period of time). The marketer knows increasing productivity can reduce the cost of producing each product, which allows the marketer to potentially lower the product's price. But increasing productivity may require major changes at the manufacturing facility that take time (and are potentially costly) and will not translate into lower price products for a considerable period of time.

♦ External Factors – There are a number of influencing factors which are not controlled by the company but will impact pricing decisions. Understanding these factors requires the marketer conduct research to monitor what is happening in each market the company serves since the effect of these factors can vary by market.

Below we provide a detailed discussion of both internal and external factors.

Internal Factors

The pricing decision can be affected by factors that are controlled by the marketing organization, including:

MARKETING OBJECTIVES AND STRATEGY

Marketing decisions are guided by the objectives established by the leaders of the organization. While we will discuss this in more detail when we cover marketing planning and strategy in Chapter 20, for now it is important to understand that all marketing decisions, including price, are impacted by the strategy formulated to meet marketing objectives. For instance, marketers whose objective is to be known as an affordable alternative to high-end products would be expected to have a marketing strategy that includes having price set at or below the price of most competitors.

It should be noted that not all companies view price as a key selling feature and, consequently, it may not play a major role in helping the marketer meet its objective. Some firms, for example those seeking to be viewed as market leaders in product quality, deemphasize price and concentrate on a strategy highlighting non-price benefits (e.g., quality, durability, service, etc.). Such non-price competition can help the company avoid potential price wars that often break out between competitive firms that follow a market share objective (discussed in Chapter 20) and use price as a key selling feature.

COSTS

For many for-profit companies, the starting point for setting a product's price is to first determine how much it will cost to get the product to their customers. Obviously, whatever price customers pay must exceed the cost of producing a good or delivering a service otherwise the company will lose money.

When analyzing cost, the marketer will consider all costs needed to get the product to market including those associated with production, marketing, distribution, and company administration (e.g., office expense). These costs can be divided into two main categories:

Variable Costs

These costs are directly associated with the production and sale of products and may change as the level of production or sales changes. Typically variable costs are evaluated on a per-unit basis since the cost is directly associated with individual items. Most variable costs involve costs of items that are either components of the product (e.g., parts, packaging) or are directly associated with creating the product (e.g., electricity to run an assembly line). However, there are also marketing variable costs, such as coupons, which are likely to cost the company more as sales increase (i.e., customers using the coupon). Variable costs, especially for product components, tend to decline as more units are produced. This is due to the producing company's ability to purchase product components for lower prices since component suppliers often provide discounted pricing for large quantity purchases (see *Quantity Discounts* discussion in Chapter 18).

Fixed Costs

Also referred to as overhead costs, these represent costs the marketing organization incurs that are not affected by level of production or sales. For example, for a manufacturer of writing instruments that has just built a new production facility, whether they produce one pen or one million they will still need to pay the monthly mortgage for the building. From the marketing side, fixed costs may also exist in the form of such expenditures as fielding a sales force, carrying out an advertising campaign, and paying a service to host the company's website. These costs are fixed because there is a level of commitment to spending that is not affected by production or sales levels. While fixed costs are normally not associated with either level of production or sales volume, marketers still must factor these into their price though, as discussed in Box 17-2, doing so is not always easy.

Box 17-2

WHAT'S THE REAL COST?

Determining the cost for an individual unit can be a complicated process. While variable costs are often determined on a per-unit basis, applying fixed costs to individual products is less straightforward. For example, if a company manufactures five different products in one manufacturing plant how should it distribute the plant's fixed costs (e.g., mortgage, production workers' cost) over the five products?

In general, a company assigns fixed costs to individual products if the company can clearly associate the costs with the product such as assigning the cost of operating production machines based on how much time it takes to produce each item or assigning advertising expense to the product an advertising campaign is promoting.

Alternatively, some firms may instruct the marketing department to automatically add a certain percentage of the variable cost as a way to cover fixed costs. For instance, final cost for products may be determined by adding an additional 20 percent on top of the per-unit variable cost.

Finally, if it is too difficult to associate costs to specific products the company may simply allocate total fixed costs by general category of product and assign it on some percentage basis. For example, for a discount retailer's website that sells many products the cost of operating the website may be distributed among the product categories (e.g., books, hardware, women's clothing, etc.) based on user traffic, category sales as a percentage of overall sales, or some other measure. Using this approach individual products may not see a fixed cost allocation, though the overall product category will.

No matter which method is used, setting price based only on the cost of the materials and labor needed to produce a product may significantly underestimate the true costs incurred. As we will see in Chapter 18, product cost is only one of many considerations that go into determining the final price.

OWNERSHIP OPTIONS

An important decision faced by marketers as they are formulating their pricing strategy deals with who will have ownership of the product (i.e., holds legal title) once an exchange has taken place. There are two basic options available:

- <u>Buyer Owns Product Outright</u> – The most common ownership option is for the buyer to make payment and then obtain full ownership. Under this condition the price is generally reflective of the full value of the product.

- <u>Buyer Has Right to Use but Does Not Have Ownership</u> – Many products, especially those labeled as services, permit customers to make payment in exchange for the right to use a product but not to own it. This is seen in the form of usage, rental, or lease payment for such goods and services as: mobile phone services, manufacturing equipment, and Internet access. In most cases, the price paid by the customer is not reflective of the full value of the product compared to what the customer would have paid for ownership of the product. It should be noted that under some lease or rental plans there may be an option for customers to buy the product outright (e.g., car lease) though this often requires a final payment.

External Market Factors

The pricing decision can be affected by factors that are not directly controlled by the marketing organization. These factors include:

ELASTICITY OF DEMAND

Marketers should never rest on their marketing decisions. They must continually use marketing research and their own judgment to determine whether marketing decisions need to be adjusted. When it comes to adjusting price, the marketer must understand what effect a change in price is likely to have on target market demand for a product.

Understanding how price changes impact the market requires the marketer have a firm understanding of the concept economists call elasticity of demand, which relates to how purchase quantity changes as prices change. Elasticity is evaluated under the assumption that no other changes are being made (i.e., "all things being equal") and only price is adjusted. The logic is to see how price by itself will affect overall demand. Obviously, the chance of nothing else changing in the market but the price of one product is often unrealistic. For example, competitors may react to the marketer's price change by changing the price on their product. Despite this, elasticity analysis does serve as a useful tool for estimating market reaction.

Elasticity deals with three types of demand scenarios:

- Elastic Demand – Products are considered to exist in a market that exhibits elastic demand when a certain percentage change in price results in a larger and opposite percentage change in demand. For example, if the price of a product increases (decreases) by 10 percent the demand for the product is likely to decline (rise) by greater than 10 percent.

- Inelastic Demand – Products are considered to exist in an inelastic market when a certain percentage change in price results in a smaller and opposite percentage change in demand. For example, if the price of a product increases (decreases) by 10 percent, the demand for the product is likely to decline (rise) by less than 10 percent.

- Unitary Demand – This demand occurs when a percentage change in price results in an equal and opposite percentage change in demand. For example, if the price of a product increases (decreases) by 10 percent, the demand for the product is likely to decline (rise) by 10 percent.

For marketers the important issue with elasticity of demand is to understand how it impacts company revenue. In general the following scenarios apply to making price changes for a given type of market demand:

- For Elastic Markets – Increasing price lowers total revenue while decreasing price increases total revenue.

- For Inelastic Markets – Increasing price raises total revenue while decreasing price lowers total revenue.

- For Unitary Markets – There is no change in revenue when price is changed.

. . . .

Many companies assume raising price will have a negative effect on sales. But if marketers offer a product perceived as providing high value to customers then the marketer is in a sense creating its own inelastic market. This situation can exist under several conditions such as when customers are very supportive and loyal to the company or if customers view the company's products as unique. Under these conditions a price increase can be passed along without too much impact on demand. (4)

. . . .

COMPETITOR PRICING

Marketers will undoubtedly look to competitors for indications of how price should be set. For many marketers of consumer products researching competitive pricing is relatively easy, particularly when Internet search tools are used. Price analysis can be somewhat more complicated for products sold to the business market since final price may be affected by a number of factors including if competitors allow customers to negotiate their final price.

Almost all marketing decisions, including pricing, will include an evaluation of competitors' offerings. The impact of this information on the actual setting of price depends on the competitive nature of the market. For instance, products that dominate markets and are viewed as market leaders may not be heavily influenced by competitor pricing since they are in a commanding position to set prices as they see fit. On the other hand in markets where a clear leader does not exist, the pricing of competitive products will be carefully considered. Marketers must not only research competitive prices but must also pay close attention to how these companies will respond to the marketer's pricing decisions. For instance, in highly competitive industries, such as gasoline or airline travel, companies may respond quickly to competitors' price adjustments, thereby, reducing the effect of such changes.

. . . .

As noted earlier, pricing is the most flexible of all marketing decisions. This allows marketers to respond quickly to changes made by a competitor. As an example, three leading U.S. wireless companies, AT&T, T-Mobile, and Verizon all introduced a flat-fee, unlimited calling within a few hours of each other. Additionally, all plans were offered at the same (US) $99 rate. Competition in the cellphone market has become so intense that some experts feel this is just the beginning of highly competitive pricing. (5)

. . . .

While gathering pricing information on products offered by competitors is research that most marketers are accustom to performing, there is other product pricing that may also affect marketers as discussed in Box 17-3.

Box 17-3

PRICING OF PRODUCTS THAT ARE NOT DIRECT COMPETITORS

In some cases pricing decisions may be impacted by products that are not considered direct competitors. Here are two examples:

Related Product Pricing

Products offering new ways for solving customer needs may look to pricing of products that customers are currently using even though these other products may not appear to be direct competitors. For example, a marketer of a new online golf instruction service that allows customers to access golf instruction via their computer may look at prices charged by local golf professionals for in-person instruction to gauge where to set its price. While on the surface online golf instruction may not be a direct competitor to a golf instructor, marketers for the online service can use the cost of in-person instruction as a reference point for setting price.

Primary Product Pricing

As we discussed in Chapter 6, marketers may sell products viewed as complementary to a primary product. For instance, Bluetooth headsets are considered complementary to the primary product cellphones. The pricing of complementary products may be affected by pricing changes made to the primary product since customers may compare the price for complementary products based on the primary product price. To illustrate, companies selling accessory products for the Apple iPod may do so at a cost that is only 10 percent of the purchase price of the iPod. However, if Apple were to dramatically drop the price, for instance by 50 percent, the accessory at its present price would now be 20 percent of the of iPod price. This may be perceived by the market as a doubling of the accessory's price. To maintain its perceived value the accessory marketer may need to respond to the iPod price drop by also lowering the price of the accessory.

CUSTOMER AND CHANNEL PARTNER EXPECTATIONS

Possibly the most obvious external factors influencing price setting are the expectations of customers and channel partners. As we discussed, when it comes to making a purchase decision customers assess the overall "value" of a product much more than they assess the price. When deciding on a price marketers need to conduct customer research to determine what **price points** are acceptable. Pricing beyond these price points could discourage customers from purchasing.

Firms within the marketer's channels of distribution also must be considered when determining price. Distribution partners expect to receive financial compensation for their efforts, which usually means they will receive a percentage of the final selling price. This percentage or margin between what they pay the marketer to acquire the product and the price they charge their customers must be sufficient for the distributor to cover their costs and also earn a desired profit.

• •

In addition to understanding how potential customers respond to price, a company may also need to consider how existing customers will respond. This is particularly important when a company is weighing a decision to decrease price. Apple faced this two months after the launch of their iPhone product. In order to reach a wider market Apple reduced the price of the iPhone by (US) $200. Customers who paid the higher price were not happy with this decision. To help calm existing customers' concerns over the new pricing strategy Apple awarded them with (US) $100 store credits. (6)

• •

CURRENCY CONSIDERATIONS

Product pricing can be dramatically altered by international monetary exchange rates. A company seeking to be a low-price market leader may find this strategy works in its home market but currency differences may move its product's price to a mid-price level in other countries. This could dramatically impact the perceived value of the product by customers in these markets. Any marketer selling internationally must be very aware of the price of its products in foreign countries once the price has been converted into the local currency.

GOVERNMENT REGULATION

Marketers must be aware of regulations impacting how price is set in the markets in which their products are sold. These regulations are primarily government enacted meaning that there may be legal ramifications if the rules are not followed. Price regulations can come from any level of government and vary widely in their requirements. For instance, in some industries, government regulation may set **price ceilings** (how high prices may be set) while in other industries there may be **price floors** (how low prices may be set). Additional areas of potential regulation include: **deceptive pricing**, **price discrimination**, **predatory pricing**, and **price fixing**.

Finally, when selling beyond their home market, marketers must recognize that local regulations may make pricing decisions different for each market. This is particularly a concern when selling to international markets where failure to abide by regulations can lead to severe penalties. Consequently marketers must have a clear understanding of regulations in each market they serve.

• •

*As we will discuss in Chapter 18, for retail products sold to the final consumer through retail outlets, manufacturers have followed a strategy of setting a manufacturer's suggested retail price (MSRP). In most cases the manufacturer not only suggests a price but also indicates that this is the minimum price at which a product may be sold by its retailers (also called **resale price maintenance**). But many retailers have chosen to ignore the MSRP and have tended to determine final price in ways they see fit, which could be lower or higher than the MSRP. However, in 2007 the U.S. Supreme Court overturned a nearly 100 year-old ruling that, in most cases, allowed retailers to set final price and instead gave manufacturers the right to set suggested prices that retailer must follow. (7) Within one year of the decision the number of manufacturers requiring retailers to abide by minimum pricing requirements jumped dramatically with one retailer reporting that 100 out of 465 suppliers set minimum price policies. (8)*

• •

REFERENCES

1. "How a $2 Bottle Transformed the Wine Industry," *MSNBC*, May 28, 2007.
2. "Free Love," *Trendwatching*, March 2008.
3. Anderson, C., "Free! Why $0.00 Is the Future of Business," *Wired*, February 25, 2008.
4. Martin, J., "Raising Prices, Keeping Customers," *Fortune*, September 13, 2007.
5. Regan, K., "Rumbles of Wireless Price War Getting Louder," *E-Commerce Times*, February 20, 2008.
6. *Apple* website.
7. Leegin Creative Leather Products vs. Psk Inc., *U.S. Supreme Court*, June 28, 2007.
8. Pereira, J., "Price-Fixing Makes Comeback After Supreme Court Ruling," *Wall Street Journal*, August 18, 2008.

Full text of many of the references can be accessed via links on the support website.

Chapter 18:

Setting Price

In Chapter 17 our coverage centered on understanding the impact pricing decisions have on marketing strategy and how internal and external factors are likely to affect price setting. With this groundwork laid, we turn our attention to the methods marketers use to determine the price they will charge for their products.

The primary emphasis in this chapter is to look at pricing as a five-step process. The process includes examination of: company objectives, approaches to setting an initial price, different types of price adjustments marketers make before settling on a final selling price, and payment options. Finally, we discuss the issues of bid and auction pricing and how these affect pricing strategy.

STEPS IN THE PRICE SETTING PROCESS

For some marketers more time is spent agonizing over price than any other marketing decision. Many times this is due to a lack of understanding of the factors that should be considered when faced with pricing decisions. To address this we take the approach that price setting consists of a series of decisions or steps the marketer makes. The steps include:

1. Examine Objectives
2. Determine an Initial Price
3. Set Standard Price Adjustments
4. Determine Promotional Price Adjustments
5. State Payment Options

While this process serves as a useful guide for making price decisions, not all marketers follow this step-by-step approach. Many marketers may choose to bypass Steps 3 and 4 altogether. Additionally, it is important to understand that finding the right price is often a trial-and-error exercise where continual testing is needed.

Like all other marketing decisions, marketing research is critical to determining the optimal selling price. Consequently, the process laid out here is intended to open the marketer's eyes to the options to consider when setting price and is in no way presented as a guide for setting the "perfect" price.

• •

*Some companies have turned to computerized methods for helping set the right price. So called **price-optimization software** programs take into consideration many of the internal and external factors discussed in Chapter 17 along with other variables, such as sales history, in order to arrive at an ideal price. For retailers using the software other variables that may be factored in include perceived image, location of competitors' stores, and seasonal consideration. (1)*

• •

STEP 1: EXAMINE OBJECTIVES

As we discussed in Chapter 17, pricing decisions are driven by the objectives set by the management of the organization. These objectives come at two levels. First, the overall objectives of the company guide all decisions for all functional areas (e.g., marketing, production, human resources, finance, etc.). Guided by these objectives the marketing department will set its own objectives which may include financial objectives, such as **return on investment (ROI)**, cash flow, and maximize profits, or marketing objectives, such as market share, level of product awareness, and increase in store traffic, to name a few (see more discussion of *Marketing Objectives* in Chapter 20.).

Pricing decisions like all other marketing decisions are used to help the department meet its objectives. For instance, if the marketing objective is to build market share it is likely the marketer will set the product price at a level that is at or below the price of similar products offered by competitors.

Also, the price setting process looks to whether the decisions made are in line with the decisions made for the other marketing areas (i.e., target market, product, distribution, promotion). Thus, if a company with a strong brand name targets high-end consumers with a high quality, full-featured product, the pricing decision would follow the marketer's desire to have the product be considered a high-end product. In this case the price would be set high relative to competitors' products that do not offer as many features or do not have an equally strong brand name.

STEP 2: DETERMINE AN INITIAL PRICE

With the objectives in Step 1 providing guidance for setting price, the marketer next begins the task of determining an initial price level. We say initial because in many industries this step involves setting a starting point from which further changes may be made before the customer pays the final price.

Sometimes called **list price** or **published price**, marketers often use this as a promotional or negotiating tool as they move through the other price setting steps. For companies selling to consumers, this price also leads to a projection of the recommended selling price at the retail level often called the **manufacturer's suggested retail price (MSRP)**. The MSRP may or may not be the final price for which products are sold. For strong brands that are

297

highly sought by consumers the MSRP may in fact be the price at which the product will be sold. But in many other cases, as we will see, the price setting process results in the price being different based on adjustments made by the marketer and others in the distribution channel (see Box 18-1).

Box 18-1

PRICING AND THE DISTRIBUTION CHANNEL

Some marketers utilize multiple channel partners to handle product distribution. For marketers selling through resellers the pricing decision is complicated by resellers' need to earn a profit and marketers' need to have some control over the product's price to the final customer. In these cases setting price involves more than only worrying about what the direct customer (e.g., retailer) is willing pay, since the marketer must also evaluate pricing decisions made by resellers.

To see how problems arise, assume a marketer sets an MSRP of (US) $1.99 for a product selling through a distribution channel. This channel consists of wholesalers who must pay the marketer $1.89 to purchase the product, and retailers who in turn buy the product from wholesalers. In this example it is unlikely the retailer will sell the product at the MSRP since the wholesaler will add to the $1.89 purchase price to increase its profit. The retailer in turn will add to the price it pays to the wholesaler when selling to consumers. In this scenario it is possible the final price to the consumer will be closer to $2.99 than the $1.99 MSRP.

As this example shows marketers must take care in setting price so that all channel partners feel it is worth their effort to handle the product (see *Trade Allowances* discussion below). In fact, resellers may balk at handling a marketer's product if they do not see sufficient value. Going back to our example, if the retailer feels the product will not sell above the MSRP then the retailer has little incentive to stock the product.

Clearly sales can be dramatically different than what the marketer forecasts if the selling price to the final customer differs significantly from what the marketer expects. For instance, a marketer's sales may be lower than forecast if the marketing organization's forecast was based on one price but resellers decided to sell at a price that is 25 percent higher than the marketer's preferred price.

When resellers are involved, marketers must recognize that all members of the channel will seek to profit when a sale is made. If a marketer seeks to sell the product at a certain retail price (e.g., MSRP) then the price charged to the first channel member to handle the product can potentially influence the final selling price.

Marketers have at their disposal several approaches for setting the initial price which include:

♦ Cost Pricing

♦ Market Pricing

♦ Competitive Pricing

Cost Pricing

Under cost pricing the marketer primarily looks at product costs (e.g., variable and fixed) as the key factor in determining the initial price. This method offers the advantage of being easy to implement as long as costs are known. But one major disadvantage is that it does not take into consideration the target market's demand for the product. This could present major problems if the product is operating in a highly competitive market where competitors frequently alter their prices.

There are several types of cost pricing methods including:

MARKUP PRICING

This pricing method, often utilized by resellers who acquire products from suppliers, uses a percentage increase on top of product cost to arrive at an initial price. A major general retailer, such as Wal-Mart, may apply a set percentage for each product category (e.g., women's clothing, automotive, garden supplies, etc.) making the pricing consistent for all like-products. Alternatively, the predetermined percentage may be a number that is identified with the marketing objectives (e.g., required 20% ROI).

For resellers that purchase thousands of products (e.g., retailers) the simplicity inherent in markup pricing makes it a more attractive pricing option than more time-consuming methods. However, the advantage of ease of use is sometimes offset by the disadvantage that products may not always be optimally priced resulting in products that are priced too high or too low given the demand for the product.

As discussed in Box 18-2, markup can be done as either a percentage of cost or as a percentage of selling price.

Box 18-2

DIFFERENT WAYS TO CALCULATE MARKUP

Resellers differ in how they use markup pricing with some using the Markup-on-Cost method and others using the Markup-on-Selling-Price method. We demonstrate each using an item that costs a reseller (US) $50 to purchase from a supplier and sells to customers for (US) $65.

Markup-on-Cost
Using this method, markup is reflected as a percentage by which initial price is set above product cost as reflected in this formula:

$$\frac{\text{Markup Amount}}{\text{Item Cost}} = \text{Markup Percentage}$$

$$\frac{\$15}{\$50} = 30\%$$

The calculation for setting initial price using Markup-on-Cost is determined by simply multiplying the cost of each item by a predetermined percentage then adding the result to the cost:

$$\text{Item Cost} + (\text{Item Cost} \times \text{Markup Percentage}) = \text{Price}$$
$$\$50 \ + \ (50 \times .30 = \$15) \ = \$65$$

Markup-on-Selling-Price
Many resellers, and in particular retailers, discuss their markup not in terms of Markup-on-Cost but as a reflection of price. That is, the markup is viewed as a percentage of the selling price and not as a percentage of cost as it is with the Markup-on-Cost method. For example, using the same information as was used in the Markup-on-Cost, the Markup-on-Selling-Price is reflected in this formula:

$$\frac{\text{Markup Amount}}{\text{Selling Price}} = \text{Markup Percentage}$$

$$\frac{\$15}{\$65} = 23\%$$

The calculation for setting initial price using Markup-on-Selling-Price is:

$$\frac{\textbf{Item Cost}}{\textbf{(1.00 – Markup Percentage)}} = \textbf{Price}$$

$$\frac{\$50}{(1.00 - .23)} = \$65$$

Why Two Methods?

So why do some resellers use Markup-on-Cost while others use Markup-on-Selling-Price? One answer is that it is a traditional way for resellers in certain industries to discuss how they arrive at price (e.g., *"We only make 5% over what we pay for the product"*). While this may explain why markup is used over other pricing methods, it does not explain why some resellers choose Markup-on-Cost while others use Markup-on-Selling-Price. The answer to this lies more with promotion than with pricing. In particular, Markup-on-Selling-Price is believed to aid promotion, especially for resellers who market themselves as low-price leaders. This is because the amount of money a reseller makes in percentage terms is always lower when calculated using Markup-on-Selling-Price than it is with Markup-on-Cost.

For example, in the Markup-on-Cost example where the markup is 30%, the gross profit is $15 ($65-$50). If the reseller using Markup-on-Selling-Price received a gross profit of $15 its markup would only be 23 percent ($50/[1.00-.23] = $65). Consequently, a retailer's advertisement may say: *"We Make Little, But Our Customers Save a Lot"* and back this up by saying they only make a small percentage on each sale. When in reality how much they make in monetary terms may be equal to another retailer who uses Markup-on-Cost and reports a higher markup percentage.

Cost-Plus Pricing

In the same way markup pricing arrives at price by adding a certain percentage to the product's cost, cost-plus pricing also adds to the cost by using a fixed monetary amount rather than percentage. For instance, a contractor hired to renovate a homeowner's bathroom will estimate the cost of doing the job by adding his/her total labor cost to the cost of the materials used in the renovation. The homeowner's selection of ceramic tile to be used in the bathroom is likely to have little effect on the labor needed to install it whether it is a low-end, low-priced tile or a high-end, premium-priced tile. Assuming most materials in the bathroom project are standard sizes and configuration, any change in the total price for the renovation is a result of changes in material costs while labor costs are constant.

BREAKEVEN PRICING

Breakeven pricing is associated with **breakeven analysis**, which is a forecasting tool used by marketers to determine how many products must be sold before the company starts realizing a profit. Like the markup method, breakeven pricing does not directly consider market demand when determining price, however it does indicate the minimum level of demand that is needed before a product will show a profit. From this the marketer can then assess whether the product can realistically achieve these levels.

The formula for determining breakeven takes into consideration both variable and fixed costs (discussed in Chapter 17) as well as price, and is calculated as follows:

$$\frac{\text{Fixed Cost}}{\text{Price} - \text{Variable Cost Per Unit}} = \frac{\text{Number of Units Needed}}{\text{to Breakeven}}$$

For example, assume a company operates a single-product manufacturing plant that has a total fixed cost (e.g., purchase of equipment, mortgage, etc.) per year of (US) $3,000,000 and the variable cost (e.g., raw materials, labor, electricity, etc.) is $45.00 per unit. If the company sells the product directly to customers for $120, it will require the company to sell 40,000 units to breakeven.

$$\frac{\$3,000,000}{\$120 - \$45} = 40,000 \text{ units}$$

Again we must emphasize that marketers must determine whether the demand (i.e., number of units needed to breakeven) is realistically attainable. Simply plugging in a number for price without knowing how the market will respond to that figure means that this method has little value.

Note: A common mistake when performing breakeven analysis is to report the breakeven in a monetary value such a breakeven in dollars (e.g., results reported as $40,000 instead of 40,000 units). The calculation presented above is a measure of units that need to be sold. Clearly it is easy to turn this into a revenue breakeven analysis by multiplying the units needed by the selling price. In our example, 40,000 units x $120 = $4,800,000.

. . . .

Major airlines have struggled in recent years in the wake of fierce competition and sharp increases in fuel costs. In setting ticket prices during turbulent times, such as when oil prices rise sharply, airlines may only focus on breakeven pricing and hope that things will improve in the long-term so they can return to realizing a profit. (2)

. . . .

Market Pricing

A second method for setting initial price is market pricing. Under the market pricing method cost is not the main factor driving price decisions, rather initial price is based on analysis of marketing research in which customer expectations are measured. The main goal is to learn what customers in an organization's target market are likely to perceive as an acceptable price. Of course this price should also help the organization meet its marketing objectives.

Market pricing is one of the most common methods for setting price, and the one that seems most logical given marketing's focus on satisfying customers. So if this is the most logical approach why don't all companies follow it? The main reason is that using the market pricing approach requires a strong marketing research effort to measure customer reaction. For many marketers it is not feasible to spend the time and money it takes to do this right. Additionally for some products, especially new high-tech products, customers are not always knowledgeable enough about the product to know what an acceptable price level should be. Consequently, some marketers may forego market pricing in favor of other approaches.

For those marketers who use market pricing, options include:

♦ Backward Pricing

♦ Psychological Pricing

♦ Price Lining

BACKWARD PRICING

In some marketing organizations the price the market is willing to pay for a product is an important determinant of many other marketing decisions. This is likely to occur when the market has a clear perception of what it believes is an acceptable level of pricing. For example, customers may question a product carrying a price tag that is double that of a competitor's offerings but is perceived to offer only minor improvements compared to other products. In these markets it is important to undertake research to learn whether customers have mentally established price points or a **reference price** for products in a certain product category. The marketer can learn this by surveying customers with such questions as *"How much do you think these types of products should cost you?"*

In situations where a price range is ingrained in the market, the marketer may need to use this price as the starting point for many decisions and work backwards to develop product, promotion, and distribution plans. For instance, assume a company sells products through retailers. If the market is willing to pay (US)$199 for a product but is resistant to pricing that is higher, the marketer will work backwards factoring out the profit margin retailers are likely to want (e.g., $40) as well as removing the marketer's profit (e.g., $70). From this, the product cost will remain ($199-$40-$70= $89). The marketer must then decide whether they can create a product with sufficient features and benefits to satisfy customers' needs at this cost level.

PSYCHOLOGICAL PRICING

For many years researchers have investigated customers' response to product pricing. Some of the results point to several interesting psychological effects price has on customers' buying behavior and on their perception of individual products. We stress that certain pricing tactics "may" have a psychological effect since the results of some studies have suggested otherwise. But enough studies have shown an effect making this topic is worthy of discussion.

Odd-Even Pricing

One effect dubbed "odd-even" pricing relates to whole number pricing where customers may perceive a significant difference in product price when pricing is slightly below a whole number value. For example, a product priced at (US) $299.95 may be perceived as offering more value than a product priced at $300.00. This effect can also be used to influence potential customers who receive product information from others. Many times buyers pass along the price as being lower than it is either because they recall it being lower than the even number or they want to impress others with their success in obtaining a good value. For instance, in our example a buyer who pays $299.95 may tell a friend they paid "a little more than $200" for the product when in fact it was much closer to $300.

Prestige Pricing

Another psychological effect, called prestige pricing, points to a strong correlation between perceived product quality and price. The higher the price the more likely customers are to perceive it as higher quality compared to a lower priced product. (Although there is a point at which customers will begin to question the value of the product if the price is too high.) In fact, the less a customer knows about a product the more likely she/he is to judge the product as being higher quality based on only knowing the price (see *Trigger of Early Perception* discussion in Chapter 17). Prestige pricing can also work with odd-even pricing as marketers, looking to present an image of high quality, may choose to price products at even levels (e.g., $10 rather than $9.99).

PRICE LINING

As we have discussed many times, marketers must appeal to the needs of a wide variety of customers. The difference in the "needs-set" between customers often leads marketers to the realization that the overall market is really made up of a collection smaller market segments (see Chapter 5). These segments may seek similar products but with different sets of product features, which are presented in the form of different models (e.g., different quality of basketball sneakers) or service options (e.g., different hotel room options).

Price lining or **product line pricing** is a method that primarily uses price to create the separation between the different models. With this approach, even if customers possess little knowledge about a set of products, they may perceive the products are different based on price alone. The key is whether the prices for all products in the group are perceived as representing distinct price points (i.e., enough separation between each). For instance, a marketer may sell a base model, an upgraded model, and a deluxe model each at a different price. If the differences in features for each model are not readily apparent to a customer, such as differences that are inside the product and not easily viewed (e.g., difference between laptop computers), then price lining will help the customer recognize that differences do exist as long as the prices are noticeably separated.

Price lining can also be effective as a method for increasing profitability. In many cases the cost to the marketer for adding different features to create different models or service options does not alone justify a big price difference. For instance, an upgraded model may cost 10 percent more to produce than a base model but using the price lining method the upgraded product price may be 20 percent higher, thereby, making it more profitable than the base model. The increase in profitability offered by price lining is one reason marketers introduce multiple models, since it allows the company to not only satisfy the needs of different segments but also presents an option for a customer to "buy up" to a higher priced and more profitable model.

Competitive Pricing

The final approach for setting initial price uses competitors' pricing as a key marker. Clearly when setting price it makes sense to look at the price of competitive offerings. For some, competitors' price serves as an important reference point from which they set their price. In some industries, particularly those in which there are a few dominant competitors and many small companies, the top companies are in the position of holding price leadership roles where they are often the first in the industry to change price. Smaller companies must then assume a price follower role and react once the big companies adjust their price.

When basing pricing decisions on how competitors are setting their price, firms may follow one of the following approaches:

♦ Below Competition Pricing – A marketer attempting to reach objectives that require high sales levels (e.g., market share objective) may monitor the market to ensure its price remains below competitors.

♦ Above Competition Pricing – Marketers using this approach are likely to be perceived as market leaders in terms of product features, brand image or other characteristics that support a price that is higher than what competitors offer.

♦ Parity Pricing – A simple method for setting the initial price is to price the product at the same level competitors price their product.

STEP 3: SET STANDARD PRICE ADJUSTMENTS

With the first round of pricing decisions now complete, the marketer's next step is to consider whether there are benefits to making adjustments to the list or published price. For our purposes we will consider two levels of price adjustments – standard and promotional. The first level adjustments are those we label as "standard" since these are consistently part of the marketer's pricing program and not adjustments that appear only occasionally as part of special promotions (see *Step 4: Determine Promotional Price Adjustment* discussion below).

In most cases standard adjustments are made to reduce the list price in an effort to either stimulate interest in the product or to indirectly pay channel partners for the services they offer when handling the product. In some circumstances the adjustment goes the other way and leads to price increases in order to cover additional costs incurred when selling to different markets.

It should be noted that many companies do not make adjustments to their list price, particularly those selling directly to final customers. There are two key reasons for this. First, the product is in high demand and therefore the marketer sees little reason to lower the price. Second, the marketer believes the product holds sufficient value for customers at its current list price and the marketer feels reducing the price may actually lead buyers to question the quality of the product (e.g., *"How can they offer all those features for such a low price? Something must be wrong with it"*). In such cases holding fast to the list price allows the marketer to maintain some control over the product's perceived image.

For firms that do make standard price adjustments, options include:

♦ Quantity Discounts

♦ Trade Allowances

♦ Special Segment Discounts

♦ Geographic Pricing

♦ Early Payment Incentives

Quantity Discounts

This adjustment offers buyers an incentive of lower per-unit pricing as more products are purchased. Most quantity or volume discounts are triggered when a buyer reaches certain purchase levels. For instance, a buyer may pay the list price when they purchase between 1-99 units but receive a 5 percent discount off the list price when the purchase exceeds 100 units.

Options for offering price adjustments based on quantity ordered include:

Discounts at Time of Purchase

The most common quantity discounts exist when a buyer places an order exceeding a certain minimum level. While quantity discounts are used by marketers to stimulate higher purchase levels, the rational for using these often rests in the cost of product shipment. As discussed in Box 10-2 in Chapter 10, shipping costs per unit tend to decrease as volume shipped increases. This is because the expenses (e.g., truck driver expense, fuel, road tolls, etc.) required to transport product from one point to another do not radically change as more product is shipped. Consequently, the transportation cost per item drops as more are ordered. This allows the supplier to offer lower prices for higher quantity.

Discounts on Cumulative Purchases

This method allows the buyer to receive a discount as more products are purchased over time. For instance, if a buyer regularly purchases from a supplier they may see a discount once the buyer has reached predetermined monetary or quantity levels. The key reason to use this adjustment is to create an incentive for buyers to remain loyal and purchase again.

Trade Allowances

Manufacturers relying on channel partners to distribute their products (e.g., retailers, wholesalers) offer discounts off of list price called trade allowances. These discounts function as an indirect form of payment for a channel member's work in helping to market the product (e.g., keep product stocked, talk to customers about the product, provide feedback to the manufacturer, etc.).

Essentially, the difference between the trade discounted price paid by the reseller and the price the reseller charges its customers is the reseller's profit. For example, let's assume the maker of snack products sells a product to retailers that carries a stated MSRP of (US) $2.95 but offers resellers a trade allowance price of $1.95. If the retailer indeed sells the product for the MSRP, the retailer will realize a 33% markup on selling price ($1.95/(1-.33) = $2.95). Obviously this percentage will be different if the retailer sells the product at a price that is different than the MSRP, but the important point to understand is that marketers must factor in what resellers' expect to earn when they are setting trade discounts. This amount needs to be sufficient to entice the reseller to handle and possibly promote the product.

Special Segment Pricing

In some industries special classes of customers within a target market are offered pricing that differs from the rest of the market. The main reasons for doing this include: building future demand by appealing to new or younger customers, improving the brand's image as being sensitive to customer's needs, and rewarding long time customers with price breaks.

For instance, many companies, including movie theaters, fitness facilities, and pharmaceutical firms, offer lower prices to senior citizens. Some marketers offer non-profit customers lower prices compared to that charged to for-profit firms. Other industries may offer lower prices to students or children.

Another example used by service firms is to offer pricing differences based on convenience and comfort enjoyed by customers when experiencing the service, such as higher prices for improved seat locations at a sporting or entertainment events.

Geographic Pricing

Products requiring marketers to pay higher costs that are affected by geographic area in which a product is sold may result in adjustments to compensate for the higher expense. The most likely cause for charging a different price rests with the cost of transporting a product from the supplier's distribution location to the buyer's place of business. If the supplier is incurring all costs for shipping then they may charge a higher price for products in order to cover the extra transportation costs. For instance, shipping products by air to Hawaii may cost a Los Angeles manufacturer a much higher transportation cost than a shipment made to San Diego.

Transportation expense is not the only cost that may raise a product's price. Special taxes or **tariffs** may be imposed on certain products by local, regional or international governments which a seller passes along in the form of higher prices.

Early Payment Incentives

For many years marketers operating primarily in the business market offered incentives to encourage their customers to pay early. Typically, business customers are given a certain period of time, normally 30 or 60 days, before payment is due. To encourage customers to pay earlier, thus enabling the seller to obtain the money quicker, marketers have offered early payment discounts often referred to as **cash terms**. This discount is expressed in a form indicating how much discount is being offered and in what timeframe. For example, the cash terms 2/10 net 30 indicates that if the buyer makes payment within 10 days of the date of the bill then they can take a 2 percent discount off some or all of the items on the invoice, otherwise the full amount is due in 30 days.

While this incentive remains widely used, its effectiveness in getting customers to pay early has greatly diminished. Instead, many customers, especially large volume buyers, simply remove the discount from the bill's total and then pay within the required "net" timeframe (or later!). For this reason many companies are discontinuing offering this discount.

STEP 4: DETERMINE PROMOTIONAL PRICE ADJUSTMENTS

The final price may be further adjusted through promotional pricing. Unlike standard adjustments, which are often permanently part of a marketer's pricing strategy and may include either a decrease or increase in price, promotional pricing is a temporary adjustment that only involves price reductions. In most cases this means the marketer is selling the product at levels that significantly reduce the profit it makes per unit sold.

As one would expect, the main objective of promotional pricing is to stimulate product demand. But as we noted back in our discussion of sales promotion in Chapter 14, marketers should be careful not to overuse promotional programs that temporarily reduce selling price. If promotional pricing is used too frequently customers may become conditioned to anticipate the reduction. This results in buyers withholding purchases until the product is again offered at a lower price. Since promotional pricing often means the marketing organization is making very little profit off of each item sold, consistently selling at a low price could jeopardize the company's ability to meet its financial objectives.

The options for promotional pricing include:

♦ Markdowns

♦ Loss Leaders

♦ Sales Promotions

♦ Bundle Pricing

♦ Dynamic Pricing

Markdowns

The most common method for stimulating customer interest using price is the promotional markdown method, which offers the product at a price that is lower than the product's normal selling price. There are several types of markdowns including:

Temporary Markdown

Possibly the most familiar pricing method marketers use to generate sales is to offer a temporary markdown or **on-sale pricing**. These markdowns are normally for a specified period of time, the conclusion of which will result in the product being raised back to the normal selling price.

Permanent Markdown

Unlike the temporary markdown where the price will eventually be raised back to a higher price, the permanent markdown is intended to move the product out of inventory. This type of markdown is used to remove old products that are perishable and close to being out of date (e.g., day old donuts), are an older model and must be sold to make room for new models or are products that the marketer no longer wishes to sell.

Seasonal

Products that are primarily sold during a particular time of the year, such as clothing, gardening products, sporting goods, and holiday-specific items, may see price reductions at the conclusion of their prime selling season.

Loss Leaders

An important type of pricing program used primarily by retailers is the loss leader. Under this method a product is intentionally sold at or below the cost the retailer pays to acquire the product from suppliers. The idea is that offering such a low price will entice a high level of customer traffic to visit a retailer's store or website. The expectation is that customers will easily make up for the profit lost on the loss leader item by purchasing other items that are not following loss leader pricing. For instance, as the price of gasoline has risen many gas stations are now using this as a loss leader in order to generate traffic to the inside of their business where customers will purchase regularly priced products, such as food and drinks. (3) While loss leader pricing is a useful option for generating customer interest, marketers should be aware of potential legal issues as explained in Box 18-3.

Box 18-3

LEGAL CONCERNS WITH LOSS LEADER PRICING

Marketers should beware that some governmental agencies view loss leaders as a form of predatory pricing and, therefore, consider it illegal. **Predatory pricing** occurs when an organization is deliberately selling products at or below cost with the intention of driving competitors out of business. Of course, this differs from our discussion which considers loss leader pricing as a form of promotion and not a form of anti-competitive activity.

In the U.S. several state governments have passed laws under the heading Unfair Sales Act, which prohibit the selling of certain products below cost. The main intention of these laws is to protect small firms from below-cost pricing activities of larger companies. Some states place this restriction on specific product categories (e.g., gasoline, tobacco) but Oklahoma places this restriction on most products and goes as far as requiring product pricing to be at least 6 percent above cost. (4)

Sales Promotions

As we noted in Chapter 14, marketers may offer several types of pricing promotions to simulate demand. While we have already discussed "sale" pricing as a technique to build customer interest, there are several other sales promotions that are designed to lower price. These include rebates, coupons, trade-in, and loyalty programs.

Bundle Pricing

Another pricing adjustment designed to increase sales is to offer discounted pricing when customers purchase several different products at the same time. Termed bundle pricing, the technique is often used to sell products that are complementary to a main product. For buyers, the overall cost of the purchase shows a savings compared to purchasing each product individually. For example, a camera retailer may offer a discounted price when customers purchase both a digital camera and a how-to photography DVD that is lower than if both items were purchased separately. In this example the retailer may promote this as *"Buy both the digital camera and the how-to photography DVD and save 25%."*

Bundle pricing is also used by marketers as a technique that avoids making price adjustments on a main product for fear that doing so could affect the product's perceived quality level (see *Step 3: Set Standard Price Adjustments* discussion above). Rather, the marketer may choose to offer adjustments on other related or complementary products. In our example the message changes to *"Buy the digital camera and you can get the how-to photography DVD for 50% less."* With this approach the marketer is presenting a price adjustment without the perception of it lowering the price of the main product.

Dynamic Pricing

The concept of dynamic pricing has received a great deal of attention in recent years due to its prevalent use by Internet retailers. But the basic idea of dynamic pricing has been around since the dawn of commerce. Essentially dynamic pricing allows for the point-of-sale (i.e., at the time and place of purchase) price adjustments to take place for customers meeting certain criteria established by the seller. The most common and oldest form of dynamic pricing is **haggling**, the give-and-take that takes place between buyer and seller as they settle on a price. While the word haggling may conjure up visions of transactions taking place among vendors and customers in a street market, the concept is widely used in business markets as well where it carries the more reserved label of negotiated pricing.

Advances in computer hardware and software present a new dimension for the use of dynamic pricing. Unlike haggling, where the seller makes price adjustments based on a person-to-person discussion with a buyer, dynamic pricing uses sophisticated computer technology to adjust price. It achieves this by combining customer data (e.g., who they are, how they buy) with pre-programmed price offerings that are aimed at customers meeting certain criteria. For example, dynamic pricing is used in retail stores where customers' use of loyalty cards triggers the store's computer to access customer information. If customers' characteristics match requirements in the software program they may be offered a special deal, such as 10 percent off if they also purchase another product. Dynamic pricing is also widely used in airline ticket purchasing where the type of customer (e.g., business vs. leisure traveler) and date of purchase can affect pricing.

On the Internet marketers may use dynamic pricing to entice first time visitors to make a purchase by offering a one-time discount. This is accomplished by comparing information stored in the marketer's computer database with identifier information gathered as the person is visiting a website. One way this is done is for a website to leave small data files called **cookies** on a visitor's computer when he/she first accesses the marketer's website. A cookie can reside on the visitor's computer for some time and allows the marketer to monitor the user's behavior on the site, such as how often they visit, how long they spend on the site, what webpages they access, and much more. The marketer can then program special software, often called **campaign management software**, to send visitors a special offer, such as a discount. For instance, the marketer may offer a discount if the visitor has come to the site at least five times in the last six months but has never purchased.

• •

Alaska Airlines is one company that uses dynamic pricing to offer different flight prices when users visit its website or are exposed to an ad on another website. The company tracks users by placing electronic code (i.e., cookies) on customer computers. Information, such as how often they have visited, where they are geographically located, and whether they have previously purchased a ticket, can be factored into determining the price. (5)

• •

STEP 5: STATE PAYMENT OPTIONS

With the price decided, the final step for the marketer is to determine in what form and in what timeframe customers will make payment. As one would expect payment is most often in a monetary form, though in certain situations the payment may be part of a barter arrangement in which products or services are exchanged.

Form of Payment

The monetary payment decision can be a complex one. First marketers must decide in what form payments will be accepted. These options include cash, check, money orders, credit card, online payment systems (e.g., PayPal) or, for international purchases, bank drafts, letters of credit, and international reply coupons, to name a few.

Timeframe of Payment

One final pricing decision considers when payment will be made. Many marketers find promotional value in offering options to customers for the date when payment is due. Such options include:

♦ Immediate Payment in Full – Requires the customer make full payment at the time the product is acquired.

♦ Immediate Partial Payment – Requires the customer make a certain amount or percentage of payment at the time the product is acquired. This may be in the form of a down payment. Subsequent payments occur either in one lump sum or at agreed intervals (e.g., once per month) through an installment plan.

♦ Future Payment – Provides the buyer with the opportunity to acquire use of the product with payment occurring some time in the future. Future payment may require either payment in full or partial payment.

OTHER PRICING METHODS

Two pricing approaches that do not fit neatly into the price setting process we've described are bid and auction pricing. Both follow a model in which one or more participants in a purchasing transaction make offers to another party. The difference exists in terms of which party to a transaction is making the offer.

BID PRICING

Bid pricing typically requires a marketer compete against other suppliers by submitting its selling price to a potential buyer who chooses from the submissions. From the buyer's perspective the advantage of this method is that suppliers are more likely to compete by offering lower prices than would be available if the purchase was made directly. Bid pricing occurs in several industries, though it is a standard requirement when selling to local, national, and international governments.

In a traditional bidding process the offer is sealed or unseen by competitors. It is not until all bids are obtained and unsealed that the marketer is informed of the price listed by competitors. The fact that marketers often operate in the dark in terms of available competitor research makes this type of pricing one of the most challenging of all price setting methods.

However, a newer form of bid pricing, called **reverse auction**, is making the bidding process more transparent. Reverse auctions are typically conducted on the Internet and in most cases limited to business-to-business purchasing. With a reverse auction a buyer informs suppliers of its product needs and then identifies a time when suppliers may bid against each other. Usually the time is limited and the suppliers can often see what others are offering. (6)

In either traditional bidding or reverse auction, the marketer's pricing strategy depends on the projected winning bid price, which is generally the lowest price. However, price alone is only the deciding factor if the bidder meets certain qualifications; thus, the low bidder is not always guaranteed to win.

Auction Pricing

Auction pricing is the opposite of bid pricing since it is the buyer who in large part sets the final price. This pricing method has been around for hundreds of years, but today it is most well known for its use in the auction marketplace business models such as eBay and business-to-business marketplaces. While marketers selling through auctions do not have control over final price, it is possible to control the minimum price by establishing a price floor or **reserve price**. In this way the product is only sold if a bid is at least equal to the floor price.

• •

While the auction pricing business model gained wide consumer acceptance in the early years of the Internet marketing, recent evidence suggests that consumer interest in this method for acquiring products may be fading. While consumers enjoyed the excitement of auctions, many now view it as more of a hassle. Instead they prefer a fixed price method where purchases are made at a set price. While this method does not offer customers the potential of receiving a product at a lower price if others do not bid, it does ensure that they will obtain the product. (7)

• •

REFERENCES

1. Bergstein, B., "Software Helps Retailers Make Sure the Price is Right," *USA Today*, April 27, 2007.

2. Caterinicchia, D., "Delta CEO: 15-20% Fare Hike Needed Just to Break Even," *USA Today*, April 22, 2008.

3. "Stations Hope You Fill Up With More Than Gas," *MSNBC*, April 1, 2008.

4. Holliday, H., "Local Retailers React to Oklahoma's Unfair Sales Act," *KTEN*, January 19, 2007.

5. Ramasatry, A., "Is It Legal for Different Customers to Receive Different, Customized Sales Offers? The Example of Alaska Airlines, and the Likely Regulatory Response," *FindLaw*, April 1, 2008.

6. Chafkin, M., "Reverse Auctions," *Inc*, May 2007.

7. Holahan, C., "Auctions on eBay: A Dying Breed," *BusinessWeek*, June 3, 2008.

Full text of many of the references can be accessed via links on the support website.

Chapter 19:

Managing External Forces

The bulk of material covered in the first 18 chapters is intended to give those new to marketing a basic understanding of the decisions marketers make as they work to successfully satisfy customer needs. Our focus has largely centered on decisions marketers control, such as product design, advertising message, type of distribution, setting price, etc. Now that we have laid out the Marketer's Toolkit, we begin a new section examining additional issues facing marketers as they manage their marketing efforts.

In this chapter we explore factors outside of marketers' control but that play a major role in shaping marketers' strategies and tactics. The external forces we discuss present both opportunities and threats with some holding the potential to dramatically alter how an industry conducts its business. Our coverage includes in-depth evaluation of seven key external forces: demographics, economic conditions, governmental environment, influential stakeholders, cultural and societal change, innovation, and competitors.

WHAT ARE EXTERNAL FORCES?

The daily routine for most marketers sees them engaging in activities related to the key marketing decisions contained within the Marketer's Toolkit we introduced in Chapter 1, namely targeting markets, creating products, establishing distribution, developing promotions, and setting price. These decisions are considered to be controllable by the marketer who has the final say on the attributes for each.

Unfortunately, while decisions in the Marketer's Toolkit are largely controlled by the marketer, these decisions can be strongly affected by external forces that are beyond the direct control of the marketing organization. By "direct control" we mean marketers lack the power to determine the direction and intensity of a change in these forces. Instead, marketers must treat external forces as something to monitor and respond to when necessary. For example, newspaper marketers in the U.S. and Europe are experiencing a major shift in how consumers obtain their news in large part due to technological innovation (an external force). Newspapers understanding this key external factor have responded by expanding their delivery of news to meet the needs of customers using these new technologies such as delivery to handheld devices. Other newspapers, that have been slow to recognize new methods for distributing news, now face serious threats to their survival as customers by-pass them in favor of new media outlets.

• •

While newspaper sales in the U.S. and Europe appear to be losing readers, research suggests that readership is rising in other areas particularly in India and China. Gains in newspaper circulation in these countries are the result of two important external factors: population growth and improved economic conditions. (1)

• •

While marketers lack direct control over external forces, in some cases they can exercise a small amount of influence over these factors. For instance, Apple's iPod has played an important role in changing how consumers listen to music and for some, how they acquire information (e.g., news podcasts). But while Apple is credited with being the catalyst for changing a social behavior (an external force) it represents just one of several organizations (e.g., music publishers, manufacturers of other music players) and others (e.g., bloggers, podcasters, news media) whose actions were necessary for behavior to change across a large group. Thus, while one company can market products and services with the intention of changing how a target market behaves, it is nearly impossible for one company alone to control the change.

For marketers the key to dealing with external forces is to engage in continual marketing research. For larger companies this may involve dedicated research personnel who watch these factors as part of their day-to-day responsibilities. A research staff dedicated to monitoring external forces may offer marketers the ability to better predict changes and respond well in advance of a change. For example, researchers may be able to predict how the economy (an external force) will change over the next one to two years and through this information allow the marketing organization to respond (e.g., new products, reduced price, etc.).

For small organizations that do not have the luxury of marketing research staff, monitoring change is difficult and often means they react after a change has occurred. However, new marketing research tools (see Chapter 2) are making the monitoring task much easier allowing small companies to respond quicker then they have in the past.

THE EXTERNAL FORCES FACING MARKETING

For our discussion we highlight seven important external forces. Each external force is described in detail though these are not presented in order of importance. In fact, the importance of each force may vary depending on the marketing organization and the industry in which they compete. For instance, a company manufacturing technology products may feel innovative forces are more important than demographic changes. While a financial services firm may more aggressively monitor and react to economic conditions.

Demographics

Demographics involves the evaluation of characteristics of a population and how these change over time. The characteristics that are of most interest to marketers fall into two categories:

♦ Total Population – These characteristics take a very broad view of the population as a whole in terms of size (e.g., number of people, number of businesses) and location (e.g., geographic region).

♦ Personal Variables – These characteristics look at how the population is changing based on individual factors such as gender, age, income, level of education, family situation (e.g., single, married, co-habitation), sexual preference, ethnicity, occupation, and social class.

We saw in Chapter 5 demographics is a key variable used to segment both consumer and business markets. In particular, demographic variables are an important component in creating customer profiles. These profiles are based on both demographic and non-demographic (e.g., customer behavior, attitudes, lifestyles) factors and are used for grouping customers into definable market segments from which a marketer then selects its target markets. Since demographics is tied directly to identifying target markets, monitoring how demographics change is critical for making marketing decisions.

Most demographic shifts do not occur rapidly so marketers will not see dramatic changes in a short period of time in the manner that other external forces can impact an organization (e.g., impact of a new government regulation). However, over the long term, demographics can reshape a target market requiring marketing organizations to rework their marketing strategy in an effort to appeal to a changing market (see Box 19-1).

Box 19-1

ADJUSTING TO DEMOGRAPHIC TRENDS

While demographic change occurs slowly, marketers can begin to see indicators of potential change by identifying small trends that may suggest a larger shift over time. By paying close attention to these trends organizations can prepare their long-term marketing strategy to be ready when the shift becomes more apparent.

To illustrate how a marketer may respond, let's consider the demographic characteristic birthrate. In some countries the overall birthrate is declining while the average age of the population is growing (i.e., people living longer). For a company targeting the youth market with sporting products this trend may suggest that in coming years it will see shrinkage in demand for its products within the youth market as the population of this market declines.

On the other hand demographic data may signal to the company that another market (i.e., older consumers), which they may not have previously targeted, may hold potential for new products. If it is predicted that the shift will occur over several years the marketer can slowly move into the new market by offering products geared toward older adults.

Economic Conditions

Since most marketers are engaged in activities designed to entice customers to spend their money, it makes sense that an important external force is economic conditions. Economic analysis looks at how a defined group produces, distributes, and consumes goods and services. These groupings can range from those defined very broadly (e.g., country) to those defined narrowly (e.g., small town).

Of course the production, distribution, and consumption of products are also of high interest to marketers and, in fact, many leading scholars of marketing first studied economics before moving to marketing. In very simple terms (and with apologies to both marketers and economists) the major difference between the marketer and the economist is that marketers are engaged in activity that make things happen to individual customers (e.g., create demand for products) while economists are engaged in activity showing the results marketers' decisions have on a group (e.g., study how much is being spent by certain groups). Additionally, economists whose job it is to study a group may use hundreds of economic variables when assessing how a group is responding. Marketers tend to evaluate far fewer economic variables preferring to concentrate on those variables that affect spending behavior of consumers and businesses including:

- Income – how much is being earned

- Spending – what consumers and businesses are doing with their money

- Interest Rates – the cost of borrowing money

- Inflation – how prices for products and services are changing

- Cost of Living – the financial requirements of living in a certain geographic area

- Employment Rates – the percentage of employable people who are working

- Exchange Rates – how the value of currencies are changing between countries and regions

IMPORTANCE OF ECONOMIC CONDITIONS

For many marketers there is a relationship between level of sales and how customers are doing financially. For most products this relationship is a direct one – as customers' financial condition improves so will selling opportunities for the marketer. A clear example of this can be seen with the sale of luxury products where marketers are likely to see their sales improve as the target market's economic condition improves. However, other products may see improvement as economic conditions decline. For instance, marketers of career preparation services, such as those offering resume development and job search assistance, may see increased interest during weak economic conditions by those who are unemployed or others who are concerned about job stability.

• •

One area of the U.S. economy that benefits from an economic downturn is classified advertising as people look to exchange personal belongs for cash. While previously the domain of newspapers, websites such as Craigslist, eBay's Kijiji, and Oodle, which hosts several sites including Wal-Mart Classified, have grown rapidly in the face of a slow growing economy. (2)

• •

Whether an organization benefits from improving or declining economic conditions, it is important it monitors changes occurring in the economy in which the organization's target markets are located. In particular, marketers should watch for changing patterns in customer spending which may indicate that a longer term change in the economy is occurring. Changes that extend over a long term (more than six months) may be part of the **business cycle** of an economy.

A business cycle is presented as a series of up (economic expansions) and down (economic contractions) measures. During expansion an economy grows and this generally leads to more jobs, higher income, and increased customer spending. However, an economy growing too quickly can present problems of **inflation** where product prices grow too fast. In this situation, even though customers have higher incomes they may not be purchasing more since product prices have increased. Such situations are a main reason an economy will contract or see customer spending decrease. If severe this can lead to marketers seeing a major reduction in sales which may indicate the presence of an economic **recession** (i.e., economic decline).

Governmental Environment

Marketing decisions must be made with an understanding of how they are impacted by international, national, regional, and local laws and regulations. For marketers, laws (i.e., acts past by governmental ruling bodies) and regulations (i.e., requirements put in place by governmental agencies) identify rules and procedures that guide certain marketing activities. Failure to conform to requirements established by the governments and their agencies may result in fines, sanctions or other legal action.

The governmental environment is a difficult external force to monitor for two key reasons. First, the number and variety of laws and regulations, can be overwhelming even for the most seasoned marketer. For instance, in the U.S. alone there are potentially hundreds of laws and regulations that are either directly or indirectly targeted to marketing decisions. Table 19-1 provides a sampling of the issues covered by U.S. laws and regulations and the primary marketing decision areas these affect.

Table 19-1: Examples of Laws and Regulations in Marketing

Decision Area	Coverage
General	unfair competition, restraint of trade, environmental
Target Market	discrimination, online registration, privacy
Product	product safety, labeling, intellectual property, warranties
Promotion	deceptive and misleading claims, advertising to children, telemarketing, email spam, promotional give-aways
Distribution	tying contracts, exclusive dealerships, transportation safety
Pricing	price discrimination, predatory pricing, consumer credit purchasing, resale price maintenance

The second reason the governmental environment proves difficult is due to the complexity inherent in understanding laws and regulations which often makes it impossible for marketers to handle these issues on their own. Seeking legal assistance is necessary (and often costly) for most marketers no matter their size.

· ·

A potential challenge facing marketers involved in e-commerce is whether their websites are accessible to blind and disabled users. While government regulation has not established minimum accessibility requirements, many feel that these will be set within the next few years. For instance, a court settlement between U.S. retailer Target and the National Federation of the Blind (3) suggests that regulations may one day be in place requiring retail websites be coded to allow site visitors with vision disabilities to utilize a "screen reader" that provides an audio read-out of the contents of a webpage. (4)

· ·

DEALING WITH THE GOVERNMENT

In addition to seeking legal assistance, marketing organizations may find value by engaging in either direct discussion with governmental personnel or indirect discussion through firms hired to serve as a representative for the marketing company (e.g., consultants, lobbyists). Representatives are particularly important when selling internationally where existing relationships between government personnel and a hired representative can effectively reduce bureaucratic red tape.

In situations where proposed legislation is likely to impact an entire industry, communication with the government may occur through a marketer's participation in an industry trade group. These groups perform many tasks on behalf of their members, including maintaining relations with governmental groups to ensure the industry's voice is heard with regard to pending legislation affecting the industry.

Finally, marketers should not view the governmental environment as always erecting obstacles. In many cases laws and regulations present marketing opportunities. For example, the U.S. Federal government recently instituted airline travel regulations limiting the size of liquid, gel, and aerosol products that may be carried on a plane. Several companies that produce personal care products (e.g., shaving cream, hair care, toothpaste, etc.) viewed the new regulations as an opportunity to market their products in new packaging that they promote as approved for airline travel.

Influential Stakeholders

Besides dealing with various governmental groups, marketers must also pay close attention to other groups that can affect marketing activity. The most important of these groups are those that have an interest or stake in the company. While such groups are not backed directly by the power of a government they can still command a great deal of power especially in terms of swaying public opinion, which sometimes leads to governmental action.

Influential stakeholders can be divided into two categories:

Connected Stakeholders

These stakeholders consist of groups that regularly interact with the marketing organization and often hold important roles in helping the marketer succeed. Examples include supply and distribution partners (e.g., distributors, material suppliers), industry standards groups, and support companies (e.g., advertising agencies). To address concerns raised by these groups often requires direct communication by management with the stakeholders.

Peripheral Stakeholders

These stakeholders consist of groups that may not routinely impact the marketer unless a specific issue arises that draws their attention. Examples include religious organizations, community activists, and cause supporters. To address concerns raised by these groups marketers often use public relations professionals as their first line of communication.

• •

Absolut Vodka found out how peripheral stakeholders can affect marketing decisions when it was confronted by calls to boycott its product after running an advertisement that depicted the Southwestern part of the United States as being part of Mexico. This was part of an "In an Absolut World" campaign showing what the ideal world might look like. The ad was shown only in Mexico but drew anger from Internet bloggers in the US. (5)

• •

Cultural and Societal Change

Society is made up of many different cultural groups. As we noted in Chapter 4, members of a cultural group share similar values and beliefs which are learned and reinforced by others within the same cultural group. These shared values and beliefs lead members of a cultural group to behave in similar ways (e.g., customs, traditions, likes/dislikes, attitudes, perceptions, etc.).

Cultural groups can be viewed on several levels. At a broad level, a cultural group consists of a very large number who share basic values (e.g., ethnicity, religious affiliation). While looking at the broad level can offer some insight into how a general cultural group behaves, marketers are much more concerned with examining cultural groups at narrower levels. Such analysis of cultural groups leads to the study of sub-cultures, which consist of individuals sharing values and beliefs that revolve around special interests. For instance, a large cultural group may exist in a certain region of a country. While they share basic cultural values with others in their country (e.g., sense of patriotism), they may also share values (e.g., work ethic, taste in food, etc.) with those in their region that are not shared consistently throughout the country. Examining these sub-cultures even more closely reveals thousands of smaller sub-cultures (e.g., sports interests, type of shopper, music preference, online gaming enthusiast, etc.).

It should be evident that a single consumer may belong to many different sub-cultures. It should also be evident that members of a sub-culture sharing similar values are also likely to have similar needs and, as we discussed in Chapter 5, this suggests that sub-cultures are natural for market segmentation.

EVOLUTION OF CULTURAL CHANGE

Cultural values and beliefs are not stagnant, these evolve and change. However the pace of change differs depending on the level examined. At the broad cultural level changes often evolve slowly. For instance, consider how people in the United States and Japan view the importance of saving money. People in the United States are more inclined to spend their earned income than they are to save resulting in a low personal savings rate for Americans. Those living in Japan are more concerned with saving and, thus, show a high personal savings rate. The difference in values toward savings has been consistent for many years and no one expects consumers from either country to significantly alter their values in the near future.

While broad cultures tend to shift values and beliefs slowly, changes within sub-cultures can occur relatively quickly. For instance, the music industry often experiences rapid shifts as a sub-culture of music enthusiasts discovers new artists. The key for marketers targeting sub-cultures is to maintain close contact with these groups through regular marketing research. In this way marketers can see how different sub-cultures behave and also spot trends, which marketers can capitalize on through new marketing tactics such as creating new products, opening new sales channels or offering more value to their customers.

. . . .

Between the 1930s and 1970s Converse was the king of basketball shoes selling a basic shoe that targeted a mass market. However, beginning in the 1980s the brand lost ground to companies like Nike and Reebok, who took a segmentation approach offering many models targeted to different needs. In 2003 Nike purchased the struggling Converse company and has reformulated the brand as a fashion shoe targeted to narrow sub-groups. A key part of this strategy includes the use of cultural figures, such as musicians, within promotion and product design. (6)

. . . .

Innovation

Arguably the external forces with the greatest potential for changing how marketers and industries compete are those associated with innovation. When most people think of innovation they immediately assume it has to do with computers and other high-tech equipment. While today the majority of innovative new products rely in some way on computer technology, it is not a requirement for something to be regarded as innovative. Instead, an innovation is viewed as anything new that solves needs by offering a significant advantage (e.g., more features, more convenient, easier to use, lower cost, etc.) over existing methods. For example, a designer of automobiles may develop a new layout for a car's dashboard using existing products (no new technologies). This new design reduces the amount of time a driver must take his eyes off the road in order to select a radio station. If this new layout is viewed positively by customers, governmental groups, and the media it may gain widespread acceptance by other vehicle manufacturers who will make similar designs available in their products.

As noted in the above example, for an innovation to be truly important it must be widely adopted within a targeted group (e.g., within an industry, by a target market). Once adopted an innovation becomes important if it leads to behavioral changes including changing how consumers and businesses satisfy their needs. These changes present both opportunities and threats to marketers.

. . . .

Over the last few years several companies, including Google, have created productivity software products (e.g., word processing, spreadsheet) that operate over the Internet. These products do not require that the software be downloaded to a user's computer. While these innovative products are not new in terms of the features they offer, they are new in terms of convenience in accessing documents from anywhere and the ability to share with others. It remains to be seen whether these products will alter behavior, though it appears that the leading maker of traditional productivity software, Microsoft, has recognized this as a threat and may soon offer its own version of web-based software. (7)

. . . .

Because of the potential innovation has in affecting products and industries it is no surprise that many marketing organizations direct significant funds to researching this external force. In fact, in many industries, such as pharmaceuticals and computers, spending on technological research and development represents a significant portion of a company's overall budget.

INNOVATION IN MARKETING

Marketers in many industries know that innovation through new product development is vital to remain competitive. But product decisions are not the only areas affected by new developments. As we've discussed throughout this book, innovation can affect almost all marketing areas as outlined in Table 19-2:

Table 19-2: Innovation in Marketing

Marketing Area	Effect of Innovation
Marketing Research	Creates new ways to conduct research, including more sophisticated methods for monitoring and tracking customer behavior and analyzing data.
Targeting Markets	Allows for extreme target marketing where micro marketing is replacing mass marketing. For customer service, technology makes it easier to manage relationships and allows for rapid response to customer's needs.
Product	Creates new digital products/services. Incorporation of innovation into existing product/service enhances value by offering improved quality, features, and reliability at a lower price.
Promotion	New techniques allow better matching of promotion to customer activity and individualized promotion. Makes it easier for sellers to offer product suggestions and promotional tie-ins.
Distribution	Creates new channels for distribution and transaction (e.g., electronic commerce) that include making it easier for buyers to place orders. Allows more control over inventory management and closer monitoring of product shipments.
Pricing	Enables the use of dynamic pricing methods.

Many of the benefits shown in Table 19-2 are driven by the evolution of the Internet. The Internet is transforming how all functional areas of an organization perform work. However, it can be argued that no functional area has been more affected than marketing (see *Marketing Strategy and the Internet* discussion in Chapter 20). Throughout this book we have seen evidence of how the Internet has impacted marketing. Over the next decade it is expected that the Internet's effect on marketing will continue to grow and marketers are well served to embrace it. As discussed in Box 19-2, the Internet has spawned innovative ideas that may be bending many established marketing rules.

Box 19-2

CULTURAL SHIFT LEADING TO INNOVATION

The accessibility to Internet communication and collaboration tools, such as instant messaging, peer-to-peer file exchange, and group development of documents, have helped enlighten many to the benefits of information sharing. In fact, sharing for the purpose of solving problems, creating new things or gaining new experiences is so rampant that it may become ingrained in this generation and may soon become an expected way to interact.

It may be wise for marketers to pay close attention to this evolving cultural phenomena, not so much for identifying opportunities to develop collaborative products (though this has and will continue to offer great opportunities), but from the perspective of "outsourcing" the development of certain marketing activities to a group of dedicated independent collaborators. Known by such names as **crowdsourcing** (8), **user innovation**, and **open development**, this concept draws from the computer industry idea of open source software development, which has produced such products as the Linux operating system, Firefox web browser, and other products.

Open Development of Marketing Activities

While product development collaboration has made its mark principally within the computer industry, marketers may soon find that it holds value in other marketing areas. Conceptually the idea of open development in marketing involves a company recruiting specialists who voluntarily agree to work together to create and possibly execute a marketing program. The open development team may be asked to follow certain guidelines established by the company, but in general the open development team would be free to develop as it sees fit.

On the surface it would appear the most likely marketing activities to be candidates for open development are in the areas of promotion and product development, though many others could emerge. Here are a few examples:

- A company planning a print advertising campaign could persuade graphic artists to provide input into the development of a series of print advertisements by offering access to an online graphics software application.

- Companies involved in event marketing could seek input from an open development group who could develop an event plan and even execute certain tasks.

- A company that markets after-market products for major industries, such as automobile, boating, and housing, could use an open development group to contribute to new product ideas and even contribute to the actual product design process.

- An online content provider could institute open development in order to solicit ideas and designs for adding new content categories.

- A marketing trade association may have an open development team design marketing research tools that would be made available to association members.

The Benefits of Open Development

Open development will go only so far if contributors do not realize a benefit from their hard work. For some the feeling of involvement and the results of their efforts will be enough reward but it is doubtful these altruistic feelings will last long. So what's in it for open development members? Again, the open source software community may offer answers. The essence of open source software projects is to develop a freely available core product that can be added to by others in ways that satisfy a particular user's needs. The developers themselves benefit by selling their services through the creation of add-on products or offering other services to facilitate use of the core product. In this way they are creating their own source of revenue through the development of a freely available core product.

Marketers may also be in a position to offer open development members after-project revenue opportunities. For example, the core group may develop an online marketing campaign that targets a specific user group. This campaign may allow for certain "build out" options that will take the promotion further. One can see this with a promotion tied to an online game that for the company's purpose attracts visitors to a website or to purchase a non-game product in stores. But the game may be created in such a way that add-on features can take users to a higher gaming level or features (e.g., characters) contained in the game can be branched out into new gaming or product promotion opportunities.

For marketers, the open development concept offers a potentially low-cost method for creating cutting-edge marketing programs. The fact that non-company employees are helping develop marketing programs may heighten the creative efforts particularly if members of the open development are also enthusiastic customers and users of the company's products. Additionally, depending on the arrangement, the company may not have to accept the results produced by the open development team. This frees the company to pick and choose from open development offerings.

On the downside, since open development members are only loosely affiliated with the company, controlling their actions can be difficult. The lack of control may be a significant hindrance to its adoption by larger companies. However, for smaller companies or decentralized units within larger firms, the open development model may be something to explore.

Competitors

For many marketers the final external force is the one most relevant to immediate day-to-day decision making. While the other external forces we've discussed tend to be examined periodically (or in some cases rarely), monitoring competitor activity is often a daily undertaking.

Monitoring competitors can serve several goals:

Competitors as Threats

The most obvious reason to monitor the competition is to see how they are responding in the same markets in which the marketer operates. Many larger companies recognize the importance of keeping tabs on their competition and create specific positions or even departments focusing on gathering and analyzing competitor data. These **competitive intelligence** programs mainly employ high-tech methods, principally the Internet, to locate information about competitors, such as news reports, government filings (e.g., patents, stock reports), and changes to competitors' websites. Even small sized marketers can track competitors' actions. For instance, there are several news and information services that will alert a marketer (usually via email) when a competitor is mentioned in the news.

. . . .

Industry trade shows make it easy for business-to-business marketers to keep an eye on their competitors. Methods used by marketers include attending competitors' presentations, picking up product literature, and, in some cases, hiring outside firms to act as secret shopping services, though some question the ethical nature of the latter. (9)

. . . .

Competitors as Partners

While many may consider competitors as the enemy, there are situations where competitors can present opportunities. This happens often to large companies that offer a broad product line serving many target markets. In some markets a company may compete aggressively with another firm but in other markets both firms may be lagging and it may make more sense for both to work together. This can be seen in the computer industry where Apple, which for many years viewed computers built with Intel processors as competitors since these run Microsoft operating systems, has now accepted these processors and is building computers powered by Intel computer chips.

Competitors of Tomorrow

In many industries and, in particular, those in technology-focused industries where there is heavy emphasis on research and development, the most dangerous competitors are the ones that have yet to emerge. Because technology-dependent industries, such as computers, consumer electronics, and pharmaceuticals, rely heavily on innovative new products, serious competitors can emerge quickly from what seems to be out of nowhere. For instance, the evolution of online video and its impact on the news and entertainment industry grew very rapidly with the introduction of online video services (e.g., YouTube), which was previously an unknown project developed in a garage. However, in less than 18 months it came to dominate the online video industry.

• •

The record industry has seen a major shift in how customers acquire music. In most cases the result has not been good as sales have dropped rapidly primarily due to technological advances that make it easy for music lovers to acquire songs via the Internet. Many of the new sources for acquiring music represent competitive threats that the music industry did not consider viable just a few years ago. While record companies are exploring other methods for making money, such as selling artist-related merchandise, their failure to recognize the new options for acquiring music could leave their long term survival in doubt. (10)

• •

REFERENCES

1. Ritter, K., "Study: Global Newspaper Circulation is Rising," *Associated Press*, June 2, 2008.

2. "Wal-Mart Enters Online Classified Advertising," *MSNBC*, June 3, 2008.

3. "Target Settles Case Over Site's Access to Sightless," *MSNBC*, August 27, 2008.

4. Klein, K.E., "Is Your Web Site Handicap-Accessible?" *Business Week*, December 17, 2007.

5. "Vodka-Maker Absolut Apologizes for Ad," *MSNBC*, April 5, 2008.

6. "Converse's All-Star Image," *Business Week*, April 25, 2008.

7. Fried, I., "Microsoft Office Heads to the Web," *CNET News.com*, September 30, 2007.

8. Boutin, P., "Crowdsourcing: Consumers as Creators," *Business Week*, July 13, 2006.

9. Armstrong, L., "The Art of Reconnaissance," *Exhibitor Magazine*, December, 2007.

10. Bachman, J., "The Big Record Labels' Not-So-Big Future," *Business Week*, October 10, 2007.

Full text of many of the references can be accessed via links on the support website.

Chapter 20:

Marketing Planning and Strategy

In our final chapter we take all that has been discussed to this point and see how marketers use this information to manage business decisions. In particular, we focus attention on the importance of marketing planning with special attention given to the role marketing strategy plays in the planning process.

We begin with a discussion of the importance of planning and show why the development of a Marketing Plan is a necessary undertaking for nearly all marketers. As part of this discussion we distinguish between strategies and tactics and see the role these play in the planning process. Next, to aid in our understanding of planning, we see how the Product Life Cycle (PLC) offers valuable guidance for marketing decisions. We cover in detail the circumstances marketers face as their products move through the PLC and why marketing decisions must be continually fine tuned to adjust to these changes. Throughout this discussion we see how the PLC can offer insight into what marketers may expect to see as the product continues to evolve. Finally, we conclude the book with a detailed look at the impact the Internet is having on marketing and offer reasons why marketing strategy must include the Internet.

IMPORTANCE OF PLANNING

As we have seen throughout this book, marketers consider many factors when making decisions. Of course the main factors are those directly associated with how customers respond to an organization's marketing efforts, such as how they react to changes in a product, new advertisements, special pricing promotions, etc.

But when making decisions marketers face other concerns that are not directly customer related. For instance, we have discussed how marketing decisions (e.g., lowering price) may place pressure on other areas of the organization (e.g., production, shipping). Other examples include:

♦ Marketers must be aware of how their decisions fit with the overall objectives of the company. For example, a company whose goal is to be the low-price leader may have concerns if the company's marketing department wants to market a very high-end product since this would go against the reputation and core strengths of the company.

♦ In Chapter 19 we showed that marketers' decisions may affect peripheral stakeholders who are not directly connected to the marketing organization but have the potential to impact the organization if issues arise that draw their attention.

♦ Marketing decisions also directly affect an organization's financial condition. Marketers' efforts generate the funds (i.e., sales) needed for the company to survive but do so while using company resources. Controls must be put in place to ensure the results of what the organization spends through marketing meet expectations (i.e., meets return on investment goals).

Because marketing decisions have both internal and external impact, marketers are wise to make their decisions only after engaging in a careful, disciplined planning process. For marketers planning is an essential task that must be continually undertaken. As we will see, shifting market conditions, including changing customer needs and competitive threats, almost always means that what worked in the past will not work in the future. This requires organizations to respond with revisions in how a product is marketed. Marketing planning is also important since it is often a prerequisite for obtaining funding, whether one is a marketer in a large corporation seeking additional money for his or her department or is part of a small startup company looking for initial funding. Finally, marketers who make hasty, off-the-cuff decisions without regard to the implications are taking risks that may lead to problems. Instead, marketing decisions should be made with consideration of how these affect others both inside and outside the organization

THE MARKETING PLAN

The central point in planning for marketing decisions is the Marketing Plan. The scope of the Marketing Plan depends on the company and industry. A small technology startup company may, for instance, have a less elaborate plan that is highly flexible (e.g., does not identify exactly where advertising money is spent) to meet the needs of a rapidly changing market. A more established marketing organization, such a large consumer products firm, may create a very structured plan that clearly identifies all activities taking place over a 12-month period.

For companies operating separate units in different international markets a different Marketing Plan is often needed for each market even though the same product is sold in each location. This is often necessary since the market conditions for one market may be significantly different than another market and, because of this, require a different marketing approach.

> *International markets are particularly susceptible to requiring different plans. For example, the tourism marketer for the city of Las Vegas found that the message conveyed to customers in the United States does not work for other parts of the world. To address the differences the city's marketers have customized plans for international markets they target. (1)*

Whether the marketer is creating a short plan intended to cover a narrow timeframe or a full-blown document laying out plans for a year or more, any plan requires undertaking significant marketing research to better understand the market. With knowledge of the market, the marketer can then begin to build the plan which will include the following six key concepts (2):

1. SITUATION ANALYSIS

The situation analysis is designed to take a snapshot of where things stand at the time the plan is developed. This part of the Marketing Plan is extremely important and quite time consuming as it looks at the current situation in terms of: 1) the components of the Marketer's Toolkit (target markets, product, distribution, promotion, and pricing), 2) the competition, 3) the financial conditions facing the organization, and 4) external forces.

2. MARKETING OBJECTIVES

The ultimate purpose of a Marketing Plan is to lead to actions that will help the organization meet a goal. The goal is reflected in one

337

or more objectives the organization expects to achieve with its marketing efforts. The objectives flow from the top of the organization down to the marketing department. Objectives can be in the form of financial goals, such as profits, sales volume or return on investment, or marketing goals, such as achieving certain levels of **market share** (i.e. percentage of market held by organization) or store traffic.

3. MARKETING STRATEGY

Achieving objectives requires the marketer engage in marketing decision making which indicates where resources (e.g., marketing funds) are directed. However, before spending begins on individual marketing decisions (e.g., where to advertise) the marketer needs to establish a general plan of action summarizing what will be done to reach the stated objectives.

4. TACTICAL MARKETING PROGRAMS

Marketing strategy sets the stage for specific actions that take place. Marketing tactics are the day-to-day actions marketers undertake and involve the major marketing decision areas. As would be expected, this is the key area of the Marketing Plan since it explains exactly what will be done to reach the marketing objectives. Box 20-1 provides insight on how strategy leads to the development of tactical programs.

Box 20-1

RELATIONSHIP BETWEEN STRATEGY AND TACTICAL PROGRAMS

One of the most important concepts of the marketing planning process is the need to develop a cohesive marketing strategy that guides tactical programs for the marketing decision areas. In marketing there are two levels to strategy formulation: General Marketing Strategies and Decision Area Strategies.

General Marketing Strategies

These set the direction for all marketing efforts by describing, in general terms, how marketing will achieve its objectives. There are many different General Marketing Strategies, though most can be viewed as falling into one of the following categories:

- Market Expansion - This strategy looks to grow overall sales in one of two ways:

    1. *Grow Sales with Existing Products* – With this approach the marketer seeks to actively increase the overall sales of products the company currently markets. This can be accomplished by: 1) getting existing customers to buy more, 2) getting potential customers to buy (i.e., those who have yet to buy), or 3) selling current products in new markets.

---

2. *Grow Sales with New Products* – With this approach the marketer seeks to achieve objectives through the introduction of new products. This can be accomplished by: 1) introducing updated versions or refinements to existing products, 2) introducing new products that are extensions of current products, or 3) introducing new products not previously marketed.

- Market Share Growth – This strategy looks to increase the marketer's overall percentage or share of market. In many cases this can only be accomplished by taking sales away from competitors. Consequently, this strategy often relies on aggressive marketing tactics.

- Niche Market – This strategy looks to obtain a commanding position within a certain segment of the overall market. Usually the niche market is much smaller in terms of total customers and sales volume than the overall market. Ideally this strategy looks to have the product viewed as being different from that of companies targeting the larger market (i.e., product positioning).

- Status Quo – This strategy looks to maintain the marketer's current position in the market, such as maintaining the same level of market share.

- Market Exit – This strategy looks to remove the product from the organization's product mix. This can be accomplished by: 1) selling the product to another organization, or 2) eliminating the product.

Decision Area Strategies
These are used to achieve the General Marketing Strategies by guiding the decisions within important marketing areas (target marketing, product, distribution, promotion, pricing). For example, a General Marketing Strategy that centers on entering a new market with new products may be supported by Decision Area Strategies that include:

- Target Market Strategy – employ segmenting techniques

- Product Strategy – develop new product line

- Distribution Strategy – use methods to gain access to important distribution partners that service the target market

- Promotion Strategy – create a plan that can quickly build awareness of the product

- Pricing Strategy – create price programs that offer lower pricing versus competitors

Achieving the Decision Area Strategies is accomplished through the development of detailed Tactical Marketing Programs for each area. For instance, to meet the Pricing Strategy that lowers cost versus competitors' products, the marketer may employ such tactics as: quantity discounts, trade-in allowances or sales volume incentives to distributors.

5. Forecasts and Marketing Budget

Carrying out marketing tactics almost always means that money must be spent. The marketing budget lays out the spending requirements needed to carry out marketing tactics. While the marketing department may request a certain level of funding they feel is required, in the end it is upper management that will have final say on how much financial support is offered. In most cases, such requests must be justified by showing what is expected to happen if the money is spent. For this marketers must develop forecasts that may include estimates of sales volume, number of customer visits, level of product awareness, coupon usage rates, and many others.

6. Implementation and Analysis

This part of the Marketing Plan identifies how and by whom the tactical programs are carried out. In many cases a timeline is presented showing when tasks will occur and who will be responsible. Additionally, the Marketing Plan shows how and when success will be measured. For instance, a retailer planning a new department within its national chain may undertake analysis of department sales once per week to see whether the marketing programs are meeting expectations.

PLANNING AND STRATEGY WITH THE PRODUCT LIFE CYCLE

As we have seen, there are many components to consider within the marketing planning process. In fact, for many marketers creating the Marketing Plan represents one of the most challenging and burdensome tasks they face. Fortunately, over the years marketing academics and professionals have put forth theories, models, and other tools to aid planning.

Possibly the most widely used planning tool within marketing is the Product Life Cycle (PLC) concept, which we introduced in Chapter 7. The PLC suggests a product goes through several stages of "life" (Development, Introduction, Growth, Maturity, and Decline) with each stage presenting the marketer with different circumstances to which they must react.

As we will see, the PLC helps the marketer understand that marketing planning must change as a product moves from one stage to another. For example, marketers will find what works when appealing to customers in the Introduction stage is different than marketing methods used to attract customers during the Growth stage.

For the rest of this chapter we offer a detailed discussion of how the PLC can aid marketing planning. The discussion is presented using the following assumptions and techniques:

♦ The chief scope of analysis is at the product form level where many companies offer products with similar benefits. In Chapter 7 we suggested that hybrid cars would be an example of a product form. In most cases a product form is a market with certain characteristics that change over time.

♦ We break down each stage and discuss the market characteristics in terms of:

- Level of Competition
- Nuances of the Target Market
- Available Product Options
- Price Level
- Promotional Focus
- Distribution Strategy
- Total Industry Profits

♦ While at the general level the PLC is divided into five main stages, we view most stages as consisting of sub-stages that result from noticeable changes in market characteristics.

♦ While market characteristics are evaluated for the product form, we offer strategy guidance for individual brands that compete within these specific markets.

♦ The PLC is tightly linked to the Diffusion of Innovation discussed in Chapter 7. It is important to keep in mind the five adopter categories: Innovators, Early Adopters, Early Majority, Late Majority, and Laggards.

Development Stage

The Product Life Cycle begins long before a product is brought to market. While technically sales do not start until the next stage, marketers must address many of the same issues they will face once the product is launched. Much of what happens in the Development stage follows our discussion of New Product Development in Chapter 7, where marketing research is the key element in planning. Most of what occurs in this stage is experienced only by companies who are on the forefront of innovation of a new product form. In our discussion, the Development stage is divided into two distinct sub-stages: early and late.

EARLY DEVELOPMENT STAGE

CHARACTERISTICS OF STAGE:

Competition	No real competition exists since the product is in early development much of which is in-house and not readily viewable to competitors. However, from a research perspective competitors are now being identified.
Target Market	The target market exists only in marketing research terms. Possibly a small number of target customers are used to assist with research.
Product	The product exists only in the form of ideas and prototypes. Inventory is not yet available.
Prices	Non-existent unless the company charges research customers a fee to be part of early product testing.
Promotion	Promotion has yet to occur as companies continue to refine their products and build their marketing plans.
Distribution	Mostly limited to internal analysis of possible distribution alternatives, though there may be some communication with a limited number of distribution partners in order to gauge interest.
Profits	At this stage there are costs only.

BRAND STRATEGY FOR STAGE:

For firms developing a new product form this stage is primarily concerned with marketing research. This stage matches the Concept Development and Testing step for New Product Development. Customers and distribution partners are only involved to aid in information gathering, often through focus group research. Because the product form is still in early development the marketer has yet to determine whether the company will move forward with a full product launch.

Late Development Stage

Characteristics of Stage:

Competition	While a marketer may not face competition in terms of sales, they may face competitive pressure from companies developing similar products, such as competition to acquire materials or technologies for product development, competition to line up product evaluators, and competition to get early word out about the product to the news media. Additionally, competition may exist in the form of other types of products that potential customers currently use to satisfy needs targeted by the new product form. If these competitors are aware that a new product form is being developed, they may increase efforts to sell their products with the intention of reducing the market's need for the new product.
Target Market	Companies may test market the product among a small group of customers or within a selected geographic market.
Product	Companies researching the product form begin to produce small quantities of the product, primarily for testing or to build initial awareness (e.g., for display at trade shows).
Prices	Initial market price is discussed and if there are active test markets the company may be testing different price levels.
Promotion	Promotion often begins prior to product launch as marketers prepare the market. Emphasis may be on public relations in an attempt to encourage the media to discuss the product prior to launch. If a real test market is used the companies may be using several promotional options including advertising and sales promotion.
Distribution	For product sold through distributors, the ground work is being laid to build the distribution network. In some cases distributor education and training will start prior to product launch.
Profits	A small amount of revenue may be generated if real test markets are used but overall marketers continue to experience substantial costs.

Brand Strategy For Stage:

Products that have moved to the late stage of development have done so because marketing research suggests there is strong potential for success. By this point a marketer has a real product (not just ideas) and is in the position to test it in the market. Consequently, this stage matches the Market Testing step for New Product Development. Firms electing to test their product in real "test markets" will do so using all their marketing tools.

Introduction Stage

This stage represents the launch of the new product form by one or more companies. It is done only after the marketer has created a detailed Marketing Plan. In many cases tactical marketing decisions (target marketing, product, distribution, promotion, pricing) have been adjusted as the product has gone through the Development stage. The Introduction stage is divided into two distinct sub-stages: early and late.

Early Introduction Stage

Characteristics Of Stage:

Competition	In many cases, when two or more companies are working to be first to market with a new product form, one company will be out ahead and for a period of time have the market to itself. However, this does not mean there is no competition. The company that launched the product still faces competition from existing products that customers previously purchased in order to satisfy their needs.
Target Market	To establish interest in the market for a new product form marketers will initially target Innovators and to a larger extent Early Adopters.
Product	From the target market's perspective, product options are limited since only one or a very small number of companies are selling products. Because of the uncertainty of whether the product will be accepted by a larger market and because of the expense involved in producing products in small volume, (primarily due to low demand) there are very few product options available.

Prices	In most cases marketers follow a pricing strategy called **price skimming** in which price is set at a level that is much higher than can be sustained once competitors enter the market. Price skimming allows the company to recover development and initial marketing costs before the onslaught of competitors eventually force prices lower.
Promotion	For products considered to be a leap ahead of existing products, early marketers may have some difficulty explaining how the product satisfies customers' needs. This is particularly an issue with high-tech products. In this situation the marketer must engage in a promotional campaign that is designed to educate the market on the product form and not necessarily push a specific brand. Additional sales promotion may be used to encourage product trial. Also, the sales force may begin a strong push to acquire distributors.
Distribution	Upon product launch marketers continue efforts to build their distribution network. As we saw in the Development stage, the focus of marketers is to find distributors committed to handling the product.
Profits	Marketers often experience low profits and most likely a loss as the cost of acquiring customers (i.e., promotion) is high and marketers also need to pay back development expense.

BRAND STRATEGY FOR STAGE:

For the early entrants in the market the most important goal is to create awareness for the product form. If customers can see that the product form holds similar characteristics to existing products then the marketers' task is easier since their job becomes one of convincing customers that this new product form is better than what they are currently using.

However, if the product form is significantly different than existing products then the marketers' job may be far more difficult. Under these conditions marketers must not only make customers aware of the new product but they must also educate customers as to what the product is, how it works, and what benefits are derived from its use. For some products, such as technology products, conveying this message can prove difficult as customers may not fully understand how the product works and, consequently, not see a need for the product. Whether customers understand the product or not, this stage requires promotional spending directed to addressing the need for customer education and building awareness. Also, education and awareness alone are not enough; customers must often be enticed to try a product through special promotional efforts (e.g., free trials).

• •

In the technology industry it is common to see companies introduce competing products that offer similar benefits but do so by employing different, often incompatible methods. Such products often confuse consumers. They fear that one product may ultimately win the battle and leave the purchasers of the other product with a product that may not be supported. The most classic example of this occurred in the early days of video players where VHS players ultimately defeated beta players. A more recent example of this can be seen in the high definition DVD player market where Sony's Blu-ray technology and Toshiba's HD-DVD were the first to launch products. After several years competing in the market Sony was able to garner enough leverage among suppliers and resellers to beat Toshiba. Unfortunately, those who purchased HD-DVD will find their players and their purchased software are not compatible with the Sony player. (3)

• •

LATE INTRODUCTION STAGE

CHARACTERISTICS OF STAGE:

Competition	By this stage any company that was alone in launching the new product form is alone no longer, as it is highly likely at least one competitor has entered the market.
Target Market	Marketers are now engaged heavily in getting a high percentage of Early Adopters to accept the product.
Product	With competitors entering the market, choices available to customers expand, though the differences between competitors' offerings are often not significant.
Prices	Product pricing remains high, though any new competitor entering at this stage may attempt to compete with the early entrants by offering a lower relative price.
Promotion	The promotional message is still one designed to educate the market on the benefits of this new product form, but with more competition there is a noticeable increase in the use of advertising that highlights a company's brand. Also, personal selling and sales promotion have increased especially targeting the channel of distribution as entrants attempt to secure distributors.

Distribution	The number of distributors continues to increase with many now offering products from several market entrants (which at this point may still be only a few).
Profits	Losses continue to mount due to high marketing cost and the need to recover development expense. Losses may be even higher than anticipated if the target market adopts slower than forecast or if more companies enter than expected.

Brand Strategy For Stage:

Early entrants continue to create awareness and educate customers, but their promotional orientation may shift to a "buy-our-brand" approach if more companies enter the market. Thus, at this stage, marketers begin to position their products with the intention of separating themselves from the competition.

Growth Stage

The Growth stage is characterized by product sales increasing often at a very rapid rate. This is seen by large percentage sales increases over previous periods (e.g., 50 percent increase in sales from one quarter to the next). This is an indication the product has advanced beyond Early Adopters and is now being purchased by the mass market (i.e., Early Majority). It is also the stage when early entrants begin to realize profits, though the fact the market is now profitable invariably leads to increased competition. It is also the time in which competitors try to actively position their brand in a way that will separate it from the onslaught of new entrants. For many products the Growth stage is represented by three distinct sub-stages: early, middle, and late.

Early Growth Stage

Characteristics of Stage:

Competition	Only a few competitors are in the market as others wait to see whether the mass market will adopt the product. However, competitors selling products customers previously purchased to satisfy needs now addressed by the new product form may be getting very aggressive in their marketing tactics as they sense the new product form to be a threat.
Target Market	Continued focus is on Early Adopters but marketers begin to identify new market segments containing the Early Majority.

Product	A basic product sold to the Early Adopters remains, but plans are underway to introduce products with different configurations such as more options (e.g., advanced models) and fewer options (i.e., stripped down model). An expanded product line may be necessary to satisfy many different potential segments of the mass market.
Prices	The average selling price may remain high especially in cases where market demand is strong and only a few competitors have entered.
Promotion	Promotions are broadened with more emphasis on mass advertising and sales promotions that encourage product trial. Also, personal selling and sales promotions to distributors continue as marketers attempt to make inroads into distributors that target the mass market.
Distribution	Marketers look for new distribution channels that enable the product to begin to reach the mass market. For instance, consumer products may look to gain distribution in large discount retailers.
Profits	The early market entrants may begin to experience profits as early development costs have been covered and overall demand is gaining steam.

BRAND STRATEGY FOR STAGE:

In the early part of the Growth stage marketers are looking to expand the market beyond the Early Adopters and into the mass market using Market Expansion strategies (see Box 20-1) such as: 1) Grow Sales with Existing Products primarily by getting new market segments to buy, and 2) Grow Sales with New Products by introducing new models containing different sets of features. The latter strategy is used not only to appeal to new customers but also to encourage repeat purchasing by existing customers. Additionally, greater emphasis is placed on using promotion to continue building awareness and driving interest in the product form. This is due to: 1) the need to reach a broader market, and 2) to maintain an effective share-of-voice (i.e., percentage of all promotions in the market) so the marketer's message is not lost among competitors' increased promotional spending.

MIDDLE GROWTH STAGE

CHARACTERISTICS OF STAGE:

Competition	More competitors are attracted to the market as they see the potential for high profits. Competitors selling products customers previously purchased to satisfy needs now addressed by the new product form may be extremely aggressive (may be entering the Maturity stage of their industry's PLC) resulting in major price reductions. This may delay the adoption of the new product form by some Early Majority.
Target Market	The Early Majority sector of the mass market begins to purchase in higher volume and, depending on the product, existing customers (i.e., Early Adopters) may be purchasing again. The Late Majority are becoming customers.
Product	Companies increase the number of product offerings in order to differentiate themselves from competitors. In most cases new product offerings improve on the performance or benefits offered by earlier products. However, the target market may begin to feel burdened by too many choices.
Prices	As more competitors enter with more product options prices may begin to fall, though the effect may not be felt as strongly if demand remains high. Pricing may be somewhat more competitive if large companies with strong financial backing are now entering or, in smaller segments, where multiple companies are trying to establish a niche.
Promotion	Emphasis has shifted to heavy advertising and promotions promoting individual brands and not just awareness and education of the product form. Heavy selling and sales promotion continues with distributors.
Distribution	Distribution reaches saturated levels as all possible channels are now handling the product.
Profits	Marketers who were early entrants to the market may begin to see very high profits as demand is increasing while the pricing levels remain fairly strong. Depending on the product, unit cost of production may be dropping as manufacturing levels increase.

BRAND STRATEGY FOR STAGE:

In the middle part of the Growth stage the objective is to continue a Market Expansion strategy. The most likely strategy is to seek out new market segments that have not been targeted. Sometimes this can be done using the same products previously introduced, though in most cases entering a new market will require revisions to existing products.

> To expand the market chocolate makers, such as Nestle and Hershey, have set their sites on the Asian market where demand is viewed as largely untapped. For instance, in India yearly chocolate consumption is only 5.8 ounces (99 g) compared to the Swiss who consume 24 pounds (11 kg). (4)

This stage is also a time to focus on product positioning. The idea is to use marketing decisions to affect customers' perceptions of a brand by trying to either: 1) separate a brand from other products (i.e., differentiate), or 2) bring a brand closer to competitors' offerings (i.e., equivalency). For the **differentiation approach** marketers use promotional methods showing why their brand is different, while the **equivalency approach** may suggest that a brand is equal to other brands but offers an advantage, generally on price.

Late-to-market competitors may use a **penetration pricing** approach to establish a position in the market. Penetration pricing intentionally sets a price that is below long-term pricing in order to capture a large share of market. In many cases the firm will raise price once the product is established.

> In markets driven by the need for status, late entrants to a market may take a different approach than entering with a low price. Their approach may be to position the product as the "latest-must-have" product that could sell at a premium compared to existing products. This is the case in the premium designer denim market where high-priced products are in high demand. The demand has lured many competitors to position the product as trend setting rather than lower in price. (5)

Finally, some marketers also determine that it is time to focus on specific segments of the market via a Niche strategy approach.

LATE GROWTH STAGE

CHARACTERISTICS OF STAGE:

Competition	As the market begins to see slower growth and companies find themselves in a highly competitive market with fierce battles occurring on some fronts such as within certain segments where demand is falling faster than in other segments.
Target Market	The overall market is still growing in terms of sales volume, especially as the product spreads to the Late Majority. But there is some evidence that while sales are increasing growth is occurring at a decreasing rate.
Product	With so many competitors offering numerous product options customers feel overwhelmed and confused by the choices available. In cases where customers do not fully understand the product (e.g., technology product) they may feel more comfortable purchasing from top brands or products sold at major distributors.
Prices	The average price is falling rapidly as market growth begins to slow and competitors struggle to maintain their market share. Price wars may break out.
Promotion	There is heavy spending on advertising and especially on sales promotions designed to offer incentives to customers to purchase and to re-purchase.
Distribution	With demand beginning to slow, some distributors cut back on the number of products they stock and persuade leading product marketers to offer more incentives to remain with the distributor.
Profits	Marketers begin to see a leveling off of profits as overall revenue flattens due to slowing demand and falling prices. However, marketing costs still remain high.

BRAND STRATEGY FOR STAGE:

Many marketers find this to be the most difficult part of the PLC. The late growth stage is a turbulent time with firms fighting just to survive. The turbulence is brought on by the slowing of growth. This is not to say that overall sales are declining but that the percentage of growth from one period to the next is declining. For instance, sales over a three-year period may show an overall increase but it is occurring at a decreasing rate compared to the previous years (e.g., 20%,15%, 10%).

The key objective for a marketer is to remain competitive by maintaining a power position (e.g., leading brand name) or by achieving an insulated position within a niche. Brands may use promotional tactics that keep existing customers happy (e.g., coupons, improved customer service) and entice new customers to try the product (e.g., rebates, extended payment, try-before-you-buy). Distribution partners are encouraged to remain loyal through such actions as special pricing, promotional assistance, and special packaging.

Maturity Stage

At some point in time sales of the product form slows. Instead of double-digit growth from one period to the next, the industry limps along with low, single digit sales increases or worse (see Box 20-2). There are two key reasons why this occurs. First, the market has become saturated and a large majority of potential customers have already purchased the product. In the case of products that have a long **buy-cycle** (i.e., time between repeat purchases)

Box 20-2

WHEN MARKET GROWTH SLOWS

Reaching the Maturity stage in the PLC means that marketers can no longer count on the growth in the overall market as the trigger for increased company sales. This can be best explained with an example.

- Period 1 – Market Size 100,000 units Market Share 10% Total Company Sales 10,000 units

- Period 2 – Market Size 200,000 units Market Share 10% Total Company Sales 20,000 units

- Period 3 – Market Size 200,000 units Market Share 10% Total Company Sales 20,000 units

As shown, during the growth stage (Period 1 to Period 2) a marketer may see product sales increase without the need for an increase in market share. Under this market condition, the marketer can still do well without having to grow its percentage of the market. In fact, if its market share dropped to 6 percent in Period 2 they would still realize an overall sales increase compared to the previous year (200,000 x 6% = 120,000 units). But in Period 3 sales have leveled off and maintaining the same level of market share no longer leads to increased growth. This situation makes things very competitive as companies fight to increase sales by increasing their market position.

---

the infrequency of repurchase results in slow sales for some time. Second, customers have moved on to purchase other products that are seen as replacements for this product form. In this situation, the growth of the product form may have been interrupted with the introduction of a new product form (e.g., CD computer drives replaced by DVD drives).

The slowing of market growth is a signal the product form may have reached the Maturity stage of the PLC. In our discussion the Maturity stage is divided into two distinct sub-stages: early and late.

EARLY MATURITY STAGE

CHARACTERISTICS OF STAGE:

Competition	By far the fiercest competition takes place at this stage as marketers move to grab customers from often weakened competitors. At this stage many competitors fail or merge with others.
Target Market	Little or no growth is occurring as the market is saturated or the target market looks to other products to satisfy its needs. Laggards may start buying but only if they can no longer purchase products they previously purchased to satisfy their needs.
Product	Many products still exist though some level of **product standardization** has occurred. Any new models introduced do not lead to major improvements in product performance or benefits offered but instead offer minor incremental improvements.
Prices	The average price continues to fall possibly below cost as competitors attempt to remain in the market. Price wars occur in many segments.
Promotion	Heavy competitive advertising and extensive promotions take place with the objective of getting existing customers to switch (for their repeat purchases) and encouraging distributors not to drop the product from their inventory.
Distribution	Distributors continue to reduce their inventory and promotional focus for the product form and become very selective on the products they will carry.
Profits	Industry profits fall rapidly and many firms lose money as they increase spending in hopes of remaining in the market.

Brand Strategy For Stage:

In the early part of the Maturity stage, the key objective is to enact strategies that enable a product to survive in the face of strong competition driven by lessening of demand. In fact, marketers may be happy following a Status Quo strategy that is intended to just maintain their market position. Unfortunately, this may prove difficult as this stage, often called the **shakeout stage**, leads to many products failing or being absorbed by competitors (i.e., companies merge, products are sold).

In order to survive marketers may need to resort to tactics designed to "steal customers" from others, which often involves significant price promotions (e.g., heavy discounting) or strong promotions intended to improve image or solidify a niche. Marketers who have avoided competing on price may be in a better position to weather the storm if they have convinced the market they have special features that few others offer. This can be the case if they have successfully established a strong position in a niche market.

A more likely scenario for companies at this stage is to investigate new ways to grow the market in an effort to extend the Growth stage of the PLC. The use of **resurgence tactics** include such measures as:

- Changing how customers use the product such as: encourage more frequent use or more consumption per usage (e.g., consume 2 units instead of 1 unit), suggest new benefits that can be obtained from using the product (e.g., has added health benefits not previously promoted) or suggest new uses for the product with messages whose tone says: *"Did you know our product can also do this?"*

- Finding new markets not previously targeted.

- Developing new product options (i.e., product line extensions) that offer more or better features (e.g., easier to use, safer, more attractive) that may get existing customers to re-purchase more quickly than they would normally.

- Heightening interest by changing image through heavy promotion and package redesign.

- Competing with lower priced brands by offering an alternative low-price product through private label branding arrangement with distribution partners (see *Private Label or Store Branding* discussion in Chapter 6).

. . . .

An example of finding new uses for an existing product is the Nintendo Wii gaming system. While many think of this product as a consumer entertainment product targeted to kids and young adults, the system is also proving to be a useful tool in the health care industry where it is helping rehabilitate those with severe injury or debilitating disease. (6)

Late Maturity Stage

Characteristics of Stage:

Competition	The competitive landscape has stabilized with the only survivors remaining consisting of a few market giants and several small niche firms.
Target Market	The market is saturated for first time buyers and focus is now on getting existing customers to remain loyal.
Product	The introduction of new models is reduced to just a few product performance enhancements, though there may be more stylistic improvements.
Prices	Overall prices stabilize and may rise due to limited competition.
Promotion	Large competitors begin to cut back on expensive promotions designed to attract new customers and focus on reminder promotions to loyal customers.
Distribution	Overall distribution has stabilized with few new distributors agreeing to handle the product. For products sold at retail stores there is a noticeable reduction in shelf space devoted to the product.
Profits	Companies see profits recover as demand stabilizes, pricing rises, and overall marketing costs drop.

Brand Strategy For Stage:

If companies have failed to extend the PLC in the early part of the maturity stage, it is very likely the product form may never again experience growth. Instead the companies will continue to market the product, albeit with little effort other than making it available to customers who have been purchasing it for some time.

By the late part of the maturity stage the companies that are still selling may no longer consider the product an important product for the future of the company, but this does not mean the product is not important. In fact, it may be very important for the profit it generates (a.k.a. **cash cow**) which is used to fund new products. Consequently, some attention is still paid to the product but only to ensure that it is still available to those who want to purchase.

Decline Stage

A product form has reached this stage when it becomes clear the market is no longer able to sustain itself. Like the Maturity stage, the Decline stage may last a long time especially for products that have been adopted by a large percentage of the market who are not inclined to change how they satisfy their needs (i.e., Laggards). Since the end of the product form is seen as inevitable, there are no sub-stages here.

DECLINE STAGE

CHARACTERISTICS OF STAGE:

Competition	As time goes on firms drop out until no one is producing the product.
Target Market	Mostly consists of Laggards who have been loyal to this type of product for a long time and have not moved on to newer products.
Product	No new improvements are introduced and some models are discontinued.
Prices	Prices may be rising as competitors drop out and companies still in the market have little incentive to engage in price competition. Also, there may be a large loyal market that may not be sensitive to price increases. However, some companies looking to get out of the market but that have existing inventory may drastically markdown product to encourage rapid sales.
Promotion	Companies limit promotions to occasional reminders to loyal customers though overall little is spent.
Distribution	With declining demand distributors are removing products. The marketer may even make the decision to remove the product from unprofitable distributors. Sales may shift to online distribution or via non-traditional channels.
Profits	For companies remaining, profits may be stable and possibly big if this stage takes a long time to play out.

BRAND STRATEGY FOR STAGE:

Marketers are faced with Market Exit strategies when they reach the Decline stage. There are two ways marketers can address this. First, companies may consider a **milking** strategy that involves getting the most out of the product in terms of sales without spending any additional funds to support the product. This strategy works best if a sizable market remains that is loyal to the product and not very price sensitive. A customer base with these characteristics allows a marketer to ride through the decline stage for some time while earning sizeable profits. Second, companies may look to sell off or divest the product. In some situations this can be done by first investing in the product in order to make the product more attractive to potential buyers.

However, discontinuing a product does not mean a company no longer earns revenue from the product form. Many discontinued products, especially those used in business and industrial settings, will continue to earn money through support services, such as selling supplies and service/repair contracts.

MARKETING STRATEGY AND THE INTERNET

We close *KnowThis: Marketing Basics* by once again focusing on the most important challenge facing today's marketers – the Internet. Throughout this book we have seen how the Internet is dramatically impacting the world of marketing. Yet, surprisingly many companies have not developed a rational Internet marketing strategy. In fact, some very large firms continue to wade into Internet waters very gingerly. (7) Considering the Internet has now been used effectively by marketers since 1994, any organization without a strategy to utilize the Internet for marketing is likely missing major opportunities while also opening itself to potential threats (see Innovation discussion in Chapter 19).

In Box 20-3 we examine reasons why marketers must make the Internet an important part of their overall marketing strategy. Much of this has been covered elsewhere in the book, but the effect of the Internet on marketing holds such importance that it is only fitting we conclude this book by concentrating these issues in one location.

Box 20-3

10 REASONS MARKETING STRATEGY MUST INCLUDE THE INTERNET

1. The Go-To Place for Information

Possibly the most important reason why companies need to include the Internet in marketing strategy is because of the transformation that has occurred in how customers seek information. While customers still visit stores, talk to sales representatives, look through magazines, and discuss product information with friends, an ever-increasing number of customers turn to the Internet as their primary knowledge source. In particular, they use search engines as their principle portal of knowledge as search sites have become the leading destination sites for most Internet users. Marketers must recognize that the Internet is where customers are heading and, if the marketer wants to stay visible and viable, they must follow.

2. What Customers Expect

The Internet is not only becoming the resource of choice for finding information, in the next few years it is also likely to be the <u>expected</u> location where customers can learn about products and make purchases. This is especially the case for customers below the age of 25. In many countries, nearly all children and young adults have been raised knowing how to use the Internet. Once members of this group dominate home and business purchases they will clearly expect companies to have a strong Internet presence.

3. Captures a Wide Range of Customer Information

As a data collection tool the Internet is unmatched when it comes to providing information on customer activity (see Box 1-2 in Chapter 1). Each time a visitor accesses a website they leave an information trail that includes how they got to the site, how they navigated through the site, what they clicked on, what was purchased, and loads of other information. When matched to a method for customer identification, such as login information, the marketer has the ability to track a customer's activity over repeated visits to the site. Knowing a customer's behavior and preferences opens up tremendous opportunities to cater to a customer's needs and, if done correctly, the customer will respond with a long-lasting loyalty.

4. Extreme Target Marketing

The most efficient way for marketers to spend money is to direct spending to those who are most likely to be interested in what the marketer is offering. Unfortunately, efforts to target only customers who have the highest probably of buying has not been easy. For instance, consider how much money is wasted on television advertisements to people who probably will not buy. Yet the Internet's unrivaled ability to identify and track customers has greatly improved marketers' ability to target customers who exhibit the highest potential for purchasing products. For example, specialized niche websites targeted to women have grown dramatically in recent years and marketers of products targeted to this demographic have responded with extensive promotional spending. (8)

5. Stimulate Impulse Purchases

Whether customers like it or not, the Internet is proving to be the ultimate venue for inducing impulse purchases. Much of this can be attributed to marketers taking advantage of improvements in technologies that: 1) allow a website to offer product suggestions based on a customer's online buying behavior, and 2) streamline the online purchasing process. But online impulse purchasing also takes advantage of the "purchase now, pay later" attitude common in an overspending credit card society. How this plays out over time as many customers become overwhelmed with debt will need to be watched and could impact online marketers' activities.

6. Customized Product and Service Offerings

Companies know they can develop loyal customers when product and service offerings are designed to satisfy individual needs. This has led many online marketers to implement a micro marketing strategy (see *Customized or Micro Marketing Strategy* discussion in Chapter 5) offering customers online options for configuring products or services. The interactive nature of the Internet makes "build-your-own" a relatively easy to implement purchasing option. An empowered customer base that feels a company will deliver exactly what they want is primed to remain loyal for long period of time.

7. Takes Prospects Right to the Sale

No other form of communication comes close to turning exposure to promotion into immediate customer action as the Internet, which enables customers to make purchases immediately after experiencing a promotion. Prior to the Internet, the most productive call-to-action was through television **informercials** that encourage viewers to call toll-free phone numbers. However, moving customers from a non-active state (i.e., watching television) to an active state (i.e., picking up the phone to call the number) is not nearly as effective as getting people to click on an Internet ad while they are actively using the Internet.

8. Conveys Perception of Being a Full-Service Provider

For distributors and retailers the Internet makes it easy to be a comprehensive supplier. Unlike brick-and-mortar suppliers who are often judged by the inventory that is actually on hand or services provided at a store, e-commerce sites can give the illusion of having depth and breadth of inventory and service offerings. This can be accomplished by placing product and service information on the company's website but behind the scenes having certain orders fulfilled by outside suppliers via shipping and service agreements. With such arrangements customers may feel they are dealing with providers that offer full-service when in reality a certain percentage of the products and service are obtained from other sources.

9. Lower Overhead, Lower Costs, Better Service

Internet technologies are replacing more expensive methods for delivering products and services, and for handling customer information needs. Cost savings can certainly be seen with products and services deliverable in digital form (e.g., music, publications, graphic design, etc.) where production and shipping expenses are essentially removed from the cost equation. Cost savings may also be seen in other marketing areas including customer service where the volume of customer phone calls may be reduced as companies provide online access to product information (see *Customer Service Technologies* discussion in Chapter 3). Field salespeople may also see benefits by encouraging prospects to obtain product information online prior to a face-to-face meeting. This may help reduce the time devoted to explaining basic company and product information and leave more time for understanding and offering solutions to customers' problems. As these examples suggest, the Internet may lower administrative and operational costs while offering greater value to customers.

10. Create Worldwide Presence

The Internet is a communication and distribution channel offering global accessibility to a company's product and service offerings. Through a website a local marketer can quickly become a global marketer and, by doing so, expand its potential target market to many times its current size. Unlike the days before e-commerce when marketing internationally was a time-consuming and expensive undertaking, the uploading of files to establish a website is all that is needed to create a worldwide presence. While establishing a website does not guarantee international sales (there is a lot more marketing work needed for the site to be viable internationally), the Internet provides a gigantic leap into global business compared to pre-Internet days.

REFERENCES

1. Voight, J., "How to Customize Your U.S. Branding Effort to Work Around the World," *Adweek*, September 3, 2007.

2. For a detailed tutorial on The Marketing Plan see *KnowThis.com's* **How to Write a Marketing Plan Tutorial**.

3. Kageyama, Y., "Blu-Ray Nears Victory in Battle Over High-Def DVD Players," *USA Today*, February 19, 2008.

4. Fishbein,J., "Chocolatiers Look to Asia for Growth," *BusinessWeek*, January 17, 2008.

5. Dickler, J., "It's All in the Jeans," *CNN Money*, February 23, 2007.

6. Miller, J., "Wii Speeds Up the Rehab Process," *USA Today*, July 24, 2007.

7. Whoriskey, P., "Brought to You by . . . Anyone?" *Washington Post*, June 18, 2008.

8. Miller, C.C., "Woman to Woman, Online," *New York Times*, August 13, 2008.

Full text of many of the references can be accessed via links on the support website.

Index

A

11390966R0023

Made in the USA
Lexington, KY
30 September 2011